CHRISTIANITY AMONG THE NEW ZEALANDERS

WAR CANOES AND MISSION BOAT.

CHRISTIANITY AMONG THE NEW ZEALANDERS

William Williams
Bishop of Waiapu

THE BANNER OF TRUTH TRUST

THE BANNER OF TRUTH TRUST
3 Murrayfield Road, Edinburgh EH12 6EL
PO Box 621, Carlisle, Pennsylvania 17013, USA

★

© The Banner of Truth Trust 1989
First published 1867
First Banner of Truth edition 1989.
ISBN 0 85151 566 5

★

Printed and bound at The Camelot Press Ltd, Southampton

CONTENTS.

LIST OF ILLUSTRATIONS.

PREFACE.

It may seem to many persons a most unfavourable time for publishing to the world a book on Christian Missions, but more particularly one which professes to give an account of Christianity among the New Zealanders. For some years every mail from New Zealand has been the bearer of intelligence respecting a war, during the course of which there have been many events recorded, showing the Maoris to be a bold and brave people, ready to fight to the last for what they consider to be their rights : but they do not tend to give a very favourable impression of the Christianity which that people are said to have received. But more particularly the development of the Hauhau fanaticism with all its horrid rites, and the cruel murder of poor Völkner, has given too much reason for the public to ask : " Is this the Christianity of the New Zealanders ? Have the large sums of money spent upon this work during fifty years, and the labours of your Missionaries—valuable men who would have done good service in any other occupation—produced no better result ? Surely it has been a mistake to think of civilizing, and of bringing over to Christianity, a race of savages, doomed by the Almighty to be shut up in utter ignorance! How much better to have bestowed these efforts in improving the condition of our own countrymen at home!" Such are the sentiments which continually meet the eye in many of the public prints, while the infidel thinks that he is able to refute the Christian by an appeal to the results of his own labours.

It is for this very reason that this little work, which was contemplated some years ago simply as a record of the past, is now given to the world, to show that those who embarked in Missionary labours have not failed in that which they undertook, and are ready to challenge a fair and calm investigation into the history of their proceedings.

The early records of Christianity lead us to expect such events as have transpired in the New Zealand Church. First, our Saviour warned His disciples that many who heard the word gladly would by and by be offended. Then, as the Churches became established in different provinces of the Roman Empire, we find St. Paul marvelling that the Galatians were so soon removed from him that had called them into the grace of Christ unto another Gospel; and after a further lapse of time, we gather from the Epistles to the Seven Churches in Lesser Asia, that their religion had begun in those early times most seriously to degenerate from its original purity. Yet there was an abundant harvest of first-fruits, and great multitudes of true believers had been received into the

Church. The dominion of Satan had been invaded, and his anger, being stirred up to the utmost, became developed in fierce persecutions, under which many sealed their faith with their blood, and in subtle temptations also, which drew aside the great bulk of professors from the simplicity of the truth.

What have we found in New Zealand but the counterpart of this? There has been a national recognition of the Christian religion; but, while there have been many nominal professors, we have undoubted evidence that large numbers of sincere Christians have been gathered into the fold of Christ. In the meantime, at the very period when the Gospel was beginning to gain a hold upon the people, there came the colonization of the country, with all the manifold temptations and changes of circumstances introduced by a new race of men. The increase of settlers led to a greater demand for land, of which there was abundance in the country unoccupied; but, as might have been expected, quarrels have arisen, some of which have been the fault of the natives, but a large proportion had their origin in our own mismanagement. The effect of all this has been most prejudicial to the progress of Christianity. The Romish priests have made use of this state of things to procure for their tenets a favourable reception, saying that they have no connexion with the English or with the English Government; and hence the notion which has been impressed upon the natives, that the Protestant Missionaries were sent by the Queen to prepare the way for the colonists. But what is the result? That, notwithstanding all these adverse circumstances, there is still a large number of faithful Christians. It was the command of our blessed Saviour that the Gospel should be preached to all nations, and it is in compliance with this command that missionary labours are carried on in the present day. God has blessed those labours to a greater extent than we had ventured to hope, and, notwithstanding all the trials and discouragements and opposition of the evil one, the Christian knows that the kingdom of Christ will be triumphantly established, and that "He must reign till He hath put all enemies under His feet."

In preparing the following pages, a large portion of the information has been gathered from the publications of the *Church Missionary Society*, and much also from personal observation.

For most of the drawings which are inserted in this book, I am indebted to the kindness of the Rev. J. Kinder and the Rev. T. B. Hutton, to whom I wish to express my great obligation.

CHRISTIANITY
AMONG THE NEW ZEALANDERS.

———◆———

CHAPTER I.

1808—1814.

CONVICT SETTLEMENT IN NEW SOUTH WALES—MR. MARSDEN'S
FIRST ACQUAINTANCE WITH THE NEW ZEALANDERS—GOES TO
ENGLAND—MEETS WITH RUATARA—HEARS THE STORY OF HIS
HARDSHIPS—MESSRS. HALL AND KING SENT TO ESTABLISH A
MISSION IN NEW ZEALAND—MASSACRE OF THE BOYD—KENDAL
AND HALL VISIT NEW ZEALAND IN THE EARLY PART OF 1814—
MR. MARSDEN CONDUCTS THE MISSIONARIES TO THE BAY OF
ISLANDS—FIRST SABBATH—DEATH OF RUATARA.

OUR first acquaintance with New Zealand is gathered
from the interesting narrative of Captain Cook
This enterprising navigator did good service in his
day by opening to our view many parts of the world,
before unknown to commercial enterprise, and thus
preparing the way for the introduction of Christianity. Among these the continent of Australia
was soon chosen by the English Government, from
its remoteness and its seclusion from the rest of the
civilized world, as a fit locality for the banishment of
that part of the community which had forfeited the

right of freedom in the mother country. A convict settlement was formed in New South Wales, under the control of a governor, supported by a guard of soldiers, and a staff of officers, necessary to conduct the affairs of the colony. A chaplain was also appointed to attend to the religious instruction of the settlement, and as his duties increased, the Rev. Samuel Marsden was sent out to his assistance in the year 1793.

In the course of time the wants of the colony brought a certain amount of trade, and as the hitherto unfrequented seas came to be better known, it was found that the whale fishery and the capture of seals could be carried on with much profit. Ships which were engaged in these occupations occasionally touched on the coasts of New Zealand, and as the natives gained confidence, many were induced to take passage in them and visit the neighbouring harbour of Port Jackson. It was in this way that Mr. Marsden first obtained a knowledge of the New Zealanders, and a growing interest was excited in their behalf, and a hope that one day the way would be open for giving to them the blessings of the Gospel. He visited England in the year 1808; and it was at this time that he laid the foundation of the Church of England Mission to New Zealand. In its consequences, civil and religious, this has proved one of the most extraordinary of those achievements which are the glory of the churches in these later times. This was the great enterprize of his life: he is known already, and will be remembered while the Church on earth endures, as the apostle of New Zealand. He had formed a high, and we do not think an exaggerated, estimate of the New Zealand tribes. "They are a noble race," he writes, "vastly superior in understanding to anything you can imagine in a savage nation." This was before the mission was begun. But he did not speak merely from hearsay : several of their chieftains and enterprising warriors had found a welcome at the hospitable parsonage at Paramatta. Sometimes, it is true, they were but awkward guests, as the following anecdote will show, which is given in the words of one of Mr. Marsden's daughters :—" My father had sometimes as many as thirty New Zealanders staying at the parsonage. He possessed extraordinary influence over them. On one occasion a young lad, the nephew of a chief, died, and his uncle immediately made preparation to sacrifice a slave to attend his spirit into the other world. Mr. Marsden was from home, and his family were only able to preserve the life of the young New Zealander by hiding him in one of the rooms. Mr. Marsden no sooner returned and reasoned with the chief, than he consented to spare his life. No further attempt was made upon it, though the uncle frequently deplored that his nephew had no attendant to the next world, and seemed afraid to return to New Zealand, lest the father of the young man should reproach him for having given up this important custom."

Mr. Marsden had succeeded in his representations to the Church Missionary Society, and on his return to New South Wales in 1809, he was accompanied by two catechists, Messrs. William Hall and John King, who were to be the pioneers of the work. His prayers and devout aspirations for New Zealand had been heard on high, and the way of the Lord was preparing in a manner far beyond his expectations, ardent as they seemed. The ship *Ann*, in which he sailed, by order of the Government, for New South Wales, carried with her one whom Providence had raised up to act an important part, as leading to the conversion of that benighted land.

The ship had been some time at sea before Mr. Marsden observed on the forecastle, amongst the sailors, a man whose darker skin and wretched appearance awakened his sympathy. He was wrapped in an old great-coat, was very sick and weak, and had a violent cough, accompanied with profuse bleeding. He was much dejected, and appeared as though a few days would close his life. This was Ruatara, a New Zealand chieftain, whose story, as related by Mr. Marsden, is almost too strange for fiction. And as "this young chief became," as he tells us, "one of the principal instruments in preparing the way for the introduction of the arts of civilization, and the knowledge of Christianity into his native country," a brief sketch of his marvellous adventures will not be out of place.

"When the existence of New Zealand was yet

scarcely known to Europeans, it was occasionally visited by South Sea whalers in search of provisions and water. One of these, the *Argo*, put into the Bay of Islands in 1805, and Ruatara, fired with the spirit of adventure, embarked in her with two of his companions. The *Argo* remained on the New Zealand coast for five months, and then sailed for Port Jackson, the modern Sydney of Australia. She then went to fish on the coast of New Holland for six months, again returning to Port Jackson. Ruatara had been six months on board, working as a sailor, and passionately fond of this roving life. He then experienced that unkindness and foul play, of which the New Zealander has often had sad reason to complain. He was left on shore without a friend, and without the slightest remuneration.

" He now shipped on board the *Albion* whaler, Captain Richardson, whose name deserves honourable mention : he behaved very kindly to Ruatara, paid him for his services in various European articles, and after six months cruising on the fisheries, put him on shore in the Bay of Islands, where his tribe lived. Here he remained some time, when the *Santa Anna* anchored in the Bay, on her way to Norfolk Island, and other islets of the South Sea, in quest of seal-skins. The restless Ruatara again embarked; he was put on shore at Norfolk Island, in company with fourteen sailors, provided with a very scanty supply of bread and salt provisions, to kill seals, while the ship sailed, intending to be absent but a short time, to procure potatoes and pork in New Zealand. On her return she was blown off the coast in a storm, and did not make the land for a month. The sealing party were now in the greatest distress, and accustomed as he was to hardships, Ruatara often spoke of the extreme suffering which he and his party had endured, while for upwards of three months they existed on a desert island, with no other food than seals and sea-fowls. Three of his companions died under these distresses.

"At length the *Santa Anna* returned, having procured a valuable cargo of seal-skins, and prepared to take her departure homewards. Ruatara had now an opportunity of gratifying an ardent desire he had for some time entertained, of visiting that remote country, from which so many vast ships were sent, and to see with his own eyes the great chief of so wonderful a people. He willingly risked the voyage as a common sailor to visit England and see King George. The *Santa Anna* arrived in the river Thames about July 1809, and Ruatara now requested that the captain would fulfil his promise, and indulge him with a sight of the King. Again he had a sad proof of the perfidiousness of Europeans. Sometimes he was told that no one was allowed to see King George, sometimes that his house could not be found. This distressed him exceedingly. He saw little of London, was ill-used, and seldom permitted to go on shore. In about fifteen days the vessel had discharged her cargo, when the captain told him that

he should put him on board the *Ann,* which had
been taken up by Government to convey convicts to
New South Wales. The *Ann* had already dropped
down to Gravesend, and Ruatara asked the master of
the *Santa Anna* for some wages and clothing. He
refused to give him any, telling him that the owners
at Port Jackson would pay him two muskets for his
services on his arrival there ; but even these he never
received."

Mr. Marsden was at this time in London, quite
ignorant of the fact that the son of a New Zealand
chief, in circumstances so pitiable, was on board the
vessel in which his passage was taken. Their first
meeting took place, as we have stated, when she had
been some days at sea. His sympathies were at once
roused, and his indignation too. " I inquired," he
says, " of the master where he met with him, and
also of Ruatara, what had brought him to England,
and how he came to be so wretched and miserable.
He told me that the hardships and wrongs which he
had endured on board the *Santa Anna* were exceedingly great, and that the sailors had beaten him very
much, that the master had defrauded him of all his
wages, and prevented his seeing the king." By the
kindness of those on board, Ruatara recovered, and
was ever after truly grateful for the attention shown
him. On their arrival at Sydney, Mr. Marsden took
him into his house for some months, during which
time he applied himself to agriculture. He then
wished to return home, and embarked for New

Zealand.   But it was not deemed prudent to allow
Messrs. Hall and King to accompany him.   Tidings
had recently been brought to Sydney of the fearful
massacre of the *Boyd* at the harbour of Whangaroa,
and it was doubtful whether the lives of the missionaries would be safe among this savage people.

Mr. Marsden believed that this outrage had been
occasioned by some great provocation; and subsequent inquiry proved that it was so.   The *Boyd*,
commanded by Captain Thompson, had taken a
cargo of convicts to New South Wales, when, having
completed her charter party, she embarked a number
of passengers for England, and then proceeded to
New Zealand for a cargo of timber.   Two New Zealanders, one of whom bore the name of George, were
together at Port Jackson, and agreed with Captain
Thompson to work their passage to their own country.
The native account states that George was taken so
ill during the voyage as to be incapable of doing
duty; and the captain, not believing this to be the
case, but imputing his absence from work rather to
laziness than indisposition, had him tied up to the
gangway and flogged.   Such treatment, it may be
readily supposed, must have sunk deeply into the
mind of a savage, and the revenge he meditated was
no less terrible than certain.   On their arrival at
New Zealand, he induced the captain to run the
vessel into Whangaroa, where he was in the midst of
his own people, promising to supply all the timber

he required. The captain, with a large party, soon left the ship, for the purpose of examining the neighbouring woods, and all were speedily overpowered and killed. The natives then arrayed themselves in the clothes of the sailors, and went off to the ship in the boats. A general massacre of the remaining part of the crew and passengers followed, and with the exception of four individuals, neither man, woman, or child, of all that had left Port Jackson, being about seventy persons, escaped the cruel vengeance of their merciless enemies.

In the face of this sad event, Mr. Marsden did not allow any direct step to be taken towards the commencement of the mission, until 1814, when Mr. Thomas Kendal, having arrived from England, he directed Mr. Kendal and Mr. Hall to proceed to the Bay of Islands, for the purpose of re-opening a communication with Ruatara, and to ascertain the general feeling of the natives. They were kindly received, and on the return of the vessel to New South Wales, several chiefs accompanied them, among whom were Ruatara and Hongi, a chief who was rising in importance, by reason of his daring acts of valour. Mr. Marsden wrote at this time to the Secretary of the Church Missionary Society :—" I am happy to inform you that the brig *Active* returned safe from New Zealand, on the 21st of August, after fully accomplishing the object of her voyage. My wish was to open a friendly intercourse between the

natives of that island and the missionaries, previous
to their final settlement among them.

"The public prejudices have been very great
against these poor heathen, both here and in Europe.
Their acts of violence and cruelty have been published to the world, but the causes that led to them
have been concealed. Many acts of fraud, murder,
and oppression, have been committed from time to
time by Europeans. The natives had no means of
redress for the injuries they suffered but retaliation.
But as they were considered such monsters of cruelty,
I did not think it prudent, in a public point of view,
to send the wives and families of the missionaries in
the first instance, but rather to bring over some of
the chiefs to Port Jackson, and to establish a friendship with them. My old friend Ruatara, with two
other chiefs and some of their relatives, are now at
Paramatta, living with me and Messrs. Hall and
Kendal. This intercourse will remove all apprehension, as a cordial intimacy and friendship will now
be formed among them." At length, on the 28th of
November, 1814, the schooner *Active* weighed anchor
from Sydney Cove, having on board the Rev. S.
Marsden ; his friend Mr. Liddiard Nicholas ; and the
missionaries, Kendal, Hall, and King, with their
wives and families, and a party of eight New Zealanders. Calling at different places along the coast,
they met with a large body of Whangaroa natives,
the perpetrators of the massacre of the *Boyd*. From
them Mr. Marsden gathered the particulars of this

sad tragedy, and their account of the causes which led to it. He spoke much to them of a better way, and of his object in bringing teachers to live among them. As the evening advanced, and the people began to retire to rest, Mr. Marsden and Mr. Nicholas wrapped themselves up in their great-coats, and prepared for rest also. " George directed me," writes Mr. Marsden, " to lie by his side. His wife and child lay on the right hand, and Mr. Nicholas close by. The night was clear, the stars shone bright, and the sea before us was smooth. Around us were numerous spears stuck upright in the ground, and groups of natives lying in all directions, like a flock of sheep upon the grass, as there were neither tents nor huts to cover them. I viewed our present situation with feelings which I cannot express—surrounded by cannibals, who had massacred and devoured our countrymen. I wondered much at the mysteries of Providence, and how these things could be. Never did I behold the blessed advantages of civilization in a more grateful light than now. I did not sleep much during the night. My mind was too seriously occupied by the present scene, and the new and strange ideas which it naturally excited."

They reached the Bay of Islands on the 22d of December, and anchored off Rangihoua, which was the village over which Ruatara was chief. The Sabbath which followed was most remarkable in its bearing on the future destinies of New Zealanders, though it was long before the anticipated fruit was to appear. Everything presented an auspicious aspect. On their arrival at the spot which had been long fixed upon, the chiefs of greatest influence came forward with strong assurances of their desire to favour the benevolent object, and the people seemed to enter into the feelings of their chiefs, all being ready to receive with gladness whatever was offered for their good. In the mean time Ruatara, who was really a man of fine character, proceeded to take a step in the right direction. He passed the remaining part of the day in preparing for the Sabbath. He inclosed about half an acre of land ·with a fence, erected a pulpit and reading-desk in the centre, and covered the whole with some cloth which he had brought with him from Port Jackson. He also arranged some old canoes, as seats on each side of the pulpit for the English. These preparations he made of his own accord, and in the evening informed Mr. Marsden that everything was ready for divine service. On Sunday morning Mr. Marsden saw from the deck of the vessel the English colours hoisted on a flagstaff, erected by Ruatara. It seemed to be the signal for better days, the dawn of religion and civilization in this benighted land ; and it was hoped that under the protection of that flag, the progress of religion and civilization might go on, until all the natives of these islands should enjoy the happiness of British subjects.

About ten o'clock Mr. Marsden prepared to go on

shore, to publish for the first time the glad tidings of the Gospel. There was no apprehension for the safety of the vessel; everybody, therefore, went on shore to attend divine service, except the master and one man. When they landed they found Korokoro, Ruatara, and Hongi, dressed in regimentals, which Governor Macquarrie had given them, each wearing a sword, and carrying a switch in his hand, with their men drawn up ready to march into the in-closure. The English were placed on the seats on each side of the pulpit. Korokoro arranged his men on the right, in the rear of the English; and Ruatara's people occupied the left. The inhabitants of the town, with the women and children, and a number of other chiefs, formed a circle round the whole. A very solemn silence prevailed, the sight was truly impressive. Mr. Marsden writes, " I rose up and began the service with singing the Old Hundredth Psalm; and felt my very soul melt within me, when I viewed my congregation, and considered the state that they were in. After reading the service, during which the natives stood up and sat down, at the signal given by the motion of Korokoro's switch which was regulated by the movements of the Euro-peans; it being Christmas-day, I preached from the second chapter of St. Luke's Gospel, and tenth verse, ' Behold, I bring you glad tidings of great joy.' The natives told Ruatara that they could not understand what I said. He replied that they were not to mind that now, for they would understand by-and-by, and that he would explain my meaning as far as he could. When I had done preaching, he informed them what I had been talking about. In this manner he Gospel has been introduced into New Zealand, and I fervently pray that the glory of it may never depart from its inhabitants, till time shall be no more."

A gloom was soon cast over the bright prospect. It pleased God that this promising chief should be removed by death, and with him for some time disappeared the hope of permanent good to the people. A few days before Mr. Marsden left New Zealand, Ruatara was taken suddenly ill. When Mr. Marsden heard of his state he went to visit him, but the superstition of the natives allowed of no interference. His people had placed a fence about him, and a certain number of persons were tatooed to attend upon him. For two or three days he tried in vain to see him. At length, partly by entreaties, and partly by threats, he succeeded, and administered a little food, which his own relatives had studiously kept from him. He was very ill, and apparently not far from death. At this awful moment he appeared not to know what to do. He had a little glimmering of light, and asked Mr. Marsden to pray with him, but the priest was always in attendance night and day, and his influence was in constant exercise to check any better feeling. Poor Ruatara seemed to be at a loss where to repose his afflicted mind. His views of the Gospel were not sufficiently clear to cause him to give up his superstitions, but, at the same time, he willingly listened to the little instruction which was given. As the period of Mr. Marsden's stay was limited, he was obliged to leave him in the midst of his affliction, and four days afterwards he expired.

A soon as Ruatara was dead, the corpse was placed in a sitting posture, according to the native custom, the forehead being encircled with feathers. On the right hand, Rahu, his wife, was on her knees as chief mourner, and on the left, his sister and two or three female relatives. When strangers arrived, the mourners commenced their usual bitter cry, beating their breasts and waving their hands. Hongi was uncle to the deceased, and as he approached, he uncovered the face of his nephew, and stood immediately before him. He appeared to be speaking to the corpse. In his left hand he held the blade of flax leaf, and waving the other he occasionally took hold of the hair of Ruatara, as if eager to snatch him from the king of terrors. Tears streamed down his cheeks as he uttered his lamentable wail. The natives all joined in the crying, but the grief of the relatives was excessive. Rahu was of all others the most inconsolable; and on the following day, while the people were still mourning and cutting themselves, according to their manner, she found an opportunity of putting a period to her own life, by hanging herself at a short distance from the body of her departed husband.

This account of Ruatara is sufficient to indicate

that the New Zealanders were a superior race of savages. Their language shows that they belong to the general family by which the greater number of the South Sea Islands are peopled, and in common with the natives of *Tahiti*, Tonga, and the Sandwich Islands, they were in many points superior to the natives of New Holland. This latter people live entirely by hunting and fishing, and raise no produce of any kind from the soil. They erect no houses, the warm climate of New Holland allowing them to sleep with impunity in the open air; and the utmost protection they seek for in a heavy fall of rain is afforded by a few short strips of bark, which are placed against a pole supported by two upright sticks. The houses of the New Zealanders are constructed with a degree of comfort, affording a sufficient shelter from the inclemency of the weather, and have often furnished a welcome refuge to the English traveller. The New Hollanders have no garment, except occasionally the skin of the opossum and kangaroo, while the mats of the New Zealanders, with which every native used to be clothed, were woven with much labour, and possessed some beauty of texture. Captain Cook mentions the cultivations of the natives as being attended to with much care when he first visited them; and potatoes and other foreign productions of the earth have always been received with much avidity, and turned at once to the best account. The natives say that the first potatoes which they obtained were carefully planted as they had been wont to plant the kumara, and the increase was distributed among their friends far and near, until all were supplied. Mr. Marsden also on his first visit to the country speaks, of Hongi's cultivations with surprise. " He had near his village one field which appeared to me to contain forty acres, all fenced in with rails, and upright stakes tied to them, to keep out the pigs. Much of it was planted with turnips and sweet potatoes, and was in high cultivation. They suffered no weeds to grow, but with wonderful labour and patience rooted up everything likely to injure the growing crop." Their agricultural tools were principally made of wood ; one formed like a spade, another which they called " ko," a stout pointed stake, with a small piece of wood firmly lashed about twelve inches from the point, upon which the foot treads to force it into the ground, in shape like a boy's stilt. This forms a powerful lever with which the ground is turned over with ease. They showed from their earliest intercourse with the English a strong disposition to increase their comforts, and gladly substituted the iron axe and the spade for their own rude implements.

In the eagerness which was shown to receive the first missionaries, it can hardly be supposed that there was much beyond a wish of obtaining a better supply of these treasures, which they saw were possessed in abundance by the foreigners. We can scarcely think that there was a real desire for any change in their religious creed. Even the gratifying

steps taken by Ruatara for the observance of the first
Christian Sabbath, may have been nothing more than
a desire to bring his people to approximate to the
English in an external rite, which his residence in
New South Wales had led him to notice as a part of
the system of civilized man.

CHAPTER II.

1815—1822.

DIFFICULTIES FROM NATIVE CUSTOMS AND SUPERSTITIONS—SLAVES
ALLOWED TO LIVE WITH THE MISSIONARIES—DISPERSION OF
THE NATIVES OVER THE COUNTRY—MARION THE FRENCH NAVI-
GATOR—DESIRE FOR FIREARMS—TEMORENGA'S EXPEDITION TO
TAURANGA—HONGI VISITS ENGLAND—INTENT ON FIGHTING—
CUTS OFF TRIBES AT THE THAMES—CRUELTY TO PRISONERS—
EXPEDITION TO WAIKATO—TROUBLESOME TO THE MISSIONARIES
—CRUELTY OF NATIVES OVERRULED TO THE FURTHERANCE OF
THE GOSPEL.

AFTER the death of Ruatara, the difficulties of the
work began to appear. Satan had obtained a strong
hold upon the people, and led them captive at
his will. They had been trained up in gross superstition, and there did not appear to them any
sufficient reason to abandon it. The New Zealanders
had no fixed religious system properly so called.
Places and persons were made sacred, but there
were no idols or temples of worship, and no priest-
hood as in India, existing as a separate class, and
depending upon their craft for support. Still there
were deities whom they thought it necessary to pro-
pitiate through fear of the evils which might otherwise befal them. There was no idea of a beneficent
Being who might bless and prosper them, but of one
who was austere and revengeful, ever ready to punish
for a violation of the accustomed rites. If a canoe

was upset at sea, it was referred to the anger of the sea god, for some act of the parties who perished.   If their crops of kumara failed, the reason was that some ceremony at the time of planting had been neglected ; and the privation suffered by the loss of the crop made them more careful for the future.   Sickness was generally attributed to witchcraft, practised by a priest of some hostile tribe, or by an unfortunate slave, whose life was sure to be forfeited.   The person of a leading chief was always sacred.   His head, his garments, the ground upon which he sat, the remains of the food he had eaten, were all highly tabooed, and his people carefully avoided them, lest some evil should befal them.

Sometimes incantation was resorted to, for the pur- pose of causing the death of a person against whom there was a hostile feeling, and an instance has been mentioned of a priest trying his power against one of the old missionaries.   The ignorant natives were in a state of alarm, but like the inhabitants of Melita, "they looked when he should have swollen and fallen down dead suddenly ;" but after they had looked a great while, and saw no harm come to him, they changed their minds, and said the New Zealand god had no power over the white man.

But besides the effect of superstition, there was the natural heart, which is enmity against God, and is not disposed to be subject to the law of God.   So long as the New Zealander did not commit an open injury to his fellow, or offer a direct insult, he was at liberty to do that which was right in his own eyes. From early infancy this principle was instilled into them. To be told, therefore, that it was wrong to indulge in their evil propensities, and that God would be angry with them, was a doctrine they could not understand. The god they believed in would rather punish them if they listened to these new ideas. The missionaries in the mean time repeated the simple message of the Gospel, though it seemed to their hearers but an idle tale. Frequently was the question asked by the chiefs, in answer to the recommendations which were placed before them—" Will you give us blankets if we believe ? " There was much excitement attendant upon their favourite pursuits. In war they could indulge the feeling of revenge, which was sweeter to them than their food; besides which it held out the prospect of gain. If they were victorious in battle, they obtained possession of valuable canoes and mats without the labour of making them; while slaves to cultivate their ground would raise them to a dignity which was always enviable.

The missionaries succeeded in gathering around them a few children, and some of the slaves also were allowed to work for them, but it was not from a wish for instruction. The children were fed and received a little clothing, which though not costly, was of great value in their estimation ; and the slaves were conducted by their master to the house of the missionary with a strict injunction that the monthly payment for their labour should be duly given over to him·

The slaves were encouraged to steal whenever they could do so without detection; and frequently were the children decoyed away from the house as soon as they had been provided with comfortable clothing. It was in vain to remonstrate; while those in authority gave encouragement, their inferiors laughed at the idea of evil consequences.

Religious instruction was only listened to for some ulterior object. It did not enter the heart nor produce any fruit. "I converse with the natives," wrote Mr. King, "on religious subjects as opportunity offers, but find it difficult to make any impression on their minds of the evil of sin, or of the love of God in Christ Jesus; but I hope and pray that we may see the Gospel have its proper effect on their hearts and lives. We must wait the Lord's good time, resting on the divine promises to make His word effectual to their salvation."

War had been the glory of the New Zealander from the earliest times. Their traditionary history tells us that they are all of one family, and that the tribes which had become most hostile to each other were still relations by blood. But quarrels arose when they were living in close quarters, and the weakest families were obliged to give place to the stronger, and seek a refuge for themselves in some distant part. The natives of Tauranga in the Bay of Plenty once lived in the Bay of Islands, while all the tribes south of Poverty Bay, now occupying from Hawkes' Bay to Palliser Bay, and various parts of the southern island, were once living in Poverty Bay, and were driven away by superior force. But they carried the natural heart with them; and as they continued to increase, the same evils were perpetuated without any abatement. The tribes becoming thus scattered over the country, did not allow the recollection of former wrongs to be forgotten, and though generations might have passed away, there was still the record handed down from father to son of some old grievance which was to be avenged whenever an opportunity should occur. Before intercourse had begun with the English at the Bay of Islands, the tribes of that part of the country were often worsted by their southern neighbours of the Thames. But the Bay of Islands became a convenient resort for shipping, and a little experience led the natives to see the great superiority of the arms of the civilized man.

In the early part of this century, a French ship under the command of Marion, visited that part of the island, and the natives massacred a portion of her crew, who were at work in the wood procuring timber. The consequence was a fearful retaliation, in which a number of natives were shot from the ship's boats. At a subsequent period, after the massacre of the *Boyd*, boats were sent from some whaling ships in the Bay of Islands, to wreak their vengeance on a tribe supposed to have been concerned in that deed. The natives were thus brought to reflect that if they could only obtain a supply of these implements of war which made the white man so powerful, they would have the means of gaining the ascendancy over their neighbours. They therefore encouraged the ships to visit their shores by treating the crews with civility, and thus by bartering their produce, they became possessed of muskets, which, though at first few in number, enabled them to gain immense advantages over their weaker enemies.

Temorenga, a powerful chief of the Bay of Islands, was thus enabled to retaliate upon a distant tribe an injury which had been done some years before. A niece of his was taken in a Sydney brig from Bream Head, and afterwards landed at Mercury Bay, where she became the slave of a chief named Hukori. She was subsequently killed and eaten by Te Waru, the chief of Tauranga. When Temorenga heard of her fate, he felt bound to revenge her death as soon as he was in a position to do so. About sixteen years elapsed, when at length he mustered a force of six hundred men, with which he proceeded to Tauranga, and landed near the mouth of the harbour. Waru came off in his canoe to know what had brought him. Temorenga replied that he was come to demand satisfaction for his niece who had been killed and eaten. Waru replied, " If that is the object of your expedition, the only satisfaction I shall give you will be to kill and eat you." The two parties met on the following day, when Temorenga directed his men not to fire till he gave the word. He had thirty-five muskets, while Waru depended upon his native weapons. Waru charged with a shower of spears, by which Temorenga had one man wounded. He then directed his people to fire, when twenty of Waru's men fell dead at the first volley, and among them two chiefs. Waru's party was at once thrown into disorder, and fled. Temorenga commanded his men not to pursue the flying enemy. He was satisfied with the sacrifice that had been made, as two chiefs were killed. His allies, however, contended that though Temorenga was satisfied with the death of two chiefs for the murder of his niece, yet that Waru ought to be punished for his insolent language ; and they recommended that the attack should be renewed. Temorenga, however, sent first to know whether Waru was inclined for peace, but was told he was not. The next day they observed that Waru had rallied his forces, and was coming down upon them. They immediately flew to arms, and in a short time made a great slaughter. Many were driven into the sea and perished. Between 300 and 400 were left dead on the field of battle, and 260 were made prisoners. Waru was now completely conquered, and fled to the woods. One day he was wandering alone at no great distance from Temorenga's people, when he saw a man approaching, and watching his opportunity, he sprang suddenly upon him, and had him in his power. " Who are you ? " said Waru. The man giving an evasive answer, Waru continued—" But I want to know your name. I am not going to kill you. I am Te Waru, and I wish to have peace." His captive then told him that he was Te Whareumu, one of the leading

chiefs of Temorenga's party. Waru then gave him
a handsome mat he was wearing, and asked to be conducted to Temorenga. . As Te Whareumu approached
the camp, apparently leading a captive, there was a
great outcry ; and when it was known that his companion was Te Waru, many were ready to fall upon
him. But Whareumu motioned them to keep at a
distance, and related the incident of his own capture
by Te Waru. This led to immediate peace. Te Waru
said he had no idea that the muskets would have
produced such an effect. He asked Temorenga if he
could give him any information about his wife and
children. Temorenga told him they were in the camp,
and should be delivered up to him. Waru was much
distressed at the death of his father, who had fallen,
and requested Temorenga to make him some compensation for his loss. This he did by giving him a
musket, with which he was well satisfied, and he
then took his departure with his wife and children.
After this the victors remained three days on the
field of battle, feeding upon the slain, and then
sailed with their prisoners and Waru's canoes to the
Bay of Islands.

This practice of cannibalism appears to have been
universal, but it was not generally practised between
tribes nearly connected, because the insult was ac-
counted so great that reconciliation afterwards would
be extremely difficult. " I have met with no family,"
writes Mr. Marsden, " but some branches of it had
been killed in battle and afterwards eaten. If any

chief falls into the hands of a tribe which he has op-
pressed and injured, by the chance of war, they are
sure to roast and eat him; and after devouring his
flesh, they will preserve his bones in the family as a
memento of his fate, and convert them into fish-hooks,
whistles, and ornaments. The custom of eating their
enemies is universal. The origin of it is now too
remote to be traced. The natives generally speak of
it with horror and disgust, yet they expect that this
will be their own fate in the end, as it has been with
their forefathers and friends. I represented to them
how much their national character suffered in the
opinion of all civilised nations from this horrid
custom. Many regretted that it should be the practice of their country, and said that when they knew
better they would leave it off. If the head of a tribe
is killed and eaten, the survivors consider it the
greatest disgrace that can befal them ; and in their
turn they seize the first opportunity to retaliate."

The success of Temorenga's expedition only stimulated the other tribes to war. Hongi was the chief
of the greatest enterprise, and wishing to obtain the
ascendancy, and particularly to make himself superior
to Temorenga, he determined to visit England, in hope
of obtaining muskets and powder. He soon had an
opportunity of doing this, in company with Mr.
Kendal, in the year 1820 ; but when he found that
there was no disposition on the part of Christian
people in England to encourage his ambitious views,
and that they recommended him to give up fighting,

and cultivate the arts of peace, he began to conceal his object. When he obtained muskets he carefully put them away, and a large portion of the many presents which he received he sold in exchange for fire-arms, which he conceived to be of greater value. In this way he accumulated a large supply, but did not succeed to the full extent of his wishes. From the members of the Church Missionary Society he had received the utmost kindness and attention, but they opposed him in his favourite object, and he took up the idea that the missionaries had used their influence to thwart him. When he went back, therefore, to New Zealand, there was a marked alteration in his manner towards them. The Committee states—" The return of Hongi wholly changed the face of things. That he should carry back with him a mind exasperated against the Society, will occasion much surprise to those who witnessed the pains taken to gratify him. But that he did return in this temper, after all the kindness shown to him, has been painfully felt by the missionaries who remained in the Bay of Islands during his absence." The manner in which he evinced his altered temper was very trying. He kept aloof for several days from the settlement at Kerikeri. The native sawyers, who had before worked quietly and diligently, caught his spirit and struck work, insisting on being paid either in the favourite articles of powder and fire-arms, or in money with which they might secure them from the whalers. With Hongi's example before them, many of the inferior chiefs began to treat the missionaries with contempt. They entered their houses when they pleased, demanding food, and stole whatever they could lay their hands on, breaking down the garden fences, and endeavouring to annoy them in every way. They seemed, in short, ripe for any mischief, and there was a continual apprehension that they would seize upon all that was within their reach; but the hand of God was over his servants for their protection.

Hongi's mind was now full of dark designs. When he arrived at Port Jackson on his way from England, he had been hospitably entertained by his old friend the Rev. Samuel Marsden, at Paramatta. He found there four chiefs from the river Thames, who had gone so far, hoping to get to England as Hongi had done. Mr. Marsden took measures for preventing them from prosecuting their voyage, and Hongi, doubtless with a view to his own interests, strongly dissuaded them from it, urging the injurious effects of the climate upon himself and his companion. He was indeed now meditating a formidable expedition against the districts with which these very chiefs were connected. While they were living together under the same roof, and eating at one common table, he told one of them, Hinaki, the chief of a tribe living at Mokai on the Tamaki, the site of the present village of Panmure, to hasten back and prepare his people for war, for that he should soon visit him. The expedition which he fitted out in the Bay of Islands was very formidable. There were at least fifty canoes, and two thousand men, a great number of muskets, and an abundance of ammunition. They intended to sweep the country before them with the besom of destruction. It was their determination to destroy men, women, and children, the party against whom they were going not being able to stand in their own defence for want of the same weapons.

These were dark days for the little band of missionaries who were come to lead them to a better way. In vain did they tell them it was an evil course they were then pursuing. They had power in their own hands, and they felt that they could exercise their savage propensities without control ; and being under the influence of the evil one, they willingly did his bidding. Their teachers could only look forward with the eye of faith to the time when all the obstacles now before them being removed, the promise should be fulfilled, that God's word should not return to him void. But the time appointed was long. Many years of anxious toil were to be passed. The bread was to be cast upon the waters, but it was not to be found until after many days.

The results of Hongi's expedition were fearful. Powerful tribes on both sides of the Thames were cut off, and for many years the whole country was deserted. The tribes attacked generally outnumbered their assailants, and rushed boldly to the conflict, being confident of victory ; while their enemies, firing upon them from a distance, soon threw them into confusion, and had them at once in their power.

Many particulars of the events which occurred upon the return of this expedition were recorded at the time. They give a melancholy picture of the extreme degradation and cruelty to which human nature may be reduced when left to itself. The details are horribly disgusting, but it seems necessary to repeat some of them, because at this distance of time some have been disposed to think that the New Zealanders were never the fierce and savage race they have been represented to be; and it was gravely asserted in an article of the *Quarterly Review*, about the year 1820, that to say that cannibalism was practised by this people was an absurdity. It is desirable, also, that these descriptions should be given, in order that the blessings communicated by the Gospel may be the more apparent, and God's name be magnified in the accomplishment of His own work.

On the 19th of December, 1821, three of the war canoes belonging to this expedition returned from the Thames, and arrived at Kerikeri. They had upwards of a hundred prisoners with them, who might generally be distinguished by their sorrowful countenances. Some of them were weeping bitterly; one woman in particular, before whom they had with savage cruelty placed the head of her brother, stuck upon a pole. She sat upon the ground before it, the tears streaming down her cheeks. These canoes brought the news of the death of Tete, son-in-law to Hongi, who was slain in fight. He was one of the most civilised and best behaved of the natives. His

brother Pu, a fine young man, was also among the
slain. This created great grief in the family. Tete's
wife, and Matuka his brother, were watched to prevent
them from putting an end to their lives. Pu's wife
hung herself on hearing the news, and Hongi's wife
killed a slave, which was a customary act on such
occasions.

The next day Hongi and his people arrived with
the dead bodies of Tete and Pu. Messrs. Francis Hall
and Kemp went to see the ceremony of their landing,
but very sorry were they that their curiosity had led
them to witness such a scene of horror. A small
canoe with the dead bodies first approached the shore.
The war canoes, about forty in number, lay at a short
distance. Soon after, a party of young men landed to
perform the war dance and "pihe," a song over the
bodies of the slain. They yelled and jumped, brandishing their weapons, and threw up human heads in
the air in a shocking manner; but this was only a
prelude to the horrid work which was about to
follow. An awful pause ensued. At length the
canoes moved slowly and touched the shore, when
the widow of Tete and other women rushed down
upon the beach in a frenzy of rage, and beat in pieces
the carved work at the head of the canoes with poles.
They proceeded to pull out three prisoners into the
water and beat them to death. The frantic widow
then went to another canoe and killed a female
prisoner.

The missionaries retired from the distressing scene,

as no interference of theirs could avail ; and they were told that after they went away Hongi killed five more with his own hand. In the whole nine persons were murdered that evening, and were afterwards eaten. The prisoners were very numerous, men, women, and children, but chiefly the latter. They were said to amount to about two thousand, and were distributed chiefly among the tribes of the Bay of Islands. The people were now more bloodthirsty than ever, and talked of going again soon, meaning to devastate the whole island. In this expedition they had done all the mischief they had threatened. Poor Hinaki, the chief to whom Hongi had given warning a short time before, was killed and eaten.

The next day Hongi was busily employed in making an inclosure with pieces of canoe, decorated with feathers and carved work, in which to deposit the bodies of the two brothers Tete and Pu. Part of the remains of the people killed the day before were roasting at the fire at a little distance, and some human flesh, ready cooked, lay in baskets on the ground. Hongi had the audacity to ask Mr. Kemp to eat some, and said it was better than pork. A part of one of the poor women killed the day before by the natives was cooked on the side of the hill at the back of Mr. Kemp's house. The head they cut off and rolled down the hill, and several of them amused themselves with throwing large stones at it, until they had dashed it to pieces. Among the slaves who were taken to Waimate on the preceding day, one of them, a woman, becoming tired or lame, could not keep up with the rest, and was therefore killed.

A few days later it was reported that Hongi and his people had killed more of the prisoners, making the number eighteen who had been murdered in cold blood since their return. Several heads were stuck upon poles near the mission dwellings, and the tattooed skin of a man's thigh was nailed to a board to dry, in order to be made into the covering of a cartridge-box.

It did not occur to this people that their relatives had fallen in fair fight, or rather that they had brought upon themselves a well-merited death by going to attack those who, by comparison, were defenceless, and perhaps, too, had given no sufficient cause for hostilities. Neither did they bear in mind how much larger a number of the enemy had fallen than the few over whom they were grieving. They had lost their nearest relatives, and they knew of no other way of moderating their grief for this than by the indulgence of brutal revenge.

One of the missionaries writes :—" These scenes of cruelty are very distressing to our feelings, and more than we could bear, were it not for the promises of God's word. We need great faith to enable us to stand our ground. At present we can do but little in forwarding the spiritual objects of the Society. The evil disposition of the natives seems to be at its height. I believe that they have a greater thirst for blood than ever; and until the Lord, by

His grace, changes their hearts, they will remain the same."

Hongi, who, when in England, left a favourable impression behind him as a man of mild and pleasing manners, was now becoming more and more inured to acts of savage barbarity, and all his family were following his example. His eldest daughter, the widow of Tete, shot herself through the fleshy part of the arm with two balls. She had intended to destroy herself, but in the agitation of pulling the trigger with her toe, she missed her aim. Another poor slave, a girl about ten years of age, was killed. The brother of Tete shot her with a pistol, and only wounded her, when one of Hongi's children knocked her on the head. The circumstance was mentioned to Mr. Hall when he went to dress the wounds of Tete's widow. He inquired if it was so, when they said with a laugh that they were hungry. Such scenes had never before taken place since the mission was established.

In less than two months, another very large armament was assembled to revenge the deaths of Tete and Pu upon the natives of Waikato, who had been in alliance with those of the Thames. In this expedition similar scenes were enacted to those which have been already related. The destruction of life was great, and many slaves were taken. On their return there was a melancholy confusion; wives crying after their deceased husbands, the prisoners bemoaning their cruel bondage, while others were rejoicing at the safe arrival of their relatives and friends. Hongi was in high spirits ; he said that at Matakitaki, on the banks of the Waikato, his party had killed fifteen hundred persons.

The natives now thirsted still more for blood. It was not sufficient for them that they had taken ample vengeance for past wrongs. The causes for a continuance of warfare were multiplied, so long as any chiefs of note might fall in their often repeated attacks. The assurance of easy victory led them forth from year to year, until every part of the island had been in like manner visited.

During all this period the native mind was in the worst possible state for the admission of the salutary influence of Christian instruction. They were the willing slaves of Satan, and the more they gave themselves up to his power, the stronger was the influence which he exercised over them. This could hardly be called the seed time of the Gospel, because there was no disposition to hear anything on the subject. The people were bent upon deeds of blood ; and it was unwelcome to them to be reminded that their whole course was wrong. The missionaries being treated with contempt by the chiefs, those of inferior rank watched every opportunity for taking advantage. Petty thefts were of frequent occurrence, and it was of no avail to seek for redress from the chiefs, where all were under a common influence. Mr. Hall writes :—" A chief came into the yard to-day, and took our iron pot and was going away with it. I happened to see him, and took it from him. He said he did it because Hongi's daughter, who had lived with us a long time, and had been treated with great kindness, and had left of her own accord, was not pleased because we had taken another woman in her room." These annoyances were particularly felt when the tribes were assembling from a distance preparatory to going to fight.* They then thought they could do any act with impunity, and broke down fences to supply their fires, and laid hands upon whatever might come in their way. It was therefore a relief to see the canoes sailing away, though going after deeds of cruelty, but then their return was looked forward to with horror. The relation of fresh acts of violence was the all exciting subject to those who had been to fight, and to those who had remained at home, while painful proofs were given of the rapid diminution of the people whom the missionaries came to benefit. It was only the year before Hongi's return from England that **Mr.**

---

* Mr. King used to tell an amusing story of an incident which took place at Rangihoua. Hongi's canoes were lying on the beach ready for departure to the south, when Titore came up to Mr. King and asked for payment for a mat which had been sold sometime before. " I gave an axe for that mat," said Mr. King, " to the person who brought it to me." "But," said Titore, "the mat did not belong to him but to me, and if you do not pay me, I will have your hat." The threat was repeated more than once, and Mr. King thought his hat was in danger, so he went back to the house and put on one which was very shabby, and again placing himself in Titore's way, it was soon snatched off his head to the satisfaction of both.

Marsden had paid his third visit to New Zealand. With untiring energy he had travelled on this occasion in various parts of the country for the period of nine months, and most of the time was spent in the neighbourhood of the Thames and Kaipara. Those districts were then well peopled. The natives everywhere received this good man with hospitality, listened attentively to his advice, and there seemed to be among them a brighter opening for missionary effort than in the Bay of Islands. But now these tribes had been cut off and scattered, and like the bear robbed of its whelps, they were ready to retaliate upon any persons from the north, whether natives or Europeans, the latter being supposed to have supplied their enemies with the means of overwhelming them. The allies of the Bay of Islanders living as far south as Bream Bay, were obliged to leave their homes and seek refuge farther north, because they felt that they had too much reason to fear a visit of retaliation from their exasperated enemies.

It may seem remarkable that God should have permitted events to take this course just at the time when he had put it into the hearts of his servants to enter upon their work, and that the benevolent plans of Mr. Marsden should thus for a time be thwarted. But we cannot understand his purposes. We only know that all is directed by unerring wisdom.

But while we mourn over these cruelties, and pity the people who were the subjects of them, we are called upon to admire the wisdom of God in making those events which seemed to be most adverse, all conspire to bring about the rescue of the New Zealanders from under the bondage of Satan. Worldly policy would not have thought of permitting the sword of persecution to be unsheathed against the infant church, immediately after the commission given to the Apostles to go and preach the gospel to every creature. But this was the means used by God for sending his servants into distant regions, who would not otherwise have been disposed to enter vigorously upon their work. And then the discipline of persecution was continued, as being best suited to promote the healthy growth of that tree which was to overshadow the whole earth. So too in New Zealand the little band of Christian teachers was to be confined to the Bay of Islands, and they were to be restrained by circumstances within very small limits, and every desire to extend their efforts was to be repressed until such instruments as God would employ had grown up. The very opposite to the course adopted towards the early Church of Christ was to be used. The missionaries were not to go to the distant natives, but the distant natives were to be brought to them. This was effected by bringing together a great body of unhappy slaves from all parts of the country, to that spot from which the missionaries were not permitted to move. It was an act which sprung from the worst propensities of sinful men, but like the slave trade on the western

coast of Africa, it was to be overruled to the furtherance of the gospel. This work of preparation however was to be very gradual. The chiefs and their
sons were elated with pride, but the abject slaves
just torn from their friends, and from all former
associations, were found to be more open to impression.
Several of them both male and female were allowed
to live in the mission families as servants, and they
appreciated the kindness and commiseration they
met with there, which was so different from the
severity of their masters. The effect of this will
be seen hereafter when the seed sown began to
vegetate.

In the meantime, as we have been led to notice
the horrible cruelties which used to be practised by
the New Zealanders in every war which they undertook, we may anticipate a remark upon their manner
in later years, when a conflict no less fierce and determined was carried on with the English government, but modified in its character by the benign
influence of Christianity. In the year 1845, when an
attack was made upon Heke's fortified village at
Mawhe by a detachment of English troops, thirteen
of our soldiers fell before the enemies' fort, and the
commander of the troops, considering that the risk of
recovering the bodies was too great to warrant the
attempt, left them in the hands of the natives. The
next morning Heke directed his people to dig a large
grave, and sent for the clergyman from Waimate to

go and bury them. On a subsequent occasion at Whanganui, one of our soldiers fell and was carried off by the natives. They deliberated as to what was to be done, and gave the poor man Christian burial, a Christian native reading over his grave the church service in their own language.

CHAPTER III.

1823, 1824.

ARRIVAL OF THE REV. H. WILLIAMS—FIRST IMPRESSIONS—WRECK
OF THE "BRAMPTON"—SETTLEMENT AT PAIHIA—TROUBLESOME
CONDUCT OF TOHITAPU—INDICATIONS OF CHANGE FOR THE
BETTER—DEATHS OF WHATU AND OF CHRISTIAN RANGI.

THE Rev. S. Marsden continued to watch over the
Mission with a paternal interest, and no personal
sacrifice was thought too great in promoting this
cherished undertaking. He accompanied the first
missionaries in the year 1814, and again in 1819 and
1820 paid two more visits, anxiously watching the
troubled state of the country, which had rendered
the cheering prospects of his first acquaintance with
the New Zealanders, dark and gloomy. On the
arrival of the Rev. Henry Williams in New South
Wales, Mr. Marsden determined to undertake another
voyage in company with him, desiring to make some
important changes in the arrangements of the Mission.
They set sail therefore on the 21st of July, 1823, on
board the *Brampton*, and anchored in the Bay of
Islands on the 2nd of August. It may be worth
while to record the first impressions produced by the
novel scenes as they appeared to those who had heard
of them only on the report of others. So great a

change has subsequently come over the country that nothing can again occur bearing any resemblance to the past. It was the Sabbath day when the ship came to an anchor, and the missionary party retired to Mr. Marsden's cabin to partake of the Lord's Supper. "They were precious moments," writes Mrs. Williams, "our feelings seemed wound up to the highest pitch. Just as the service was about to commence, a canoe full of natives was seen through the portholes, hailing the ship, and endeavouring to get alongside. The sight affected us all, and moved our hearts in prayer, for that time speedily to come, when these strangers should come in to partake. We anchored about six o'clock, half-way between Rangihoua and Kerikeri, when we sat down to dinner, after which, though dark, some natives came on board, from whom Mr. Marsden learnt that most of the chiefs were gone to East Cape to fight. Early the next morning Mr. Marsden was on deck rubbing noses with some of his old friends, and while I was dressing Mr. Marsden put into our cabin a pretty little naked New Zealand boy, about two years old, to the no small astonishment of our children. The little fellow did not relish our company, for he set up a great cry, so we let him go out to his father and mother, to whom I was shortly introduced, and to many others, all in their native dress. As they squatted down on the deck, they reminded me of a print in Captain Cook's voyages of the natives of Nootka Sound, except that their mats were mostly fringed, and rough all over. The animation and energetic expression of these noble natives cannot be described. We were surrounded by chiefs as we sat at breakfast, all earnestly begging to have missionaries. I could have gone with all or any of them. Both my husband and myself felt a desire to satisfy the wishes of three disconsolate-looking chiefs from the river Thames, had Mr. Marsden thought it prudent. They were the relatives of Hinaki, a chief of the Thames, who was killed and eaten by Hongi. After a wearying day I retired to rest to prepare for our removal to Kerikeri ; but the tall and muscular forms of the New Zealanders flitted before me, whenever I endeavoured to close my eyes. I felt a wish to convey every look and every conversation to our absent friends, and several times in the course of the day I said to Mr. Marsden, " I wish our English friends could peep in upon us." Indeed it seemed worth all we had undertaken, to behold with our own eyes the scenes of this day. I felt a fervent thankfulness that we and our little ones had been brought to this scene of labour. We are now in the way, and the Lord of the harvest can give us employment, and teach us how to work, and in his own good time, if not in our day, cause the seed to spring up. At present this noble though cannibal race of men are fast bound in the chains of Satan, and what can be a nobler ambition than to enlist them beneath the banner of the King of kings, and in his strength to rescue them from their subtle foe ! Often had I, in

THE FALLS, KERI-KERI.

the course of the day, pictured in idea our ancestors at the time of the Roman invasion, and many a noble Caractacus might we fancy amidst these warlike yet kingly-looking savages. The following morning the natives again flocked around us. Amongst the first was Taui, who was very angry when he found that Waitangi was chosen for our settlement in preference to his place. I could hear him from our cabin, stamping and talking with great vehemence. He was however satisfied by Mr. Marsden telling him that he would send another missionary to live with him, and he set to work immediately to collect raupo to build him a house.

" On our arrival at Kerikeri, our friends told us we were come at a happy time, for that New Zealand is a paradise when the chiefs and fighting men are absent. The missionaries can look out of their high paled yards and gardens in perfect quiet, and are free from angry visits of parties of naked savages. I heard many dismaying accounts of the past ferocious conduct of the natives, most of which were confirmed by Mr. Kemp's experience, but from none of them, taking all circumstances into consideration, did I gather any cause for personal dread. There is only the greater need of missionary labours and earnest prayer for the outpouring of the Holy Spirit. In God's own time the little leaven will spread, and the surrounding mass may even now be in a state of preparation."

In the meantime Mr. Williams had been occupied

in making preparation for the reception of his family
at Paihia, and Mr. Marsden had taken leave, intending to return in the *Brampton* to New South Wales.
The day following was fixed for their departure from
Kerikeri, when a new cause for excitement occurred.
The household was engaged at family prayers, when
some natives with unusual earnestness, which could
not be repressed, spoke to Mrs. Butler through the
back window, which they persisted in opening,
regardless of what was going on within; and upon
some words being spoken to her, she hastened out of
the room. Scarcely had they risen, when Tom, one
of the boat's crew, pushed forward, and with up-
lifted hands, and native vehemence and energy of
action, seemed determined that he would be understood. Before there was time for further inquiry,
one of the domestic natives exclaimed, "The ship is
broken to pieces, and Mr. Marsden is come back
again!"

It was too true. The *Brampton* was lying upon a
reef of rocks, in the middle of the Bay of Islands, to
which she has given her name. This catastrophe
served to show that there had been some impression
produced upon the natives since the residence of missionaries among them. "We were all," says Mr.
Marsden, "both on shore and in the vessel, as well as
our property, completely in their power. They could
have taken our lives at any moment, and it cannot be
doubted they would have done so if the missionaries
had not been among them, and gained their confidence

and good will." The captain subsequently stated that he had got all his stores landed on the island of Moturoa, and that the chiefs had behaved well; that on one occasion between five and six hundred men came around the ship, and appeared as if they intended to be troublesome, but a leading chief desired the captain to be still and not interfere, and in a speech of more than an hour long he pointed out the fatal consequences of committing any act of plunder or violence; and then, taking the captain's sword, he told them he would cut down the first man who should attempt to come on board. By his firmness order and quiet were restored, and the captain removed from the wreck everything of importance.

The necessary preparations being made at Paihia, Mrs. Williams gives an account of her first landing there:—"The beach was crowded with natives, who drew me up while sitting in the boat, with great apparent glee, exclaiming, 'Te wahine,' 'the wife,' and holding out their hands, saying, 'Tena ra ko koe,' and, 'Homai mai te ringaringa,' 'How do you do; give me your hand.' I cannot describe my feelings; I trembled and cried, but joy was the predominant feeling. The cultivated land, on which was springing up our crops of oats and barley, extended close down to the fine flat beach, bounded on either side by a projecting point of rock, overhung by clumps of the noble pohutukawa tree. Within an inclosure of paling stood our raupo hut, which

had, except in shape, the appearance of a bee-hive.
By the side stood the store, and scattered about were
the cart, timber carriage, goats, fowls, and horse, and
near the beach were the saw-pits. Behind was a
large garden, already partially green with numerous
rows of peas and beans. The entrance to the house
was dark, and within were two rooms with no floors,
and boards nailed up where sash lights are to be
placed. The carpenter and my husband laid me a
boarded floor in the bedroom before night, and I
never reposed more comfortably." On Sunday Mr.
Williams opened another raupo hut for a chapel.
The day was fine. The bell was rung for a quarter
of an hour, and sounded sweetly as the congregation walked along the beach. The natives carried
the chairs and planks for benches. The Union Jack
was hoisted in front of the settlement as a signal to
the natives that it was the sacred day. The whole
scene was delightful."

The events which pass at a missionary station,
while yet the people are not under the influence
of higher principles than they have received from
their forefathers, must continually vary. There
will be a frequent alternation of circumstances to
discourage and to cheer, the former being more numerous than the latter. And in order to draw a
balance between the two, there must of necessity be
a large amount of faith and Christian courage to make
up the deficiency. The Rev. Henry Williams writes
to the Secretaries of the Church Missionary Society

at this period:—" When I consider the natives, their dignified appearance, their pertinent questions and remarks, their obliging disposition, with the high sense of honour which they possess, I cannot but view them as a most interesting people, whom our Almighty Father will ere long adopt for His own. They are desirous to have missionaries, and they will occasionally listen to instruction. Men, women, and children have the greatest confidence in us, and there are many who wish to leave their little ones with us, but for want of means of support we cannot receive them at present. They distinguish the Sabbath by abstaining from work, and wearing their English clothes. Our settlement on that day is quiet, and the head chief, with his wife and many others, generally attend our services. There are certainly a few trying circumstances, which for the time are painful, but by letting matters rest, the evil will often remedy itself. We were never more comfortable in our lives, nay, I will say, happy; and nothing interrupts our happiness but the knowledge of our own unworthiness."

An animated description of some of these trying circumstances is given by Mrs. Williams in a private letter:—" Freed from wars and rumours of wars, which have distracted our ears and perplexed our thoughts, and put an entire stop to all business, we are enjoying a quiet afternoon. I feel exactly as when relieved by calm weather after a succession of storms at sea. I have long been wishing to give you some home scenes now that the novelty of our situation has begun to wear off. The continual excitement of Mr. Marsden's visit has subsided, and we have acquired some experience of the troubles and numerous petty discouragements of the missionary life. It is now that the steady light and firm support of missionary zeal requires to be kept alive by constant supplies from the source of grace and light. We feel that the strength that is in Christ Jesus can alone give us patience, firmness, hope, and never-dying faith in the accomplishment of all the promises. But to give you a week's history.— On Sunday we had a fine day. At our morning service no natives were present except those of our own household. After service the native girls, who have the London fashion of keeping the Sabbath, went, some with and some without leave, off to their friends, so that I had not a moment to sit down and read till I had cleared the tea-things away, washed the children, and all except our eldest boy were asleep, and it was time for our evening service. After dinner, Mr. Williams went out as usual to visit the natives of a neighbouring village, and had some interesting conversation with them. Our evening service was closed, as usual, with the hymn for Sunday evening, when we always think of our Hampstead friends. This is a season I always much enjoy, for I never through the week sit still so long together. Monday morning Riu was unusually long in preparing to wash the clothes. Just as she was beginning her work at her old spot in the yard, a boat from one of the ships came to look for men, eleven of their crew having left them. This event unsettled our whole establishment. The moment a boat arrives, down scamper all the natives, servants, men, boys, and girls, to the beach. If there is anything to be seen, or anything extraordinary occurs in New Zealand, the mistress must do the work while the servants gaze abroad. She must not scold them, for if they are rangatiras, they will run away in a pet, and tell her she has too much of the mouth. Having been forewarned of this, I wait and work away till they choose to come back, which they generally do at meal times. After dinner a most troublesome chief, named Tohitapu, who lives about a mile from us, put us all in confusion. The carpenter, who was at work at the bench, saw him coming, and called to some one to fasten the gate. Instead of knocking in the usual manner for admittance, Tohi sprang over the fence. The carpenter told him he was a bad man for coming in like a thief, and not like a gentleman. He immediately began to stamp and caper about like a madman, attracting all around by his vociferous gabble, and flourishing his "meri" (green stone weapon), which every chief carries concealed under his mat, and then, brandishing his spear, he would spring like a cat, and point it at the carpenter, apparently in earnest. Mr. Williams, upon joining them, told him his conduct was very bad, and refused to shake hands with him. The savage, for so in truth he now appeared, stripped for fighting, keeping on only a plain mat, similar to those worn by the girls. Mr. Williams and the carpenter beheld his capers with great appearance of sang froid. At length they left him, and he sat down to take breath, and upon their going to the beach he went out. Engaged with the children indoors, I did not hear all that passed; you will therefore have only parts of the scene. When Mr. Williams returned he saw some mats, apparently thrown down in haste, which he imagined to belong to Tohitapu, and putting them outside, shut the door, and went to the back of the house. Shortly after the furious man returned from the beach, and, snatching up a long pole, made a stroke at the door, but it not yielding to his violence, he sprang over the fence, resumed all his wild antics, and when Mr. Williams appeared, he crouched and aimed his spear at him. Mr. Williams advanced towards him, not heeding his threats, but though Tohi trembled with rage, he did not throw the spear. He said he had hurt his foot in jumping over the fence, and demanded payment for it, and said a great deal more, which we did not understand. Mr. Williams said it was well for him to hurt his foot, when he came in that manner, and that he should have no payment. He then walked towards the stove, and having snatched up an old iron pot in which pitch had been boiled, was springing towards the fence, but, retarded by his unwieldy burden, was making for the door, when Mr. Williams darted upon him, snatched the pot out of his hands, and set his own back against the door to stop his retreat. He then called to some one to take away the pot, which Tohi made several attempts to seize, at the same time brandishing his spear over Mr. Williams's head with furious gestures, while the latter, folding his arms with a look of determined and cool opposition, resisted his attack upon the contested iron pot, occasionally exclaiming, " Kati emara, heoi ano," " Gently, sir, that is enough." As I looked through the window with no little feeling of trepidation, the scene reminded me of a man attacked by a furious bull, who steadily eyes the monster, and keeps him at bay. The blacksmith now came forward, and shoved his shoulder against Tohi, who seemed to relax a little, though he still flourished about in a way which I can scarcely describe. The agility of this huge man astonished me. He ran to and fro with his spear in his hand, something like a boy playing at cricket, except that the New Zealander dances sideways, slapping his sides, and stamping with a measured pace and horrid gestures, every now and then squatting down and panting, as if trying to excite his own rage to the utmost before he made a fatal spring. Tohi continued to demand his payment, and said he should stay here to-day and to-morrow and five days more, and make a great fight, and to-morrow ten and ten and ten men, holding up his fingers as he spoke, would come and set fire to the house. During prayers he was more quiet, and seated himself at the fire, at the back of the house. His wife and some natives who came with him were looking in at the window, and one or two chiefs sat

in the room. When prayers were over, he came to
the window, and, without any ceremony, put his leg
in, pointing to his foot, and demanded payment for the
blood which was spilt. Mr. Williams told him to go
away, and come again to-morrow like a gentleman,
and knock at the gate as Te Koki did, and then he
would say, "How do you do, Mr. Tohitapu," and
invite him to breakfast with us. He answered his
foot was so bad he could not walk, repeated his intention of staying here many days, and burning the
house; and after talking some time, again worked
himself into a terrific passion, and stripped for fighting.
It was now about eleven o'clock at night. Tohi had
thrown off his garments, and by the imperfect light
looked like some wild animal, running to and fro
in furious rage. I sat down to attempt to write. Our
friends looking in at the window, one and another
called to me, "Mother, to-morrow you see a great fire
in the house. Oh yes, children dead, all dead, a great
fight, a great many men, plenty of muskets." Mr.
Williams now came in, and desired me to go to bed,
and left Tom with strict orders to keep watch, and
give the alarm immediately in case of any outrage
being committed. The friendly chiefs wrapped themselves in their shaggy mats, and went to sleep upon
the ground, while we were preparing for rest. Tohitapu, who is a great priest, now began to chant a
horrible ditty, which the carpenter told us was for the
purpose of bewitching us. This poor victim of superstition, the slave of Satan, imagined he could by these

means secure our death. The natives said he had "karakiad" us, a term they apply to our religious worship, and said he had killed a man on board the *Active* schooner in this way. We were awakened early in the morning by the noise of Tohi and others who were continually arriving, until our premises were surrounded. At breakfast I made some tea for several of our friends, and having the curiosity to see how he would act upon it, we sent a pint pot full to him outside the gate, where he was sitting on the ground in sullen majesty, surrounded by a number of his followers. We saw him through the paling drink his tea, and I hoped it might have proved a quieting draught, but before long he was again prancing about inside the yard, with many of his followers, all hideous figures, armed with spears and hatchets, and some few with muskets. They looked more formidable to me, as I caught occasionally a glimpse, feeling that my husband was in the midst of them. Our native girls were all out, and I had to remain close prisoner with my children, the windows being blocked up the whole day by ranges of native heads looking in. The poor children began to pine for air and liberty, and at about five o'clock Mr. Williams came to the window and said that things were more tranquil now, and the natives dispersing. I then put out the children through the window, but scarcely had the feet of our little girl touched the ground, when a sudden noise was heard of loud strokes, apparently against the store, and it seemed as if they were making a breach through the wooden walls for the purpose of forcing an entrance. Mr. Williams put back the children head foremost through the window, and ran to the spot. The noise and clamour now became very great. A chief brought our little boy in his arms, screaming and looking pale. I asked where he was hurt. The poor child exclaimed, " No, mamma, I am not hurt, but they are going to kill papa. We shall be all burnt, and they will kill poor papa ; I saw the men, I saw the guns." As I sat in the centre of the bedroom, the infant at the breast, and the three others clinging around me, I saw, through the little back window, the mob rushing past, and a man pointing his gun at the house, and immediately Mr. Williams stepped in between. My feelings were now excited to the utmost, yet I felt an elevation of soul it is worth much suffering to possess, even for a few moments. Oh that we did not so soon drop down to earth again ! The dear children, sobbing and crying, fell on their knees, and repeated after me a prayer prompted by what was passing. The noise continued. They repeatedly shook our slight walls, but the house remained unbroken, and the children grew more calm. The younger ones soon began to be troublesome, trying to get to the windows to look out. The women outside kept coming to the window, exclaiming, " E mata tena ra ko koe ?" " Mother, how do you do !" Po at length put up her good-natured face, telling me in her own language that there would be no more fight to-day, and that all the men were gone away, and that she had been making a great fight for us, for women fight in New Zealand. I gladly unbolted the door for my husband to enter. He told me all was over, and that this second disturbance was quite distinct from the first. Tohitapu had remained quiet during the whole affray, and was rather inclined to take our part. In compliance with the request of the friendly chiefs, the iron pot had been given to him, with which he had departed. It seems that in the course of the day, the son of one of the chiefs who came as our friend had stolen a blanket from the carpenter's window. Some of our people charged him with it unknown to us, and this second disturbance was made by him because he was annoyed at the exposure of his conduct."

It will be allowed that such trials as those here described were not of a trifling character ; moreover they were of very frequent occurrence, while there was but little encouragement to place in the other scale ; and yet the missionaries were enabled to regard them without much concern, as a part of that which was to be endured for the accomplishment of a great object. Troublesome visitors were to be expected occasionally, and a good deal of patience and prudence was required at these times, But notwithstanding all uncomfortable circumstances, they were able to lie down in peace every night without fear of molestation, the windows not secured, and in a raupo hut, which would burn to the ground in less than ten minutes.

During this period the natives continued as indifferent as ever to the instructions which were pressed upon them. They did not regard the white man and the New Zealander as having anything in common. They had their own traditions about the origin of the world. Their language, their customs, and their gods were different, and their superstitions led them to believe that it would be fatal for them to neglect any of those rites which had been handed down to them, and exchange them for those of a foreign race. They were dead in sin, and it was only the power of God which could give them life. Hence therefore, when a chief was asked why the people did not attend when they knew the white man was coming, he would reply that they did not care about such things; all they thought of was eating and fighting; he had called his people, but they would not come. When told that should they die in their present state, they must for ever be banished to the place of darkness and misery, they were unconcerned about such tidings; and as to the work of redemption, they said they could not understand it. The dominion of Satan was never more visible. If the time had not arrived for this people to receive the Gospel message, certainly the time was come for the servants of the Lord to pour out their prayers to him in humble supplication to remove the veil from the eyes and hearts of this people.

The greatest desire of the natives was to possess muskets and powder, and in order to procure these they laboured hard to grow potatoes for the whaling vessels, where the supply of these commodities was to be had. Their ambition was that the whole tribe should be well equipped for their wars, which now engrossed their whole attention. And yet there was encouragement for the missionaries, inasmuch as they were able to hold their ground against so much indifference and opposition. The natives, too, upon the whole were kind to them, and while they cared not for instruction, they liked to have the missionaries living with them. Some, too, began to be dissatisfied with themselves. They acknowledged their inferiority as a people, and a few desired that their children should be educated. These indications were worthy of notice, but the exercise of faith was required to look forward to a substantial change, and to the realization of God's promises respecting the efficacy of His word—" So shall my word be that goeth forth out of my mouth : it shall not return unto me void, but it shall accomplish that which I please, and it shall prosper in the thing whereto I sent it."

How frequently do we see in God's dealings with His Church that He allows His people to be reduced to the lowest extremity, bordering almost on despair, to the end that they may be led to lift up their voices in fervent prayer to Him who alone can order the unruly wills and affections of sinful men. There is a never-failing store of mercy in the treasury of grace, but it is God's will that the need should be felt, and the petition offered before He will bestow it. It was a season of anxious suspense, but prayer was being offered up by the Church on the behalf of New Zealand, and God vouchsafed a ray of hope, like the faint glimmering light which is the harbinger of the rising sun. First there was the case of Whatu, a native who had been to New South Wales, and, when suffering under a fatal illness, came under the care of the missionaries at Kerikeri. He said that when he was in New South Wales he had heard Mr. Marsden talk about Jesus Christ, but he could not understand him. But now he was brought low, his thoughts were not so much distracted by external objects, and being prepared in that way in which God is pleased to bring the careless to a state of reflection, he was glad to hear of another hope beyond this world, which is secured to the helpless sinner through that Saviour who died for him. There was good reason to hope that poor Whatu was a brand plucked from the burning,—a part of the first-fruits, which showed that at no distant period an abundant harvest might be expected.

But another instance of the power of the Gospel soon followed. After the devastations committed by Hongi at the river Thames, the people of Bream Bay, a little further north, who were Hongi's allies, felt insecure in their position, which was a sort of border land between the hostile tribes ; and through fear of the vengeance of the Thames natives, they came to live at the Bay of Islands. Rangi was a chief of some rank in this tribe, and he, with his small party, took up their abode about a mile from Paihia, where they came under the frequent instruction of the missionaries. While indifference marked the character of most of his friends, old Rangi listened with attention to the new instruction. This was during the year 1824. He impressed upon his people the propriety of observing the sabbath day, and he was in the habit of hoisting a piece of red cloth for a flag, as a signal to his neighbours that it was God's sacred day. At length it pleased God to bring him very low by sickness, and he was gradually falling away under the ravages of an insidious cough. But as the body wasted his mind was becoming light, for the rays of the sun of righteousness had evidently beamed upon him. About two months before his death, when he was under much bodily suffering, he was asked what he thought of death. "My thoughts," he said, "are continually in heaven, in the morning, at mid-day, and at night. My belief is in the great God and in Jesus Christ." "That is very good," he was told; "for there is no pain in heaven either for the mind or the body, no fear of the enemy coming to kill you, but a quiet rest for ever. But do you not at times think that our God is not your God, and that you will not go to heaven?" "That is what I sometimes think when I am alone. I think I shall go to heaven, and then I think perhaps I shall not go there; and possibly this God of the white people may not be my God; and then, after I have been thinking in this way, and my heart has been cast down, it again becomes more cheerful, and the thought that I shall go to heaven remains last." "These are the temptations of the devil," he was told, "to prevent you from thinking of heaven; but you must ask God to give you His Spirit to enlighten your heart, that you may discover this to be a device of Satan. Do not think that God will not give it to you, for He gives His Spirit to all who ask for it." "I pray several times a-day," he replied. "I ask God to give me His Spirit, that He may dwell in my heart and remain there." About a fortnight afterwards he was asked, "What is your idea of the love of Christ?" "I think of the love of Christ, and I ask Him to wash this bad heart, and to give me a new heart. When I think of heaven and of Jesus Christ I am glad, because when I die I shall leave this flesh and these bones here, and my soul will go to heaven." The subject of baptism was then brought before him, and he was told that those who believe in Jesus Christ are all called by one name after Him; they are Christians; but those who do not believe are called heathens. The New Zealanders are heathens, but those who believe in Christ take His name, as a sign that their hearts are washed in His blood. The old man appeared to be much pleased with this idea, and expressed a wish to be called after Jesus Christ.

Three days before his death his mind seemed to derive a cheerfulness from the increase of light vouchsafed to him, by which he was assured of perfect happiness in another world. "I think I shall soon die," he said; "my flesh is all gone off my bones, but I think I shall go to heaven above, because I have believed all that you have told me about God and Jesus Christ." "But what payment have you to bring to God for the sins you have committed?" "I have nothing to give Him, only I believe that He is the true God, and I believe in Jesus Christ." "Do you not know who was the payment for our sins?" "I do not quite understand that." "Have you forgotten that Jesus Christ is the Son of God, and that He came into this world and suffered for us?" "Yes, yes, I remember you told me that before, and my whole wish is to go and dwell in heaven when I die." "Have you any fear of death?" "Not altogether."* He was told that the man who believes in Jesus Christ with all his heart, and sees death approaching, will feel glad that he is shortly to leave this body of pain and misery, and that his spirit is to take its flight to heaven. "I have prayed to God," he said, "and to Jesus Christ, and my heart feels full of light."

His end was now drawing near. He had maintained a steady course for many months; he professed his faith in Christ as his Saviour, and appeared to rejoice in hope of eternal life. Every proof of sincerity which could be looked for was given, and he was now admitted into the Church by baptism.

---

* His answer was a natural one for a person who was only feeling his way towards the experience of a Christian.

To those who had been the means of leading him to a knowledge of Christ, it was a season of gladness, a period to which they had been looking with great interest. Surrounded by those who would willingly have drawn him back, he, in the presence of all, boldly renounced the darkness which once hung over him, and he was able to profess the sure and certain hope of soon being in glory.

This was the first Christian baptism, the earnest of a large harvest, which in God's appointed time was to be gathered in. Whatu, and perhaps one or two others, may have gone before, but now was Christ acknowledged in a more open manner, and with those attendant circumstances which he had directed his disciples to use. It was a time of rejoicing among the angels of heaven when the tidings were there announced that another of the tribes of this lower world was being added to that vast company, which is made up of all people and nations and tongues and languages. But this little band had to wait long before many were added to their number. There was yet a dreary season of labour to be passed through, the great enemy was determined to hold his dominion to the last, and every inch of ground was to be fiercely contested. The baptism of Rangi served to cheer the drooping spirits of the missionaries ; and although it did not appear that any even of his own family were likely to follow his steps, yet there was about this time a manifest improvement in the conduct of many of the New Zealanders. Mr. Davis writes in allusion to this fact:—"The spiritual prospects of the mission brighten much; superstition seems to be giving way, and a spirit of inquiry is visible." "We are treated with much respect," writes another, "and the people receive us with kindness wherever we go."

CHAPTER IV.

1826, 1827.

BUILDING OF SCHOONER "HERALD"—VOYAGE TO BAY OF PLENTY—
STUDY OF NATIVE LANGUAGE—WESLEYAN STATION AT WHANGA-
ROA — HONGI ATTACKS WHANGAROA — MISSION STATION DE-
STROYED — HONGI WOUNDED—FLIGHT OF MISSIONARIES TO
PAIHIA—BRIG "WELLINGTON" SEIZED BY CONVICTS, AND RE-
TAKEN IN BAY OF ISLANDS—VISIT TO HONGI—DEATHS OF LUCY
AND RURERURE—TE KOIKOI—A PLUNDERING PARTY THWARTED—
BOOK OF TRANSLATIONS PRINTED—AKAIPIKIA—DEATH OF HONGI.

WHEN Mr. Marsden visited the river Thames, he was
full of hope that the labours of the missionaries would
be extended to that part of the island. We have seen
how this benevolent design was brought to naught by
the devastating wars of the Bay of Islanders. The
savage thirst of the natives had been in some measure
satiated, and it was hoped that now at length there
would be an opening for intercourse with the southern
parts of the island. The Rev. H. Williams had spent
the early part of his life in the navy, and Mr. Marsden
thought that his nautical knowledge might be turned
to good account. He proposed, therefore, that a small
schooner, of about sixty tons burthen, should be built
under Mr. Williams's direction. Communication with
the colony of New South Wales was not frequent at
that period, and as a large portion of the supplies required for carrying on the mission was procured

from thence, the proposed vessel would secure the
advantage of having these necessaries conveyed with
regularity.   But the chief benefit which was looked
for was the means of intercourse with the southern
tribes.   This vessel was immediately commenced by
two carpenters, one of whom was a regular ship-
wright.   It proved to be a very laborious work, and
the missionaries at the station felt it necessary to
render as much assistance as they were capable of
undertaking; and on her completion, in the year 1826,
the first voyage was made to New South Wales.
After this Mr. Williams made two visits to the Bay
of Plenty, accompanied by Mr. Davis and Mr. Clarke,
where they had much satisfactory intercourse with
the natives of Tauranga, though at another place they
narrowly escaped destruction from a party who pulled
off to the ship with the intention of seizing her, a fate
which befel the brig *Haweis* two years after, when
several of her crew were killed.   On every part of
that coast there seemed to be a large population, and
a strong desire was expressed that missionaries should
go and live among them, and several sons of chiefs
were allowed to return in the vessel, in confidence
that under the care of the missionaries they would be
safe from their old enemies of the Bay of Islands.

At the stations in the Bay of Islands much attention was given to the study of the native language,
with a view to the translation of portions of the
scripture; and the young persons who were conveyed
from the south in the schooner *Herald*, together with

the natives living in the mission families, chiefly slaves from the distant tribes, were brought under regular instruction, which was gradually to prepare them to communicate a benefit to their countrymen. The general plan pursued at Paihia at that time was as follows:—At five in the morning the large bell was rung to arouse the settlement. At six the natives and the mission families assembled for prayers; at seven instruction was given to the natives; and from nine till eleven the native language was studied, and an attempt was made to translate portions of scripture. By carrying on this work in a body, there was mutual benefit derived. They had also the valuable help of Mr. Puckey, who had lived in the island from his youth.

The native congregations had hitherto been so small that they met together without difficulty in the dwelling houses of the missionaries. It now became necessary to erect a separate building of larger dimensions, which might serve the double purpose of church and schoolroom. "It cheers us," it was observed, "to be obliged to enlarge the place of our tent, to stretch forth the curtains of our habitation, to lengthen our cords, and strengthen our stakes; and we feel assured that the Gospel will here break forth on the right hand and on the left, and that this barren desert will become a fruitful field." This was a pleasing indication, but still deep-rooted superstition and every evil disposition continued to hold undisturbed possession of the body of the natives.

Towards the end of the year 1826 Hongi had been seized with a violent pain in the knee while on board a ship in the harbour. His people fancied he had been bewitched by a chief of the river Thames, whose destruction consequently was determined on. Some bloodthirsty creatures proposed to kill all Hongi's slaves, who were very numerous,* but he protested strongly against the sacrifice of any life on his account, and told the slaves to fly for their safety. But Ururoa, his brother-in-law, seeing one pass with a load of firewood on her back, shot her dead on the spot, and another chief immediately killed a boy.

Mention has been already made of Whangaroa, the scene of the massacre of the *Boyd.* It is necessary again to recur to it, because some events of painful interest happened there at this time. The harbour is approached by a narrow entrance between rocky cliffs, which are formed by the disruption of a mountain range. The hills are broken into every variety of form, evidently the effect of some violent convulsion of remote ages. There are two remarkable rocks on the opposite shores, to which navigators have given the names of Peter and Paul, and by a singular coincidence, the former of these has been subsequently occupied by a Romish priest, the latter by a catechist of the Church Missionary Society. Within the heads the harbour expands into a basin, which affords safe

---

* The usual mode of showing respect to a great man when any calamity had befallen him, was to carry off all his property, or kill his slaves.

anchorage for shipping, and on every side the ground rises to a great elevation, and is covered with forest of kauri and other trees. Several small rivers fall into the bay from the surrounding hills, the banks of which are cultivated, always yielding to the natives a rich return for their labour. Up one of these fertile valleys, not far from the spot where Captain Thompson was killed, a Wesleyan station was established in the year 1823. It was most romantically situated upon a rising ground, looking towards the opening harbour on the one side, and on the other to the village of Kaeo, where the son of George and his other relatives were still residing. His tribe Ngatipo had lived some years before in the Bay of Islands, and it was they who cut off the French navigator Marion with part of his crew. Subsequently, in consequence of some domestic quarrel with their neighbours, they were driven away to Whangaroa. It seemed, however, that a retributive justice was still to follow them. They received the missionaries to live among them, but they treated them so harshly, that for a time they were glad to take refuge in the Church Mission station at Kerikeri. The Gospel was taken to them, but they did not accept it. In the summer of 1826 this beautiful valley was teeming with the fertility of native crops, and the wheat sown by the missionaries for their own support was now white for the harvest. Not so the moral field of the native inhabitants. In three weeks the restless spirit of Hongi, who had been annoyed by the misconduct of a near relative,

THE CUPOLAS OF ST. PETER AND ST. PAUL, WHANGAROA HARBOUR.

stirred him up to undertake some expedition, no
matter where, for the relief of his own excited feelings. A pretext was never wanting to a New
Zealander. If there was not one of late occurrence, it might be sought for in the past generation. He went to Whangaroa with a body of
chosen followers, and without much previous notice
destroyed two fortified villages, while the natives
who lived at Kaeo fled away to their friends at
Hokianga. The missionaries were thus left without
native protection, and although Hongi had strictly
charged his followers not to molest them, a straggling
party went off without his knowledge, attracted by
the prospect of plunder, and pillaged the missionary
premises, and then burnt them to the ground, obliging
the occupants to fly for refuge to the Bay of Islands.
The missionaries had hitherto been kept from harm
for the space of twelve years, and though continually
living in the midst of dangers, they had never met
with any serious obstruction in their work. There
was a sort of reverence paid to them and to their
object ; but now a breach had been made, and those
who had possessed themselves of the property at
Whangaroa exulted in the act.

While Hongi was in pursuit of some of the fugitives, he received a serious wound through the lungs.
It was soon reported that he was dead, and although
this turned out to be incorrect, the feelings of the
natives were expressed without disguise. They all
agreed that if Hongi's wound should prove mortal,

the mission station at Kerikeri should share the same
fate with that at Whangaroa. "It is beyond doubt,"
wrote Mr. Williams, "that according to the present
disposition of the natives, as soon as Hongi dies, our
brethren at Kerikeri, who are considered to belong to
him, will be plundered. This is according to the
custom of the country. We have also been told that
when our chief Te Koki dies we must expect the same
fate." In this unsettled state of things, the missionaries considered themselves merely as tenants at will,
who might be ejected at any hour. The rumours
were of such a character that it seemed not improbable
that they all might be obliged to leave the island together, though it was their intention to continue as
long as they could keep their ground. Four days
afterwards news was received which led to the suppo-
sition that Hongi was either dead or very near his
death. If this had been true, all that was anticipated
respecting the settlements was likely to have come to
pass. At nine o'clock in the evening a messenger
from Kerikeri arrived at Paihia, stating that Hongi
was dead, and that the missionaries hourly expected
to be turned out of doors, and plundered of everything.* The boat was sent up immediately to fetch
Mrs. Clarke, who was in ill health; the rest were to
stand their ground to the last. During this great excitement the minds of the missionaries were preserved
from that anxiety which might have been expected,

* This report turned out to be incorrect, but still a strong ground
for apprehension continued.

believing that whatever might happen, God would overrule all for good.

In the meantime the Rev. H. Williams and Mr. Davis had gone off to Whangaroa upon the first intimation of the troubles of the Wesleyan missionaries, and met the forlorn party midway between Kerikeri and Whangaroa. It was a mournful sight, when on the 11th of January, 1827, the large boat of Paihia was seen on its way from Kerikeri, with as many passengers crowded into it as it was capable of carrying. It contained all that remained of the mission station of Whangaroa, Mrs. Turner, with her three little children, and the rest of their mission party. Their clothes were contained in a few small bundles, which they had carried in their hands the distance of twenty miles. Arriving at Kerikeri, the natives would not allow them to remain, fearing that that place would be the next to fall. They were thankful, therefore, to proceed onward to Paihia.

It is not easy to describe the effect of this breach which had been made upon the mission body. The first thought was to comfort and relieve our friends who had lost their all, those friends whom some of us had visited in peace and security not two months before : the next was apprehension for our brethren at Kerikeri. Then, too, it was felt that every one must immediately pack up all they could send away by the ship *Sisters*, which was about to sail to New South Wales. News from every quarter showed that all the tribes were more or less involved in this horrible civil war, and the fate of Whangaroa opened our ears to listen to reports we had before disregarded, and showed us we were all exposed to a like danger. During this interval the boat at Kerikeri was kept in a state of readiness, and in a back room of Mr. Kemp's house, which was contiguous to the water, there was a heap of small bundles containing changes of linen for each of the little children, with as many paddles as could be used in the boat, so that on the first alarm their faithful natives might snatch up all that could be carried in addition to the children, and place them safely in the boat.

But to return to Whangaroa. After Hongi was wounded another pa was taken, where a great number of the natives had sought refuge, and men, women, and children were all massacred without any regard to age or sex. Hongi gave orders that not one should be spared except the slaves, who were to be incorporated into his tribe. Some messengers had been sent from Kerikeri to inquire the particulars of Hongi's wound, and while they were there several of the Whangaroa natives were dragged from their hiding places and killed. The scenes of cruelty exceeded description, and the messengers said they could not have conceived the horrible sights they were obliged to witness.

A remarkable event had occurred at this time, which, under God's providence, proved to be a great relief in a season of extreme anxiety. The brig *Wellington,* having on board sixty convicts, bound from

Sydney to Norfolk Island, had been seized by the
prisoners and came forward to the Bay of Islands for
a supply of water, the convicts hoping to make their
way to the coast of South America.   She arrived on
Friday, and the next day a strong breeze from the
north-west not only prevented her from getting under
weigh, but drove her close up to two whaling vessels
which were lying at anchor, the crews of which came
to the bold determination not to allow her to escape.
At daybreak on Sunday morning they opened fire
upon her, and when their few round shot were
expended they loaded their guns with coopers' rivets,
and nails, for the purpose of cutting up the rigging.
After a few hours the convicts proposed to capitulate,
on condition that they should be allowed to go on
shore, taking with them their clothes, which were no
doubt the property of the soldiers and the seamen.
This proposal was agreed to, and instruction was at
the same time given to the natives, who were in great
numbers on the shore, to secure them on landing,
and not to allow any two of them to be together.
On the following morning they were all brought back,
and the payment of a musket or a cask of powder
was given for each.   It was then arranged that one
of these whalers should go to New South Wales with
half of the prisoners, and this circumstance furnished
a conveyance to the Wesleyan missionaries, who left
the island for a season.*   The Church missionaries

---

* After a sojourn of a few months in New South Wales, they
returned again to re-establish their mission' at Hokianga, on the
western coast.

also were able to send off a part of their property, which might still be preserved for their use if they were driven to extremities. When these arrangements had been made, the missionaries were in a position to await quietly the result, ready to follow out the path to which God might direct them. They were now prepared to depart or stay, according to the behaviour of the natives; but it was their united determination to remain until they should be absolutely driven away. When the natives should enter the houses and plunder their contents, it would then be time for them to take refuge in the boats. There seemed now to be great indifference on the part of the chiefs as to whether the missionaries remained or not; and many of those who had been kind in their behaviour had taken a prominent part in the late scenes of depredation. It seemed possible that it might be the will of God that the missionary work should be interrupted for a season, in order to its being carried on with greater vigour at a future time. Of this there can be no doubt, that a change would soon take place, and a proof of this was the great opposition stirred up by the wicked one.

Two weeks after Hongi was wounded, he sent a request to the writer to visit him. It was somewhat dangerous at that time to travel through the woods, and the party of mission natives who went in company requested that they might carry hatchets with them for their own protection. Night overtook the party in the dense forest, not many miles from Kaeo.

We withdrew from the path into a secluded spot, that we might not attract the notice of any straggling foe. When the day dawned, the tent, and whatever was carried by the natives in the way of baggage, was securely hidden in the forest, each one marking the spot where he had deposited his load, and then we proceeded towards Hongi's encampment. As soon as the valley of Kaeo opened, there were seen the abundant crops of Ngatipo, who had now forsaken the place for ever, and the natives began to regale themselves upon the water melons, which were lying in great profusion. Suddenly a movement was observed among the foremost natives, which showed that there was an apprehension of danger. The rest all rushed forward, when five or six men armed with muskets and hatchets, were seen among the bushes standing at bay, gazing silently on our party. It was soon known that these were Hongi's followers, and about 150 more presently came up all armed. They had come to forage for the rest of the army. As we passed up the valley we saw the work of desolation on every side; the dwelling-houses were all burnt to the ground, and all moveable property had been taken away. But the sight of the late mission station was still more melancholy. The black ashes of the wooden buildings and of the stack of wheat alone remained to mark the spot, while the grave of Mrs. Turner's infant had been disturbed, and the coffin broken open, in hopes of finding some relic of value. Hongi was encamped

about five miles further on, within one of the pas
he had taken.   How different was the state of things
a few weeks before, when its former inhabitants were
dwelling in security.   Not one of them was now
remaining.   Those who were not killed had fled for
their lives, and it was in pursuing the fugitives in
the woods with a very few followers that Hongi
received his mortal wound.   He had never been hit
before, and he fancied that he was invulnerable, but
now a ball had passed through his lungs, and he was
lying helpless, with a very slender prospect of
recovery.   The people around were careless and
secure, elated with their recent victory, but Hongi
was cast down and thoughtful, feeling perhaps that
it was doubtful whether he would ever be able to
resume his former career.   He appreciated, however,
the attention which was shown to him, and a few
weeks after he directed his people to convey him by
canoe to Paihia, hoping that he might recover from
the effects of his wound.

The anticipations of danger to the missionary
stations in the Bay Islands were happily not realized,
but the excitement continued, and there seemed to
be little prospect of any change for the better.
There were so many circumstances on all sides to
keep alive the feeling of bitter hostility, chiefly dependent on the death of relatives who had been killed
in battle, even though at a remote period, that a
cause for going to war was never wanting ; and were
it not for the assurance from the word of God that

there is to be a glorious period, when the inhabitants of the earth shall learn righteousness, and war be no more known, it would have been hopeless to expect an improvement. If the chiefs were asked when their wars would be at an end, they replied never, because it is the custom of every tribe which loses a man not to be content without satisfaction, and nothing less than the death of one individual can atone for the death of another. Hongi returned to Whangaroa, and determined to make that place his residence. There seemed to be a prospect of his recovery, and he was hoping to go again to fight. His restless spirit was stirring up a desire within him to obtain satisfaction for the wound which he had received the preceding summer, and he had already requested different chiefs to join him.

Among the surrounding tribes there did not appear to be one gleam of hope of the progress of the Gospel, but God granted from time to time in the missionary stations a few indications of improvement, which were received as an earnest of future good. In June, 1827, the Rev. H. Williams writes from Paihia :—" It appeared evident that our little native girl Lucy, who had been with us three years, was at the point of death. We conversed with her on the love of Jesus and the delights of heaven. She listened with great attention, and expressed an earnest desire to go there. She extended her feeble hand to us, and leaned her head against me. We left her at eleven in charge of her brother and a faithful slave, and at two o'clock I was told she was dead. We think there is ground of hope in her death, and that she was looking to Christ for the pardon of her sins."

Shortly after this a still more satisfactory case occurred at Rangihoua, the oldest mission station. Rurerure had been long under the instruction of Mr. King. His own account of himself was that he formerly used to disbelieve all that was said about Jesus Christ, and thought Jehovah to be a very angry God; but now, for about five months, the word of God had made a deep impression upon him, and he was much afraid. The natives who lived with him reported that he often prayed that his soul might be washed in the blood of Christ, and that God would not permit him to go to hell, but take him to himself. The Rev. H. Williams visited him shortly before his death, when the following conversation took place :—" What do you think concerning death?" " I have so much pain that I cannot give you a correct account of my thoughts." "Whither do you think you will go when you die?" "To heaven." "Why do you expect to go to heaven?" " I believe that God will take me there." "How can you look for that, seeing you are a sinner?" "Jesus Christ came into the world to save sinners, and I believe in Jesus Christ." He inquired if he were right, and if he should go to heaven? He was assured of the love of Jesus, and that he came down from heaven to gather to himself and to purify from sin all persons from every people who should flee to him. The subject of baptism was

now mentioned, but as it was new to him, it was proposed to visit him again in two days, but in the
interval his spirit was removed to another world, and
was doubtless received by him who said to the thief
upon the cross, " To-day shalt thou be with me in
paradise." This case was the more encouraging
because, as Mr. Williams remarked at that time, he
was not aware that there was even a single instance
in the whole mission of a native who was really
earnest in his inquiries. In the midst of many trials
God was pleased to grant that there should be an
occasional gleam of light. The Gospel message was
constantly delivered, but most frequently it appeared
to be the seed which fell by the wayside, and sometimes it aroused the hostile feelings of those who
heard it.

It was in the month which followed the peaceful
death of Rurerure that the Rev. H. Williams went
to the neighbouring village at Te Haumi, where a
powerful chief from the interior, named Te Koikoi,
was on a visit. Tohitapu, the old priest, requested
that nothing might be said about the place of fire
and brimstone, as a place for wicked people, while
this man was with him, because he was a very great
man. But this was a challenge which could not be
passed by. Te Koikoi was asked if he had never
heard of that place, and he replied, " No." He
was then told that God had declared that the wicked
should be turned into hell, and all the nations that
forget God, and was exhorted to flee from the wrath

to come, and to lay hold on eternal life. It was of
the more importance to speak plainly to this man,
because he was a great chief, and a great savage, and
the natives had said the missionaries would be afraid
to speak on these subjects to him and to Hongi.
The old man appeared to be attentive and not at all
offended. He asked Tohitapu if this was the usual
mode of address, and was told it was. Whether this
chief was really offended, or only thought it a favourable opportunity for extorting something in the way
of payment for an alleged insult, this conversation
was made a pretext for a hostile attack. A few
weeks afterwards news arrived that a large party was
on its way, with Te Koikoi at its head, with the object
of plundering the mission station. There came, however, three friendly chiefs who had travelled by night
in order to gain time. They said that they had
directed their own people to follow them for the protection of the station. Soon after Te Koikoi was at
hand marching at the head of his people towards the
gate. The old man paid Mr. Williams the compliment
of rubbing noses with him. He was accompanied by
an excellent native, Wharerahi, who had been with
him all the night trying to moderate his anger, and it
seemed likely, from his manner, that no serious mischief would ensue. Te Koikoi told his people to sit
down. He stated to the chiefs present that Mr.
Williams had invited him to his house some time
before, and had not given him a present, and that
when he saw him at Te Haumi he told him he would

be cast into the place of fire and brimstone, and that he was now come to obtain satisfaction. He was told it was a mistake to imagine that he was entitled to any present, and that he had better direct his anger against Tohitapu, who had led him to expect one. In answer to the second charge, he was reminded that the words spoken were the words of God to him, and to all men, and that it was for the purpose of declaring these things that teachers had come to their country. To this he could not answer a word, and the chiefs acknowledged the truth of what was said. He then intimated that he had come to make peace, and wanted something to be given him. This, however, was refused, as the precedent would have been bad, considering that the grievance originated entirely with himself. In a short time he turned away in a rage, and some of the natives looked on with astonishment, wondering what would follow. In the afternoon he returned again, but his appearance and that of his people was very different from what it had been in the morning. They came in procession without arms, and some were carrying baskets of cooked food, which were distributed to each of the houses; and thus ended peaceably a device which had been intended by the evil one for great mischief.

On another occasion, the simple declaration of the objects for which the missionaries had come to the country, together with that influence which God was pleased to grant for their protection, had the effect of turning from their purpose a body of men who had evidently come in quest of plunder. A large party had arrived from the coast for the purpose of committing depredations upon a tribe near Paihia. On Sunday, towards the conclusion of English service, the natives came to say that a number of strangers were in the settlement, and beginning to be very troublesome. They had empty baskets with them, and seemed bent upon taking a crop of potatoes which were nearly ripe. The people were entire strangers, and were vociferating in a most angry mood, and striking the fence with their hatchets. They appeared to be ready to make a rush for general plunder. The missionaries, however, went out into the midst of them, and after a little while, persuaded them to sit down on the ground. They were in number about a hundred and fifty. It was thought that the most likely way to quiet them, would be to speak boldly concerning the great message. Instead, therefore, of expostulating with them for coming on the errand which it was clear they were bent on, they were told of their own condition, their danger, and the remedy. They listened quietly, and though they frequently cast a wistful eye upon the potatoes, and spoke of taking them, they at length walked off and gave no further trouble. The same tribe a year before had plundered the garden of the Wesleyan missionaries at Whangaroa, and threatened their house also, a few weeks before their mission was broken up, and there is not the least doubt that their intention was most mischievous when they now came to Paihia; but there was a restraining hand upon them. A friendly chief was sitting at a distance, anxiously waiting for the result. He observed, that though the people were pacified at present, they would soon rise up and be very angry, and carry off everything. He was not aware of the Christians' confidence, that stronger is he that is for us than they who are against us; but the result quickly proved this to him.

About the close of the year 1827, after a season of unusual trouble, it became evident that there was a more general diffusion of that divine influence, which was to extend on the right hand and on the left. In the missionary stations there were a few who began to pay more serious attention. It was noticed that some met together for prayer and reading the Scriptures. A small book was printed at this time in New South Wales, consisting of the first three chapters of Genesis, the twentieth of Exodus, the fifth of St. Matthew, and the first of St. John's Gospel. This was a small matter in itself, but it was a beginning, and the little book was of great use among the few who were disposed to profit by it.

In some of the villages also there were a few who gave reason to hope that the leaven of God's word was working in their minds. Wini, a brother of Christian Rangi, was of this number. On being told that unless the hearts of men are changed they cannot see the kingdom of heaven, Wini replied that they had called upon God frequently to give them new hearts, and to forgive their sins; "but perhaps," he added, "God will not hear us; we have called upon him for a long time, without perceiving any great change." He was reminded of the declaration of our Saviour, "If ye, being evil, know how to give good gifts," &c. "Ask and ye shall receive, seek and ye shall find." "Aye," said he, "God will hear if we ask him, but perhaps he is like us, when anyone asks for a thing, and we say, 'taihoa,' by-and-bye I will do it." In explaining the scheme of salvation through Christ, there are always at hand illustrations of the vicarious satisfaction of the Gospel, in the universal practice among this people of demanding payment for every offence done to them. Wini seemed to have some insight into the way of salvation, and desired to learn more. He said in conclusion, that "he was vexed with himself on account of the excessive hardness of his heart." At another village the head of the family, who had only been visited once, said, "I have forgotten the words you directed me to make use of in prayer, when you came here last." He was told he must pray for the pardon of his sins, and for a new heart, and while a few particulars of our Lord's history, and his future coming to judge the world, were related, the people seemed to listen as attentively as any Christian congregation.

It was at this time that communication was held with an interesting old man who subsequently lived at Paihia, a most consistent Christian till the day of his death. Akaipikia was a chief of some note, possessing a remarkably fine countenance, with much natural intelligence; but he had for many years lost the use of his lower extremities, it was said, through eating the poisonous berries of the karaka-tree. Three weeks had elapsed since a former visit had been paid to him. He said he had observed Sunday, though he had looked in vain for any one to teach him during the two preceding weeks. "Here is my mark," said he, pointing to the roof of his little shed, which was constructed with seven sticks as rafters "I count one for each day, and when I come to the last, I make the day sacred." He then said a few words to one of his children, who was living at Paihia, and had accompanied the missionary. But recollecting himself, he said, "I have been talking to to her on another subject, but let us proceed with our conversation." He said he had prayed according to the direction given him, and repeated a petition, which was for pardon; but he added that he did not know whether God heard him. "If he would 'whakao mai ki a au,' (that is, if he would make a sound, such as a man makes when called by another at a distance,) I should know that he heard me." He asked if he was not very good to remain quiet and not go to war. On being reminded that he only remained at home because he was lame and could not go, "True," he said; "I used to be an angry man formerly, and very bold, but now I am obliged to sit still."

Great apprehensions had been entertained for the safety of the missionaries in consequence of the expected death of Hongi, but this event did not take place for fifteen months after he had received the wound which was to terminate his life. Time was thus given for the excited feelings of the natives to wear off. The manner in which this event was ordered was a loud call for thankfulness. Had he died when he received his wound at Whangaroa, there is not a doubt that the natives would have proceeded to very great lengths; he was, however, permitted to live at Whangaroa so long, that his connexion with the missionaries who resided at Kerikeri was in a great measure broken off, and when his death did take place, the only party from whom mischief could be apprehended was absent on the western coast. Hongi died as he had lived, a heathen. His behaviour towards the missionaries was always friendly, with the exception of a short interval after his return from England, and his last moments were spent in requesting his survivors to treat them well. Respecting his state of mind, and views of eternity, all was midnight darkness, though he was sensible that his departure was near at hand. He had often heard of the glorious Gospel of peace, but it interfered too much with his ambitious plans: he consequently rejected the offer of mercy held out to him to the very last.

CHAPTER V.

1828—1830.

QUARREL AT HOKIANGA—PEACE MAKING—ESCAPE OF PANGO FROM PAIHIA—RANGITUKIA KILLED AT THE THAMES—"HERALD" WRECKED—EXAMINATION OF SCHOOLS—NATIVE MARRIAGE—BAPTISM OF TAIWHANGA'S CHILDREN—EXAMINATION AT KERI-KERI—BAPTISM OF TAIWHANGA—INCREASED DESIRE FOR IN-STRUCTION AT MISSION STATIONS—BATTLE AT KORORAREKA.

SHORTLY after the death of Hongi, an event took place which threatened general confusion. A chief of the Bay of Islands having been shot in a quarrel at Hokianga, a party set off from the Bay to investi-gate the affair. At the very time when they seemed on the point of an amicable arrangement, a mis-understanding arose which led to a general battle, in which Whareumu, a chief of note, and several of his followers were killed. The natives rose in all quarters, and the missionaries were under the dread of a bloody and desolating war. But it pleased God to incline the chiefs who were most nearly interested to a course of peace. The principal of them came and stated to the missionaries that they did not wish to fight with the other tribes, as they were one people and nearly related. They were aware that much evil would befal them if they did fight, and yet their customs required them to avenge the death of their chief. They could not make peace of themselves, but proposed that the missionaries should accompany them to the scene of action, in order to close the breach. Such a request as this, proceeding from the natives, was a new thing. It was quite contrary to their principles, when any chief of consequence had fallen, to make peace without fighting. For this reason many said that peace would not be made until a number had been killed. Still, however, though there was but a bare possibility of success, a path was opened which it was a duty to follow.

In compliance with this invitation, the Rev. Henry Williams, with Messrs. Kemp, Clarke, and R. Davis, accompanied the chiefs, and had the satisfaction of bringing about, under the blessing of God, a complete reconciliation of the hostile parties. The negotiations were opened on Saturday, and both parties, being equally desirous of peace, agreed that it should be settled the next day. To this the missionaries, fearful lest anything should occur to prevent the accomplishment of the object which they so much desired, offered no objection ; but on stating that it was the sacred day, the chiefs readily agreed to postpone the business till Monday, and preparation was made for a suitable observance of the day. Tohitapu and other chiefs directed the army to sit down in a compact body, leaving a small open space in the middle for the missionaries. The congregation consisted of at least 500 people, and was remarkably attentive. The afternoon was spent in conversing

with the people in their huts, and in this way the
Sabbath was passed without any cause for apprehension, in the midst of a body of men who had
never before submitted to such a restraint even for a
few hours. It was evident that there was a powerful
influence acting upon their minds. God inclined
them not only to be civil to their best friends, but
also to pay a degree of deference and respect which
was a new thing in an army of savages. The next
morning was ushered in by a heavy fall of rain.
The course of proceeding having been arranged
among the chiefs, it was agreed that Tohitapu should
accompany the missionaries to the enemy's pa. But
he was a timid man, and for a time drew back. At
length, however, he made up his mind to whatever
might await him, and prepared to move, requesting
that a white flag might be hoisted by the side of the
broad ditch which divided the two armies. The
arrival at the pa was greeted with the usual for-
malities. After a short parley the natives of the pa
moved towards the entrance of their fortification, and
several persons of distinction, including the eldest
son of Patuone, came forward, upon which Rewa
crossed over from the Ngapuhi camp, and rubbed
noses with them. Much noise was now heard in the
camp, and in a short time the various tribes were
observed marching out in order. The sight was im-
posing for this part of the world. When they were
within the distance of a hundred and fifty yards,
they rushed forward, uttering a horrible yell. There

were about 700 men under arms. Rewa then conducted the chiefs of the pa towards his own people.
The two armies successively danced the war-dance,
and fired volleys of musketry. Rewa was the first
to speak, and in an energetic address expressed his
desire that peace should be made. All the leading
men followed in the same strain. The great danger
on these occasions, where neither party is under much
control from their leaders, is, lest through mischief or
by accident a musket might be discharged, and a
person of the opposite party wounded, which would
occasion an immediate renewal of hostilities. Both
parties fired off their muskets in the air, but when
the chiefs noticed that many were loaded with ball,
they abruptly ordered their people to disperse. The
public business was soon at an end, and the mission
party withdrew by way of the pa of the Hokianga
natives. On their way many balls passed over their
heads, but providentially no one was wounded. As
soon as they had entered the pa the firing ceased ;
and the natives, released from further restraint, took
to their canoes and dispersed.

Satan was thus disappointed in his efforts, but he
forthwith tried to create mischief in another quarter.
A leading chief from the powerful tribe of Rotorua
was on a visit at the Bay of Islands, with a number
of his people. A short time before they had been
at war with the Islanders ; but now peace was
established, and there was a hope that Rotorua might
soon become a field for missionary labour. But two

great chiefs had died recently—Hongi, from the effects
of his wound, received fifteen months before at
Whangaroa; and now Whareumu in the late conflict
at Hokianga—and the great enemy put it into the
minds of the Islanders that Pango, the Rotorua
chief, was the author of this evil, and that he, by
the power of witchcraft, had directed the course
of the balls by which these two warriors had fallen.
No sooner, therefore, had the army returned from
making peace at Hokianga, than mysterious reports
were circulated, threatening his safety. Pango,
with several of his followers, made an immediate
application at Paihia for a passage home in the
mission schooner; but she was undergoing repair,
and could not quickly be ready for sea, while the
danger was most imminent. Happily, there was
another vessel in the bay, about to sail to the south,
and passage was at once procured in her, and they
were embarked under cover of the night. The native
who gave most cause for apprehension was Tohitapu.
He had already shown a desire to have these people
killed, and a word from him would have been sufficient to ensure the perpetration of the act. The next
morning he went to Paihia, and inquired whether
they had gone on board by the sanction of the missionaries, and being told that it was so, he said it
was very wrong. The old man refused to eat, and
he seemed ready for the commission of any act, however desperate. The exciting cause of this temper of
mind was some improper conduct of his wives during

his absence at Hokianga, and he would gladly have wreaked his vengeance on the people of Rotorua. He declared his intention to hang himself, and sent for his friends to witness his death. In the afternoon, Mr. Williams went to see him at his house. He was apparently in great sorrow, and said he had not eaten food since his return, neither could he do so unless he were to kill some one; then his heart would be at ease; but that, as he was restrained by the missionaries, he must die. The next morning he went again to Paihia, but declined the food which was offered to him; and, holding up a hatchet in his hand, he said, " Sixteen persons have been sent by this to the shades below, and unless I can kill and eat some one now I shall have no rest." Mr. Williams reasoned with him upon his wicked madness, and, after a little while, he cast away the deadly weapon, saying, " I will use it no more."

The dangers which had threatened at Hokianga were scarcely passed, when there arose another cause for alarm at the south. Rangitukia, a chief from the Bay of Islands—who had been in the affray with Whareumu, and had carried him, when wounded, some distance upon his back, until the close pursuit of the enemy obliged him to relinquish his burden— set sail, with three canoes, in the direction of the Thames. His object, it appears, was to revenge the death of a relative, who had been killed two years before. But in the interval peace had been made, and his present expedition was undertaken without

the concurrence of the other tribes. He killed one
or two persons, and was, in the end, overpowered by
superior numbers, and only three or four individuals
escaped to carry news of the disaster. The tribes of
the Thames and of Waikato were very indignant at
this unprovoked attack, and it was soon reported
that, with their combined strength, they were about
to make an attack upon the Bay of Islands. The
natives were in great alarm, and it was thought expedient to take some means of providing a place of
safety near Paihia, as that would be the first point of
attack. There was high land at the back of the
mission station, which was favourable for this purpose; and the whole strength of the settlement,
assisted by natives from the neighbouring villages,
was, for a time, given to this object. Happily,
the apprehension of danger was speedily removed.
Whereraki, the great peace-maker of Ngapuhi, went
off to the Thames for the purpose of bringing about
a reconciliation, and, on his arrival, sent up a large
party from thence for a like object, which put an end
to the alarm.

The Society's schooner *Herald* had been of great
service ever since her completion, and was likely to
prove a valuable auxiliary in promoting the extension
of the mission. A part of the Rotorua natives, who
had not been able to obtain passage in the same
vessel with their chief, Pango, were subsequently
conveyed in safety to their home. The schooner
was then sent to Hokianga, to obtain a cargo of

potatoes for the schools, but in a few days news arrived that she was a total wreck. At the mouth of the river Hokianga is a bar of sand, over which vessels may generally pass with safety ; but at times the sea breaks with dreadful violence. The *Herald* had been off the harbour two days, waiting for a favourable opportunity, as a high sea was running. A little before sunset she was making for the bar, with a fair wind, and a prospect of being shortly at her anchorage ; but as soon as she reached the bar, the wind suddenly failed, and being left to the power of the breakers, she was carried into shoal water, and let go her anchors. Night coming on, and there being a most awful prospect before the crew, each began to think of his own safety. In the meantime, the boat which had been lowered was washed away by the surf, and two men who were in her had to swim ashore. The master and the remainder of the crew clung to the rigging till morning, when the tide had left her sufficiently to allow them to walk ashore. When they reached the land, however, they met with little mercy at the hands of the natives, who took much of their clothing from them, and threatened to go to still greater lengths. As soon as the tide was sufficiently out, the natives proceeded to the vessel, and completely ransacked her of every thing which was moveable. Nor were they content with this, but hacked the vessel itself in a most shameful manner, cutting away all the rigging, together with the lining of the cabin, and left nothing but the hull. The loss thus sustained was most serious, and it showed also how extremely uncertain were the minds of the natives, whenever a circumstance might occur of which they could take advantage.

The close of the year 1828 was marked by an event which was new in the history of the mission, and indicated an onward and steady progress, which was preparatory to a more general movement. It had been determined that an examination of the three schools of Rangihoua, Kerikeri, and Paihia should be held at the latter place. The numbers present were 170. The proceedings were opened with a part of the Liturgy in the New Zealand language, omitting the Psalms, which were not yet translated. The first classes of the three schools were then examined together in the catechisms, reading, arithmetic, &c. and so on with the rest of the scholars. In the afternoon they were all feasted, with about sixty strangers, principally friends of those in the schools. The result was highly satisfactory as a first trial, and was likely to have a good effect on the strange natives, who appeared pleased, and some talked of sending their own children for instruction.

There was a circumstance which took place at Paihia at this time, which indicated an improvement upon the old customs of the people. The manner in which matrimonial connexions were wont to be arranged was most objectionable, and it was desirable that a change should be introduced. It was not

customary to ask the consent of the bride. If only
that of her relations or friends could be secured, it
was sufficient. But those who had lived for any
length of time with the families of the missionaries
felt that this course was improper; and though as yet
there were no Christian natives upon whom the
marriage service would be binding, yet it was desirable that some other way should be followed, more
in agreement with the Christian rule. Poutu, who
had lived in the settlement from its first commencement, delivered a note to Mr. Williams, in which he
expressed a wish to take one of the native girls to
wife, but said he could not ascertain the lady's mind
upon the subject, and asked that the question might
be put for him. The suit was favourably received,
and in the course of a few days, on occasion of the
arrival of the lady's father, he requested that his
bride might be delivered to him. Tauwehe was
accordingly sent for, and asked if she were willing
that the ceremony should take place. Her manner
on the occasion excited much amusement. She commenced by whimpering; but after some time she
gave her consent, and, by her permission, the bride-
groom and groomsman were called in and informed
of what had passed. It was explained that it was
much more proper that their mutual consent should
be written on paper, than that they should follow
their native custom. Pen and paper, therefore, having
been prepared, Tauwehe was asked if she were willing
to become the wife of Poutu. It was long before the

wished-for "Yes" could be obtained. A similar question was then put to Poutu; and he, considering it necessary to take as much time for reflection as the young lady, allowed a pause of more than ten minutes to elapse. At length Hori, the groomsman, said he would speak for him, but he was told that would not answer the purpose. Poutu at length spoke for himself. The formal signature was then made, which it was hoped would have some effect in binding the parties to their engagement.

Among the natives living at Paihia was a chief named Taiwhanga, a great warrior, and a frequent follower of Hongi to the field of battle. His reputation stood so high that, after he had come to the determination to join the missionaries, he was frequently solicited to accompany the fighting expeditions, and when he steadily refused, a request was made that he would allow them to take the musket, with which a celebrated chief at Kaipara had been killed. As the time passed on he had many temptations to contend with, and on one occasion his property was all placed in a canoe, and he was about to turn his back for ever upon those instructions he had begun to receive. The difficulty was, a determination on his part to take a second wife, a slave belonging to himself. His countenance was dark and lowering but there was a better principle contending within, and he suddenly renounced his intention, and carried his goods back to the house. After this he maintained a steady course, and though not as yet in a state to receive Christian baptism, he was desirous that his children should be given up to the care of the missionaries, and that like their children they should receive the holy rite. He addressed a letter to all the missionaries at the station, which describes powerfully the working of his mind. "Here am I thinking of the day when my son shall be baptized. You are messengers from God, therefore I wish that he should be baptized according to your customs. I have left off my native rites, and my native thoughts, and am now thinking how I may untie the cords of the devil, and so loosen them that they may fall off together with all sin. Christ is near perhaps, beholding my sinfulness ; he looks into the hearts of men. It is well for me to grieve in the morning, in the evening, and at night, that my sins may be blotted out." It having been considered that this application should be attended to, his four children were baptized, together with the infant son of the writer, all the missionaries at the station being sponsors. The service was most affecting, and the attention of the natives marked ; and the public celebration of this baptism in their own language could not fail, under the divine blessing, to bring some of them to reflection. It was explained to the natives that by baptism a believer is admitted into the visible church, and that without it none can be considered members of the same ; while, unless the outward sign be accompanied by inward grace, it will be of no avail.

The year 1829, like that which preceded it, was closed by a general examination of the schools of the three stations, which was held at Kerikeri. At an early hour on the day appointed the whole population of Paihia was in motion, and a little after seven o'clock the English families and the natives embarked in four boats and one large canoe. On the passage up the river they fell in with Mr. King's boat and one canoe, and then, proceeding together, arrived at Kerikeri at about eleven o'clock. The native mode of salutation at such times is a rush upon each other and a sham fight; but this was exchanged for the more sober welcome of three English cheers. The numbers met together were about 290. In the afternoon the mission families assembled in the chapel, and partook together of the Lord's Supper. The next morning, after prayers, the examination was conducted as on the former occasion, and it was evident that good progress had been made. The closing business was the most interesting to the greater number of the natives. It was a dinner consisting of pork, beef, potatoes, and bread, served up in little baskets which answered the purpose of plates. They had not been eating many minutes, when all with one consent left their seats and scampered off with the remainder of the food; it being the native practice never to leave anything which is set before them, but to carry off what they cannot consume at the time. The needlework of the girls was afterwards examined, when some creditable specimens were shown, and the next day a few prizes were awarded to the most deserving. Work done by the native carpenters was also brought forward, which would have done credit to workmen in a civilized country. This gathering gave an opportunity of drawing a contrast between the present and the past. Here were a number of cannibals collected from the tribes around, who a few years before were ignorant of every principle of religion, many of them, like their fathers, had feasted on their fellow-creatures, and gloried in the practice, but now there was not an individual who was not in some degree acquainted with the truths of the Christian religion, which, with the blessing of God, might be the means of his conversion. Not long before they had commenced on the simple rudiments of instruction ; now many of them could read and write their own language with propriety, and some were masters of the first rules of arithmetic. But a few years before a chisel made of stone was their only implement ; now they had not only the tools of civilized man, but were learning to use them. It is true that this was but a day of small things ; still greater and more permanent blessings awaited New Zealand. The Gospel was preached ; the Bible was being translated ; scriptural precepts were taught, and would, it was to be hoped, be soon practised ; and then the whole train of blessings which follow a preached Gospel would be theirs also.

The progress which had been made in the work of

evangelization was very slow up to this period, but it was a steady advance. The tender sapling which was afterwards to become as one of the trees of the forest, and whose branches were to cast their shadow to a wide extent, was carefully nurtured by the Lord of the vineyard, though before its roots should strike deep into the soil beneath, it was to be exposed to many a rude blast which would threaten its destruction. A spirit of inquiry was now at work in the missionary stations. A little band was beginning to feel its way after those doctrines which they had long heard without effect. Taiwhanga, whose children had been committed to the care of the missionaries the preceding year, was among this number. Early in the year 1830 he was received into the Church of Christ with two others, a man and his wife. The latter promised well at the time, and there have been few cases in which there was less reason for hesitation, but they subsequently fell away and dishonoured their Christian name. Taiwhanga alone continued in the onward course. His baptism was calculated to produce an important effect upon the natives. He was a man of strong natural passions, who had not taken this step hastily, but after long deliberation and in the face of much opposition. When he advanced from the further end of the crowded chapel, with firm step but subdued countenance, an object of interest to every native as well as to every English eye, and meekly kneeled where six months before, at his own request, his young children had been dedicated to God, it was a sight which would call for joy among the angels in heaven, and filled the hearts of those who were present on the occasion with joy and thankfulness. This mission, from the first, had excited much interest, but had hitherto been carried on with great expense and very little fruit, while the minds of those employed in it had been continually cast down, and their faith had long been in exercise, waiting for the fulfilment of that which had been written. But now the time seemed to have arrived when the New Zealanders were about to receive the Gospel. The interest manifested by a few of those in the settlement at Paihia now became almost general, and the cry as soon as evening prayers were concluded was, "May we not come to you and talk?" One youth observed, that a fortnight before, in the house in which he lived, there was nothing but bad language. He went away to his friends for a week, and on his return this language was no longer heard. All the quietly disposed first came forward, and their example drew others after them.

One evening, when the natives had shown marked attention during an address at prayers, Mr. Davis invited all who might be disposed to attend to come to his house for conversation. About thirty men and boys responded, and an interview of deep interest followed. After a prayer for God's blessing, one of the natives stood up and spoke in a very affecting manner. He requested all present to be attentive to what was told them by their teachers, to forsake all sin, and to go to God continually in prayer for strength to enable them to believe, that they might be saved. Another said, " Let us all do as you say ; let us live to God, and then we shall be happy." Some said that they had a great desire, others that they had a little desire, to believe in God. A suitable word of advice was given to each, and there was reason to hope that it was not in vain.

It was a time of peculiar encouragement, a season of peaceful calm, and it seemed as though the hour of triumph was at hand; but it was a treacherous calm, like a cloudless sky in summer, which is the precursor of a storm, when all nature rejoices in its grandeur, as though nothing could disturb its settled course. Satan had withdrawn into his stronghold, but it was that he might gather strength for a renewal of the conflict. Only two days had passed away, when the natives were assembling at Kororareka under Pomare, about two miles distant from Paihia, expecting an attack from the tribes of Whangaroa, Rangihoua, and Kerikeri. The cause of this was the dissolute habits of a whaling captain. Whenever he came to the Bay of Islands, he had living with him the daughter of Morunga, a leading chief of Te Kawakawa, upon whom, with her friends, he was in the habit of lavishing a large amount of property. He had lately taken a second woman, the daughter of Rewa, a powerful chief of Kerikeri. A quarrel ensued between the two females, and much abusive language was uttered by the daughter of Morunga; and it was to revenge this insult that Rewa's friends were now coming together. It was soon apparent that a serious commotion was expected; for all the tribes connected with the Kororareka party came flocking together from the interior, and from all the neighbouring rivers. At Waitangi, about a mile distant from Paihia, the people had been occupied in the completion of a large fishing net, and the old chief, Te Akaipikia, who was skilful in this work, had been carried from the interior to lend a helping hand. But now the canoes were crossing the Bay from all directions, and old Aka, being afraid to be left alone, requested a native to carry him upon his back to the mission station. The excitement was so great, that a number of the natives living in the settlement, declared that they must of necessity go and join their relatives, and either live or die with them. The next morning, Ururoa, the brother-in-law of Hongi, having arrived from Whangaroa, at a bay near Kororareka, it was thought well to visit both the contending parties, and endeavour to restrain them from mischief. Landing at Kororareka, where those expecting the attack were gathered together, we passed over the hill to the army of the assailants. They were feasting on kumara, which they had just pulled up from the gardens at which they landed. They gave us a hearty welcome, and at the time, Tohitapu, our neighbour, was in the act of making an harangue, the object of which was to restrain Ururoa from going to any greater lengths, and to content himself with having plundered the kumara gardens, as a satisfaction for the insult received; but Ururoa seemed to be resolutely bent upon crossing the hill to Kororareka on the following day. They desired us then to express our opinion upon their proceedings. We spoke as freely as we had ever done, and they received well our remarks. They afterwards turned out their forces, which were marshalled according to their respective tribes, that we might see their strength. Tohitapu, who properly belonged to this party, though he had also much connexion with the other, greatly admired them, and with a feeling of pride, pointed to the different companies, exclaiming, " Those are mine! and those are mine!" We returned after a time, hoping that there was no reason to apprehend mischief. The next morning there was much firing, and by our glasses we could observe persons running in all directions, and canoes also pulling off to the ships filled with people. The Rev. Henry Williams immediately pulled over in the boat, and after communicating with Captain King, on board the *Royal Sovereign*, went on shore to endeavour to put a stop to the firing. He landed at the scene of action, but could not see any person of rank, though the combatants were only twenty yards apart, as all were concealed by fences and screens. He called out as loudly as he could, but with no immediate effect. He then passed on to Tohitapu, who was at the extremity of the beach, out of harm's way, and tried to persuade him to accompany him to the opposite party, but he was not to be moved, and deputed a young chief to go instead of himself. The firing ceased shortly afterwards, and it was found that many had been killed and wounded. He proceeded at once to Ururoa, who was scarcely able to speak through excessive excitement. Numbers, however, flocked around, and were all ready to listen to what was said. They acknowledged that the advice which had been given them was good, and that they were urged to this act of madness by Satan. Many were dead, others dying, and the number of wounded no one knew. Within a quarter of an hour after the firing ceased, very many of each party were dispersed indiscriminately among their opponents, and it was found that fathers and sons and brothers had been fighting against one another. When there was time to gather more particular information, it was learnt that Ururoa had crossed the hill without any intention of fighting, and that the leading chiefs of both parties were close together holding a parley, not very far from the spot where Captain Robertson, of H.M.S. *Hazard*, afterwards engaged Kawiti's party in the year 1845. There was a prospect of the difference being quickly settled, when a musket was discharged at random by a native in the rear of the Kororareka natives, towards the rear of the other party, and a woman was wounded. As soon as the mischief was known, the two parties fired upon each other, in much closer quarters than they would have

chosen if they had known what was going to happen.
Hengi, a great chief of Ururoa's party, soon after the
firing began, rushed forward with merely a wand in
his hand, to try to stop the combatants, when he was
deliberately shot through the body. The death of
this man caused much subsequent difficulty.

Many of the wounded men from Pomare's side
were carried on board the *Royal Sovereign*, and the
deck of the vessel presented a fearful spectacle. The
surgeon was employed dressing the wounds, assisted
by some of the seamen. As it was expected that the
village would be taken, and that the natives might
fly to the ships for protection, they were put in a posture of defence, and the worst prepared for; but in
the meantime the assailants returned to their former
encampment.

A breach was now made which was extremely
difficult to heal; for though many of Pomare's men
had fallen, there were several chiefs of rank killed on
the side of the assailants. The people of Kororareka
remained in possession of the field, but they were
afraid to continue there, believing that their enemies
would make a vigorous effort to obtain satisfaction
for the slain. On the following day, which was
Sunday, they set fire to the village, having determined to withdraw to a favourable position up the
river Kawakawa. But their plans were hardly
understood by themselves, and some of the canoes
landed at Paihia, and were carrying their goods
ashore, and then, finding that the greater number

were proceeding up the river, they embarked again and followed in the same direction. In a few days peace began to be talked of, but Pomare's people were doubtful whether their enemies would listen to any terms, because their loss had been so serious. In the meantime a vessel came in sight, which proved to be from New South Wales, having the Rev. S. Marsden on board. The combatants being removed some miles apart, there was a favourable interval for holding communication with them, and Mr. H. Williams, accompanied by Mr. Marsden, went from one camp to the other to bring about a reconciliation. It was unanimously agreed that Kororareka should be given up as a payment for Hengi, and for the other chiefs who were slain. The general cry was for peace. This proposal came from Pomare's party, but their opponents were at first doubtful about the sincerity of it. The next day Mr. Marsden and Mr. Williams, with the chief, Rewa, went to see them. A white flag was hoisted in the boat. On landing, all the people came together, and were satisfied with the answer from the opposite party, but they said that Ururoa must depute some chief to visit them, and that they would afterwards send a deputy to his camp. Ururoa agreed to this, but he waited for the arrival of Mango and Kakaha, the sons of Hengi; as the duty of seeking revenge for the death of their father now devolved upon them. Five days were thus spent in settling the preliminaries; and both parties equally manifesting a disposition to put an end to hostilities, it was fixed that the meeting should take place. At an early hour on the day appointed, several canoes were in motion from Kororareka towards Te Kawakawa, and were joined by the boats from Paihia. The party amounted to about three hundred, and advanced till within a mile of the place of meeting, when the ambassadors, three in number, proceeded with Mr. Marsden and the missionaries to Otuihu, where Pomare's forces were now encamped. On landing they were conducted towards the principal chiefs. All sat upon the ground, leaving a narrow space as a sort of platform for the speakers. The first man who rose was one of Pomare's men. He intimated that peace would not be lasting, because a chief of his people had not been killed, as an equivalent for Hengi, and that he should be afraid to remain in this part of the country, and should go to live at Kaipara. After several others had spoken, the different tribes mustered for the war dance, when about a thousand men were under arms. The three ambassadors remained in the Pa for the night, which was considered to be an important part of the proceedings. The next morning they returned, accompanied by Pomare's deputies; and calling at Paihia for the missionaries, they proceeded to Kororareka. A similar scene occurred to that of the preceding day. The concluding act in the ratification of the peace was the following:—A chief of Ururoa's party repeated a song, the purport of which it was difficult to understand, holding a small stick in his hand which as he concluded he broke, and threw it down at the feet of one of Pomare's ambassadors. The meaning of this was that hostilities were broken off. The latter chief then repeated a similar form of words, and cast down his broken stick at the feet of the former speaker. Thus was healed one of the most serious ruptures which had ever occurred among the northern tribes ; and where danger had been apprehended, good was made to appear, for it raised the missionaries in the estimation of all the natives, even of those who were not disposed to listen to their instruction. They felt that they had been placed in extreme difficulty, and that they could not have made peace in their own way, without having protracted their warfare to an indefinite period ; while at the same time they were heartily glad that the effusion of blood should be stayed. This was the second time this influence had been exercised, and it disposed the natives to look up to the missionaries as their best friends.

CHAPTER VI.

1830.

EXPEDITION OF HENGI'S SONS TO MAYOR ISLAND—RIPI, CHIEF
OF MAWHE—DEATH OF RAPE—SECOND BOOK OF TRANSLATIONS
PRINTED—HAPPY DEATH OF PETI—INCREASED ATTENTION IN
THE MISSION STATIONS—SCHOOL EXAMINATION.

THE sons of Hengi were not satisfied with this peace,
but they could not go contrary to that which had
been agreed upon by all their friends and allies.
They therefore adopted the extraordinary expedient
of getting up a small expedition to attack any party
of natives they might meet with to the south of the
Bay of Islands. They went as far as the Mercury
Islands, their number being about one hundred, and
fell upon a defenceless tribe with which they were not
at war. It was blood they wanted, and if they could not
exact it from those who had slain their father, they
were content to have it elsewhere. Returning home
they were still dissatisfied, and on a second expedition, they destroyed a large body of natives, belonging
to Tauranga, living on Mayor Island. They killed as
they thought every person, but two escaped under
cover of the night, and pushed off to the mainland, a
distance of twenty miles. The Bay of Islanders then
passed on to Moliti, an island lying off Maketu, and
killed all the people they found there. They re

mained a few days feasting upon the slain, and then began to think of their return. Haramiti, their great priest, had been consulting the augury, which he declared to be inauspicious. At grey dawn the next morning, the Tauranga natives were upon them in great force. They fought desperately, but all were killed excepting one youth, who was afterwards restored to his friends by the Rev. T. Chapman. It was a just retribution they received, but the consequences, as we shall see hereafter, were most disastrous, involving the people of the Bay of Islands in a long war with those of Tauranga. This did not occur till the following year, and in the interval there was a gradual work going on which became the foundation of a great change.

Ripi, the chief of the tribe living at Mawhe, was one of the first of those in authority who favourably received the instructions of the missionaries. He had been on board a ship in the harbour to purchase muskets, and had just landed with his people at Paihia on Sunday evening, when Mr. Davis fell in with them. They seemed to be much occupied with their muskets, and the manner in which they had made their bargains. Mr. Davis remarked—"We do not object to your possessing muskets and powder, but we wish that you should use them with discretion. At the same time while you are thinking of the means of protecting your bodies, we desire you also to think of your souls' welfare." Taiwhanga, who was related to Ripi, said—" Yes it will be well for you to think of these things and to pray to God." Ripi said, "God will not hear." Taiwhanga told him that God would hear, and that he would even listen to his thoughts, and that though he might find his desires small at first, yet God would enlarge them. "Did you not," said Taiwhanga, "get that musket, which you have in your hand, from the ship by asking for it? In like manner God will give you his Holy Spirit, if you ask for it." On subsequent occasions, Ripi came to Paihia, and always attended service when there. Preparations were now being made to form a station at Waimate, and frequent intercourse was kept up with Ripi and his tribe. Aperahama, a Christian native, visited them regularly on Sunday, and, as far as his knowledge went, preached the Gospel to them. When Mr. Davis afterwards removed to Waimate, he went to see Ripi at his own village, and found both him and his people apparently attentive worshippers. A congregation, varying from one hundred to a hundred and fifty persons, was always ready to welcome the visits of their teacher, and as the convictions of his own mind became stronger, Ripi gave proof of his sincerity by a desire to bring others to the same way of thinking. As a chief of rank, his words carried weight, but still he was not protected from those trials which are incident to a warfare between the kingdom of Satan and the kingdom of Christ. He succeeded in introducing daily prayer into many families in his tribe; and then he turned nis attention to the natives of the village of Kaikohe. Here he was well received by the principal chief, but in a little while he was forbidden to continue his visits.   Wharepoaka, the chief of Rangihona, and two chiefs of Waimate had sent to desire that the people of Kaikohe would not listen to anything which either native or European teachers might tell them, but that they should continue in the course their fathers had followed before them.   The reason of this was that many of the natives were meditating an expedition against Tauranga, and a large piece of lead had been sent to Ripi that he might make bullets and be ready to join them ; but Ripi returned the lead, telling the messengers that his mind was altogether altered as to those proceedings, and that it was not his intention to go.   The cry therefore was raised that their craft was in danger by this new teaching.

At Paihia a native named Rape, who had lived in the station some years, was lying very ill, and to all appearance his illness was likely to end in a speedy dissolution.   He had always manifested a careless indifference to religious instruction, as well as inattention to what was taught in the school, so much so that he contrived to be absent as often as possible. At length, however, he showed a disposition to listen, and this change was to be attributed, under God's blessing, to the instrumentality of those natives about him who had received the truth.   As his illness increased, he said that he thought much of Jesus Christ, and hoped that he would take him to heaven when he died. "I pray to him to come and take care of me, lest the devil should tempt me. My body," he observed, "has not been baptized, but Jesus Christ will baptize my soul by his Holy Spirit." He was told that if he was sincere in believing in Jesus Christ he might be baptized now, for that Christ has directed that those who believe should be baptized. A week afterwards he was admitted into the Church. He gave every evidence, of which in his situation he was capable, that his profession was sincere. His language was that of an earnest inquirer, and religion was the only subject on which he cared to converse. A few hours before his departure, mention was made of the blessed prospect he had before him, and after the missionary had engaged in prayer, seeing that he was about to leave him, he pressed him to stay longer and talk with him. He seemed to rejoice in the hope of deliverance from this world of sin, and soon he was released to join the company of the blest above.

The work of translation was proceeding gradually, and the increasing wants of the natives were now in some small measure supplied by a second little volume which was printed in New South Wales, during the time of the commotions which were going on in the Bay of Islands in the early part of the year 1830. It contained the first three chapters of Genesis, portions of the Gospels of St. Matthew and St. John, a part of the first Epistle to the Corinthians, and parts of the Liturgy and Catechism. These little books were at once caught up by all those who were religiously disposed, and tended much to help them forward in their inquiries.

Another happy death occurred at Paihia in the month of September this year. About five years before a girl named Peti was left at the house of Mr. Davis by a Kaipara chief, who had fled to Te Kawa-kawa for protection, at the time the Ngapuhi tribe first began to make inroads into that part of the country. When first brought into the house she was a sickly-looking girl, and withal rather stupid ; but regular living had a good effect upon her constitution, and she became valuable as a servant. After a time she appeared unusually thoughtful and steady, but said nothing about her views on religious subjects. At length she expressed a wish, in common with other girls in the house, to hear more about the great love of Christ in dying for sinners. They met regularly for this purpose twice in the week. After further instruction she was baptized in the month of April, 1830, and from that time till her death she maintained much consistency of character. Soon after her baptism she became unwell, and it was soon evident that her complaint was consumption, which had carried off so many of the natives. She was much attached to two of her companions, Tuari and Rama, and prayed with them every evening for a long time previous to her death. She would often cry over Tuari and say, " Oh Tuari ! Tuari ! it will not be long before I shall leave you, and why do you not believe? Do you think that God will not listen to your prayers? Yes, he will listen to all who pray to him from their hearts. He is not like the Maoris. He does not bear malice towards believers; his love is great, it is not like the love of the world, which soon dies away, but it lasts for ever." During her illness Tuari was very attentive to her, and she would say, "Tuari, you are very kind to my body, but you do not care for my soul. I used to pray with you, but as I can do that no longer, I will now pray for you." She would also talk very seriously to Rama, who had made a great profession of religion, and said, "Rama, you say you believe, but your works do not correspond with your profession. Do pray often and earnestly that God may preserve you when you are tempted. Mind you cannot deceive God. No. He can see everything, and he knows everything."

As her illness increased, her anxiety for the welfare of others increased also. But Peti was not without her trials. In the beginning of August a copy of the little native book was given her, which she much valued. This excited Rama's jealousy, and she said it was thrown away upon Peti, a sick girl. As these words were spoken in her hearing, they grieved her much, and she wished to return the book. In the evening she was asked, why she took so much notice of what Rama had said? She answered, " Because I had not prayed in the morning, and consequently not having been fed with food from heaven, I was not strong, but as Rama prays for me, why did she say those bad words to vex me?" Being asked if she was angry with Rama, she said, "No; God has forgiven my sins, and shall I be angry with my friend for one word? No! no! I forgive her."

Towards the end of August her pain became more severe, and her cough was very troublesome, but she was never heard to repine; on the contrary, she would often rejoice in the prospect of her release. On the 14th of September there was reason to think that she would speedily be removed. She was evidently suffering much, and said, "My pain is great, but it is nothing to what my Saviour suffered. I feel happy." Being asked if she was not afraid to die, she replied, "No, I am not afraid; Christ is waiting at the end of the road. I want to go. Do not let the girls make a noise to disturb me, I shall soon be gone." She then requested to be read to, but during the reading she fell asleep. When she awoke she said, "Why did you let me sleep? It is but a little while, and I shall hear you read no more." Seeing her attendant much affected, she said, "Do not grieve, we shall be separated only for a short time."

On the 17th it was evident that her end was near; the pain was very great, but she bore it with much patience. During the afternoon she took leave of all the members of the family, and when Miss Davis said to her, "Farewell, Peti, you are now going to Jesus," she said in a whisper, "Yes, I am happy, I am happy," and after this she spoke no more.

In the settlement at Paihia there were nine baptized natives, and many who were candidates for the rite. This was a small party, but the time had been when that number of natives would not have remained with the missionaries. Now the influence of Christianity was extending, and there were nearly 200 persons in the station. The power of God was manifestly with his servants, and the stronghold of Satan was giving way. The inquirers after truth often gave expression to their feelings with much simplicity and force of language, and sought frequent opportunities for religious conversation. The following was written in the blank page of a book by a native youth living with Mr. King :—" Oh Jesus, we cannot perfectly believe in thee. We are bound by the evil spirit, and he will not let our hearts go free, lest we should believe in thee, lest we should be saved by thee, Oh Jesus, Son of God ! Oh, Jesus, how great is thy love to us. Thou didst descend from heaven, when thou didst understand the anger of thy Father to all man kind. They were going to the place of punishment ; they were not seeking after God. Thou didst say to thy Father, ' Let thine anger to mankind cease ; I am the substitute, I go to the world to be slain as a satisfaction for their sins ; I will purchase them with my blood.' "

The year 1830 was concluded, as the two preceding years had been, by a general gathering and examination of the natives belonging to the three missionary stations. This period had been by much the most eventful since the commencement of the mission. Disturbances among the natives had been frequent, and the missionaries had been sometimes exposed to danger; but never before had the contest taken place immediately before their eyes, as had been the case ten months before. This quarrel had been amicably settled. In the meantime a spiritual change was going on, having sprung, as it were, from the wreck of Satan's schemes of mischief. Many were shaking off the iron fetters; and, feeling the sweets of liberty, were ready to invite others to share it with them. It was thought to be a good opportunity of bringing together the people who were well disposed, under circumstances which might lead them to see more forcibly .the blessings of peace. The natives in the schools were most anxious to prepare themselves for the examination. A day or two before the meeting which took place at Paihia, the strange natives began to assemble, although invitations had been carefully avoided to any not belonging to the Christian party. Two canoes came from Whangaroa, the old chief Ururoa observing that Mr. Williams had paid him a visit some time before, and that he was now come to return it. The number of natives went on increasing, and by night it amounted to not less than eight hundred men, women, and children. At an early hour of the following day, the natives of the settlement were on the alert making preparations for the feast. Owing to the large number to be provided for, they cooked in the native mode in sixteen ovens, which were holes dug in the ground five feet each in diameter, and about eighteen inches deep. The process of cooking is to make a large wood fire in the cavity ; a proportionate number of stones, about one or two pounds weight each, are then thrown upon the wood, and the fire kept up until the stones are nearly red hot. A sufficient number to cover the bottom of the hole is then left, the rest being reserved. Upon the lower stones is placed a layer of grass or green herbage of any kind, and upon this the pork or potatoes are heaped up. A layer of grass similar to the first covers the food, and upon this the remainder of the hot stones are placed, which again are covered with more grass. The heap is then profusely sprinkled with water for the purpose of creating steam, and the whole is closely covered up with earth. Food thus prepared is exceedingly well cooked, and by no means to be despised even by an English palate. To carry on this part of the proceedings, which to the majority was by much the most important, it was necessary to retain some of the natives, while the rest were assembled at the chapel for prayers and examination.

At nine o'clock the business commenced, when the whole of the classes, arranged in three divisions, were respectively examined in the catechisms, writing, reading, and arithmetic. Their improvement since the last examination was not so great as might have been wished, but where a deficiency was made manifest it was more easy to apply the remedy. The numbers present were 270, being 178 men and boys, and 92 girls.

At two o'clock a plentiful supply of food was laid out, consisting of beef, pork, potatoes, and bread. That for the natives in the schools was arranged in Mr. Williams's garden, in green baskets made for the occasion, while a portion for the principal chiefs, together with a large supply of boiled flour sweetened with sugar, was carried out and divided according to the respective tribes. The number of strangers was larger than had been known to visit the settlement on any former occasion, but it is worthy of remark that they were never more peaceably disposed : there was no attempt (with one solitary exception), to be in any way troublesome, while all were satisfied and pleased with the repast provided for them. As soon as the dinner was ended, the two parties of strangers, representing those who had been engaged in conflict at Kororareka some months before, danced in the native style, and in a little while dispersed to their respective homes.

CHAPTER VII.

1831, 1832.

NEWS OF THE DEATH OF HENGI'S SONS—QUIET INTERVAL BEFORE
WAR BREAKS OUT—MESSRS. H. WILLIAMS AND CHAPMAN VISIT
TAURANGA AND ROTORUA—NATIVES IN THE BAY OF ISLANDS
PREPARE FOR WAR—EXPEDITION SETS OUT, ACCOMPANIED BY
THE MISSIONARIES—SLOW PROGRESS—CONSULTING THE AUGURY
—ARRIVAL AT TAURANGA—FREQUENT SKIRMISHING—MISSION-
ARIES RETURN TO THE BAY OF ISLANDS—MR. WILLIAMS SAILS
AGAIN TO TAURANGA—FRUITLESS EFFORTS TO MAKE PEACE—
PERILOUS VOYAGE BACK—NGAPUHI RETURN HOME, HAVING
FAILED IN THEIR PURPOSE.

IT was not till the month of March, 1831, that
tidings reached the Bay of Islands that the expedition under the sons of Hengi against the natives of
the south had met with a disastrous fate, and the
first feeling of their relations was to rise up and
avenge their death. The tribes assembled to delibe-
rate, and one spirit seemed to animate the whole;
but the season of the year was unfavourable : it was
now autumn, and they agreed to put off further steps
until their crops should all be in the ground for the
ensuing year. Here was again the prospect of a terrible storm. Not one tribe only, but all the tribes from
the North Cape, with those of Hokianga and the Bay
of Islands, were involved ; and they were to attack
the tribes of Tauranga, who were now well provided
with fire-arms, since the trade in flax had been

carried on with New South Wales. It was in vain to tell the natives that their relatives had brought this disaster upon themselves, and ought not to be avenged. They said that according to their customs they were bound to require blood for blood.

In the interval there was opportunity for the quiet progress of the Gospel, though as yet there were not many of the rulers who had believed. It was among persons of little note, principally slaves living at the mission stations, that the power of the Gospel began to appear. One of the missionaries writes :— "Edward came this evening and said he had a question to ask. His countenance brightened up as he was about to speak. At length he said, 'Will it be correct for the baptized natives to have a meeting to themselves on the night of your prayer-meeting, for there is one of us who says it will be wrong, because it will be making ourselves like the missionaries ?' He was told that they could not employ their evening better. He then inquired, 'How does the Spirit work upon the heart?' 'He brings sin to our knowledge, and enables us to overcome it.' 'And does it return again ?' 'Yes, and again we must fight with it.' 'Aye,' said he, 'this is my case.'"

About this time a man from Rotorua visited Paihia, saying that he was sent by the principal chief to ask for a missionary, and that the people were wishing to live quietly and to be instructed. Rotorua is situated a few miles from Tauranga, in the Bay of Plenty. A part of the tribe was cut off some

years before by Hongi, but it still numbered as many
people as the whole of the Bay of Islands. Tauranga was also populous, and the two districts
together had as many inhabitants as were to be found
from the Bay of Islands to the North Cape.

In the month of October the Rev. Henry Williams
and Mr. Chapman set out for Tauranga and Rotorua
in a small vessel, named *Te Karere* (messenger), which
had been built at Paihia, with a view to the extension of missionary operations. Several tribes were
visited, and it was sufficiently apparent that the field
of labour was of great importance. On their arrival
at Ohinemutu, a large village on the banks of the
Rotorua lake, the natives soon gathered around to
talk. One young man began to ask the use of
letters. They were written down for him, and in
half an hour he knew them all, and was teaching
those about him. Others again applied for copies,
until there was no paper left. At length they
brought some small pieces, and about two hundred,
old and young, were soon engaged in learning, first
the letters and then the Catechism, repeating it after
one who was already acquainted with it. They
continued at this employment till the time for evening
prayer, when they were told that the next day was
the Christian Sabbath, and it was proposed that they
should remain quiet and listen to what the missionaries had to tell them. Conversation was kept up
till dusk. The interest which was shown by old and
young was something altogether new. It was the

day on which the Gospel message was first delivered to them, and all was fair and promising. How easy might be the progress of true religion if there were no let or hindrance !

In the morning a white flag was hoisted as a signal for the natives that it was the Christian Sabbath. The natives were assembled in a house about fifty feet in length ; a partition in the centre was removed, and some holes were cut to admit light and air. After prayers, they were addressed on the necessity of the new birth, and an interesting conversation on this subject followed. The young people came together afterwards for catechism, and repeated their letters. At the evening service the subject brought before them was the fall of man, and his salvation by Christ. This must have been an astonishing day to these natives. Many new things did they hear, surprising to their savage understandings. The word was put forth to await the blessing of him who sent it.

On the return of the missionary deputation, it was found that Ngapuhi were all on the alert making preparation for war. They were elated with the hope that their forces would be numerous enough to overpower all opposition, and their evil passions led them back to the scenes of former days, when they were able to destroy their enemies at pleasure. The missionaries determined to attempt to bring about a reconciliation, but the chiefs at first would hear of no interference with their plans. On the 24th of November I accompanied the Rev. H. Williams to Kororareka, to ascertain whether Ngapuhi were inclined to make peace with Tauranga. We found Wharerahi and several other chiefs busy preparing their canoes, but they all left their work to come to us. On asking what their intentions were, Rewa rose up and made a violent harangue, saying that they intended to fight and take slaves, and that it would not be well for any of the missionaries to go with them, because they would only be offended with the sights they would witness. When he had concluded we obtained a quiet hearing, and he told us privately that it did not rest with him to make peace, and that we were at liberty to go with them if we liked. They had been somewhat disconcerted the day before by a report that the natives of Te Kawakawa, who the year before had abandoned Kororareka, intended to go and kill their wives and children during their absence, and they requested us to go and speak to them. The next day we went up to Otuihu, when the chiefs disclaimed all idea of attacking the families at Kororareka. By thus interesting ourselves in their temporal welfare, we were permitted to obtain great ascendency over them, which could not fail to work for good.

About a week after this we saw the chiefs at their respective residences, and were grieved to hear some of their expressions relative to the war. They were respectful, however, and gave their sanction for some of us to go with them. But the intentions of many

were very bad. They contemplated nothing less than
the utter annihilation of their enemies. Were it not
for the still small voice of God heard amidst all this
confusion, encouraging us in our efforts, we should certainly have given up in despair. Those who were
about to engage in the expedition were our most inti-
mate friends, men who had distinguished themselves
latterly in the promotion of peace, but now they were
influenced by another spirit, and were ready for all
kinds of wickedness. They were told that if they
were strangers we should not say so much, but that
since they were our friends, if they persisted in their
determination to go, we must accompany them.

On the 7th of December we observed several
canoes under sail standing for Kororareka. Tohitapu
came and invited us to go over, which we immediately did. He observed on the way that we must
be very urgent with the natives, and not regard their
objections to our interference. We met the principal chiefs at Moka's house. Their manner was
much more friendly than it had been previously.
After some conversation we all went to Ururoa, the
Whangaroa chief. He certainly did not show much
desire for fighting, and seemed willing either to go or
stay, according to the wish of the majority. Titore
was the reputed leader of the expedition, and it was
necessary to know his mind. He did not like to speak
publicly, but coming over to Paihia, he said that the
natives must proceed, but that when we approached
near to Tauranga something might be done to bring

about peace. After thus gathering the opinions of the most influential persons, we concluded that there was a sufficient opening for us to act, and that it would be right for some of us to accompany them, with a view to influence them by every means in our power.

A week afterwards, three canoes came over from Kororareka, in which were Tareha, Rewa, Moka, and others. Their language was totally changed. They expressed a desire that both the mission vessels should go in company with their canoes. Not a word was now said about killing and eating their enemies, but all was for peace, if the opposite party should be so disposed. We could not but thank God for this change. Day and night had our hearts been lifted up to Him, that He would confound their wicked imaginations, and bring their devices to naught.

It was now arranged that the missionary deputation should consist of the Rev. H. Williams, Mr. Kemp, and Mr. Fairburn ; and on the 3d of January, 1832, they set sail in a boat from Paihia with two of the canoes, for the purpose of joining the main body at the general place of rendezvous. There was a prospect of a tedious voyage, because the various little tribes of which the armament was made up were each independent of the other, and those who were disposed to linger on the way would oblige the rest to wait for them, before they reached the enemy's territories. Notwithstanding the improvement which had been noticed in the language of some of the chiefs, the body of the people was under the influence of the worst passions of our nature, and impatient of restraint, their chief desire being to carry destruction among their enemies. It was a novelty to have any in their company who did not enter into their wicked schemes, but now they had consented to allow missionaries to go with them, whose presence they knew would often prove an inconvenient check. Yet there were many who thought that this arrangement might prove advantageous, having experienced the good effects of the reconciliation which had been brought about on former occasions at Hokianga and at Kororareka, when much evil was avoided, which they could not otherwise have escaped. Moving slowly down the coast, the fleet reached the beautiful little harbour of Tutukaka on the afternoon of the 7th, and on the following day, which was Sunday, they consented to remain quiet. At eight o'clock all the natives within reach were assembled. It was truly pleasing thus to meet a congregation of New Zealand warriors, called aside from their usual horrid conversation to sing the praises of God, and to hear of a Saviour's love. They all acknowledged that it was a good thing thus to meet together. Some of Titore's people, contrary to his wishes, were in the woods shooting pigeons. In the afternoon, by the special request of Rewa and Wharepoaka, who were encamped at a little distance, another service was held with their party.

A fortnight passed without advancing very far on

their way. There was a large body of natives, but there was no leader of sufficient authority to influence the whole. Those from Hokianga began to talk of going up the Thames to fall upon the women and children of the Tauranga people, making an attack by an inland road. Food was now becoming scarce, and on the 22d of January there was much exclamation at the sight of some excellent fern-root, which had been dug up the day before, and Moka at once gave orders to launch his canoe, for the purpose of going in quest of some. There was great confusion, and it was felt that to speak to him would be of little use. Mr. Williams, however, sent to him to say that it was the sacred day, that he must not resist the command of God, and that on the next day they would all go. Contrary to expectation, he at once told his people to remain. Thus there was an encouragement to use the means, with simple trust in God to accomplish the end. This Moka was brother to Wharerahi and Rewa, a daring, impudent, self-willed savage, of much influence, always ready for mischief, and possessing no one good quality. At 8 A.M. there was service, and the natives behaved well; but later in the day many felt the restraint irksome. Huke, a leading chief, was busily occupied at his work at the further end of the beach, but he immediately stopped on seeing Mr. Williams approach. In the evening Moka and Tohi-tapu put their canoes in order for moving in the morning, and, from a few expressions that escaped them, it was evident that their intentions respecting any straggling natives they might fall in with were bad. They said they were hungry, and they must go and dig fern-root, and cross the Thames at a narrower part, and that the missionaries had better remain with Tareha and Titore ; but as they seemed to be disposed for mischief, Mr. Williams determined to keep close to them.

After the lapse of another month, the main body of the fleet had only reached the Mercury Isles. There was no appearance as yet of Ururoa's party, who had separated from them ; and there was reason to apprehend that they might have passed on, and perhaps commenced their murderous proceedings. Poor creatures ! how greatly they needed all that could be done for them ! Every man's hand was against his brother. Surely the land was polluted with blood. Places were continually pointed out where recent conflicts had occurred. The only hope of their deliverance from the cruel bondage under which they were held was in God.

Superstition, as well as every other evil, still kept a firm hold upon their minds. An instance of this was given on the 4th of March. " It was Sunday morning, and the natives were making a great noise on every side long before daylight. When in want of his breakfast, Mr. Williams was told that fire and water were ' tapu '—that none were to eat or drink until the oracle had been consulted, and that the priest was preparing for the ceremony at a short distance from them. He went, and found about eight

chiefs in a retired shady spot, and was at first forbidden to approach; but after a little consultation,
he was permitted to join them under the plea that he
was a white man. They were all naked, and were
fixing sticks about a foot long in the ground, in rows,
according to the number of the canoes. There were
other sticks also to represent the chiefs of the enemy.
Against each of these were placed two others of the
same length, each stick having a piece of flax leaf
tied to it. When all was duly arranged, they were
required to withdraw, and the old wizard alone remained, who had scarcely five pounds of flesh upon
his bones. In about half an hour, the old fellow,
with an air of great self-importance, came out, and
sat down in the midst of the expectant host. He
inquired of Tohitapu his dreams, and related his own
of the preceding night. The chiefs then approached
the scene of action, where the old priest had been at
work, and found the sticks in the greatest disorder.
About a third of them lay on the ground, which were
said to indicate those who were to fall in battle. He
had one set of sticks for the boat,—that is, for Mr.
Williams and his crew, which were all safe. In a
few minutes a large body of natives rushed up to
learn their impending fate, each making inquiries
about himself, with so much vociferation and earnestness that it was impossible for any to hear. At
length partial silence was obtained, and the old man
began to relate particulars; but did not advance far
before he was confused, and the ceremony had to be

gone over again. The sacred spot was again cleared, and no one was allowed to be there but the old man. Inquiries were made whether Mr. Williams had had any breakfast, and they were much pleased when they found he had not. They appeared to place implicit confidence in what this priest should disclose to them. At ten o'clock, the ceremonies being concluded, the bell was rung for service. This bell had been sent from Paihia, in a native schooner, and was now used for the first time. It was a pleasant sound in this wild place, and in the midst of a still wilder mob. About a hundred came together. Rewa and Te Koikoi were the only chiefs of note present, but all were attentive. After service, Rewa remarked that they should all soon become believers.

On the 6th of March the fleet of canoes entered the heads of Tauranga, and prepared an encampment at Matakana. Here an old woman belonging to Ngatimaru was taken by Tareha's people. She stated that great deeds had been done by Wharerahi, and the party who accompanied him up the Thames, against the allies of the Tauranga natives. There was every probability that her story was false; but it was painful to see with what eagerness her tale was listened to. She said, moreover, that Ururoa, who had preceded the main body, was only a few miles distant, on the opposite side of the river. In a short time five of the canoes went over to learn the news, and it was ascertained that several skirmishes had taken place, but none were killed or wounded on either side. At midnight the camp was alarmed by the discharge of four guns close to the beach. It not being known whether they were fired by friends or foes, all were at once under arms. It was a messenger from Ururoa. The silence with which he stood for a time cast a degree of awe over the assembly, who were all gathered around the fires they had hastily kindled. The native was a stranger, a fine-looking man, though wild in his appearance. He stood leaning upon the top of his musket; a billhook, bright as silver, in his belt, and a handsome dogskin mat thrown carelessly over his shoulders. By the light of the fires, he presented a fine specimen of savage nobility. He gave some particulars of Wharerahi and his party, and also of their own encounter the same afternoon with Ngatiawa, which is the general name of the Tauranga natives.

At daylight on the 7th of March all were in motion launching their canoes, and at ten o'clock they embarked, but in closer order than before, and presented a formidable appearance, each canoe displaying its separate flag. The number of canoes and boats was about eighty. They took up a position about two miles from Otumoetai, the Pa of Ngatiawa. At low water, all the people set off for the professed purpose of foraging in the plantations; some few, however, went directly towards the Pa, which was separated from them by a deep stream of water. Several of the opposite party turned out to meet them, and they carried on a brisk fire till dusk; but none were hit on either side. This affair supplied subject for conversation through the night. It was painful to witness the spirit which was shown. Tohitapu was among the worst, and was very angry when Mr. Williams spoke to him of the deceitful course he was pursuing.

On the 10th, at daybreak, a landing was effected near Otumoetai. The Ngatiawa were soon out to receive their enemies, and a brisk fire was kept up. Mr. Williams ascended the summit of an old Pa, from whence, with the help of his glass, he had a good view of their movements, and soon perceived that the Ngapuhi were driven out from some bushes where they had taken up their position. The firing lasted about three hours, and various reports were brought of the killed and wounded. They then returned to the camp, having expended their ammunition, and bringing with them one of their party killed. A second had been struck by a ball on his cartouche-box, which saved him. There was now a great clamour made by the Ngapuhi relating their great deeds during the action. Mr. Williams retired to his tent, over-whelmed with the gloomy prospect, and he determined to take up his abode on board the Mission schooner, considering that his counsel was rejected, and that the natives had better be left for a while to them-selves. On going out of his tent, he was much sur-prised to observe the enemy in possession of the heights, about half a mile distant, and firing down upon some wild fellows who were exchanging shots with them, in full view of the main body, occasionally dancing and brandishing their muskets in defiance.

As he passed down to the boat, several of the chiefs were sitting by their canoes, and appeared to be much crestfallen. None spoke but Moka, who desired that the wounds of their enemies should not be dressed. They were told that all the Maoris throughout the island were alike the missionaries' friends, and that the same attention would be given to all. Several of the Ngatiawa were on the side of the river as the boat passed ; but none attempted to offer molestation, being aware of the object for which the missionaries were there.

The skirmishing parties were now out daily, and there seemed to be very little hope of bringing about a reconciliation. Ngatiawa would gladly have made peace, but the Ngapuhi were averse to it. On the afternoon of the 14th, Mr. Williams and Mr. Kemp went to their camp. Some were friendly, as before ; others would not speak, and appeared to be quite elated with a fresh supply of ammunition they had obtained from a vessel then lying at anchor. It was determined, therefore, to ascertain their real intentions ; but every voice was for war, and all their wicked feelings seemed to be let loose. Tohitapu was very violent, and Tenaana, a Waimate chief, tried to stir up a hostile feeling by saying that Mr. Williams had been giving a description of the principal men to Ngatiawa, in order that they might be picked off ; but he was soon put to silence. On the 15th of March it was concluded that as much patient exertion had been now used for many weeks, but all to no purpose, the best course would be to leave the people to themselves. The missionaries accordingly passed through the camp, and, returning on board the *Active*, prepared for sea. Several of the Ngatiawa went on board, and expressed a desire that they would soon come back, and bring teachers to live among them ; but there seemed to be little hope that they would be able successfully to oppose an enemy much superior to them in numbers, and supported by an English trader, who supplied them with ammunition. In the evening the *Active* put to sea, and, after a voyage of three days, reached the Bay of Islands in safety.

After a lapse of eight days Mr. Williams and Mr. Fairburn again sailed for Tauranga, anxious to observe any favourable opening that might occur for the restoration of peace. They entered the harbour of Tauranga on the night of the 31st of March. The next day was the Sabbath, and at sunrise upwards of a dozen canoes full of men were observed pulling towards them from the Ngapuhi camp. They landed at some distance, and continued running along the beach until they came abreast of the vessel. A white flag was hoisted, but they were not satisfied what the vessel was until they had hailed her, when they danced the war dance, and invited the passengers to go on shore. They said they thought it was the schooner with which they had been engaged ten days before, and they had now come to take her, and had brought with them six great guns. They related their proceedings during the interval of Mr.

Williams's absence, and appeared glad to be again visited. Titore, with three canoes, remained till the tide flowed, for the purpose of conducting the missionaries to the camp. At ten o'clock there was service on board, and in the afternoon they went on shore. They met a canoe in which were the principal Ngapuhi chiefs. They were very friendly, and returned with them. Tohitapu with much self-importance related their great deeds, magnifying the loss of the enemy. As they passed through the camp it was gratifying to see a change in the tone of the people. Many shook their heads, signifying that they were tired; and others complained of want of food. Their attempts had failed. They found their opponents were not backward to meet them: their great guns had been brought into action, but had proved useless, and news had just arrived that a large reinforcement had joined Ngatiawa from Waikato. There was thus some reason to hope that peace might be brought about. On the next day the camp was visited, and it was found that many of the natives were wishing to return home, but others were obstinately bent on fighting. They went also to see the Ngatiawa, who were in good spirits. They were willing to make peace, but were also prepared for war. Upon further intercourse with Ngapuhi, finding that they were still averse to peace, it was determined again to take leave and return to the Bay of Islands.

They set sail on the 7th of April. The wind was fair, and was freshening up to a gale, and it was thought advisable to proceed to the Barrier Island, where there are two good harbours. As they drew under the land, the gusts were so violent that it was feared that either the masts or yards would be carried away. The vessel became unmanageable, and with much apprehension they were obliged to take in sail, and let the vessel drift. As the darkness set in, so did the fears of those on board increase. They could not keep the weather shore—what were they to expect from a lee one? It was an iron-bound coast, with rocks and small islands scattered in all directions. At first dawn of day there was a dark hazy loom of high land close on the lee beam, like the king of terrors frowning upon them, as he sat brooding over the storm, ready to snatch his victims. They wore the ship and made sail, under the impression that it was Cape Colville; but it was soon seen to be the north head of Port Charles, in which there was no shelter. They stood on under all sail to endeavour to weather the point which presented itself on their lee bow, but despairing of this, as the sea was setting them fast to leeward, they determined to try and stay the ship, as the only alternative, there not being room to wear. She had missed stays several times the preceding day, which had brought them into their present position. Every countenance spoke alarm, and it was declared to be impossible to save her. But what is impossible with man is possible with God. They watched a smooth of the sea to put the helm down, and at that interval there was a lull.

The vessel came round in a surprising manner, though to all human appearance it was impossible she could weather the land owing to the heavy sea which was running. After a short time they were relieved by perceiving that they gradually drew off the shore. They stood on, wishing to regain the islands to windward of Mercury Bay, but still the weather was so very thick, they could scarcely see the vessel's length around her. After standing with intense earnestness on the look-out, for the danger was not yet over, land was announced on the lee bow, close to them, which they perceived was the desired point. They bore up and were soon in smooth water, under the lee of the Mercury Isles, and discovered what had not been before seen, though they had often been in this neighbourhood—a commodious bay in which they anchored, to the unspeakable relief of both body and mind. They all assembled in the cabin, to offer up praise to the God of all mercies for their great deliverance. As soon as the gale broke the vessel proceeded back to the Bay of Islands.

" On reflecting upon the circumstance of this voyage," wrote Mr. Williams, " I was overpowered with gratitude. We had sought for shelter in a known harbour, but were prevented from reaching it, though close to the entrance, and were exposed during a long night to danger on all sides. Land was around us, but the weather was so thick that we could not see it till we were close upon it. But at the moment when it became needful for us to act the day dawned ;

our danger at that instant was pointed out by a break in the haze, and we were enabled to do what alone could save us. The captain gave orders to wear, which would have been inevitable destruction. This was overruled, and the ship was thrown into stays as the last and only resource. Oh, may it be a Sabbath long remembered with gratitude!"

The attempts thus made to bring about a reconciliation between the contending tribes were unsuccessful, but still it was believed that the proceedings of the natives were much influenced by this interference. Little mischief comparatively was done on either side, and on the return of Ngapuhi to the Bay of Islands, the chiefs acknowledged that their expedition had been a failure, and that they believed the God of the missionaries had made them listless, and had prevented them from carrying out their purposes. Some said their guns would not shoot straight, for though they were frequently quite close to the enemy, the shots flew off from the object aimed at. They brought with them, however, a few of those trophies over which they most exulted—the heads of their enemies. The following scene took place at Kororareka when Mr. Williams and Mr. Brown went with Tohitapu to see Titore. After a good deal of ceremony on the part of Tohi they walked towards Titore and his party, who were all tapu, and consequently sitting by themselves, in an open space, with the heads of their friends and enemies arranged before them. There were fourteen heads of the Nga-

tiawa, and three of Ngapuhi. The latter were at a short
distance from the others, being worthy of more honour.
The sight was most disgusting. The heads were dressed
with feathers, and the teeth exposed to view, which
gave them a most ghastly appearance. The countenances of all the natives seemed to partake of the
image of their father the devil. They were truly
Satanic; a grin of satisfaction was on every face.
Tohitapu walked towards the three heads belonging to
Ngapuhi, and addressing "Tu," the god of war, from
whom the art of war, bravery, and cunning is considered to proceed, he extolled the heroic deeds of these
warriors; and looking to the payment, the fourteen
heads of Ngatiawa, he expressed his approbation. He
then turned to Titore, and falling on his neck, they
joined in a New Zealand lamentation. This lasted
a few minutes, after which they proceeded to talk
over the events of the late campaign.

The return of the natives without effecting the
object for which they went was regarded by the
missionaries as a cause for thankfulness, inasmuch as
the hand of God was distinctly manifest, and acknowledged too by the natives. A day of general thanks-
giving was therefore set apart to commemorate this
event. On that occasion many natives assembled at
the places of worship, and while some secretly
maligned the good cause, and would willingly have
set themselves in direct opposition, they were con-
strained to confess that the missionaries were right
and they were wrong.

CHAPTER VIII.

1832, 1833.

PROGRESS AMONG THOSE WHO REMAINED AT HOME — RIPI—BAP-
TISMS—MISSIONARY VISIT TO KAITAEA—PANAKAREAO—MISSION
STATION FIXED UPON — POLYGAMY—TITORE LEADS ANOTHER
EXPEDITION AGAINST TAURANGA—MESSRS. WILLIAMS AND CHAP-
MAN ACCOMPANY IT—FRUITLESS EFFORTS TO BRING ABOUT
PEACE—A PARTY OF EAST CAPE NATIVES BROUGHT TO THE
BAY OF ISLANDS.

DURING the interval in which the principal chiefs
of Ngapuhi had been thus employed at the south, a
good work was gradually proceeding among those they
had left behind. Not only in the mission stations,
but in all the surrounding villages, the seed which
had been scattered was beginning to vegetate, and it
was an advantage no doubt that most of the restless
spirits were away for a time, and unable to exercise
their pernicious influence upon the community. At
Waimate the chapel was far too small for the congregation, and numbers could not gain admittance.
At Ohaiawai there was an average attendance of
from sixty to seventy, and sometimes there were more
than the house could hold. At Kerikeri the desire
on the part of the natives to read the Scriptures was
increasing. Those who made a profession of religion
discovered great earnestness, and the senior baptized
natives rendered much assistance in giving instruc-

tion. There was great cause for thankfulness in the progressive state of the mission towards the great object in view. It seemed as if Satan was retreating from his stronghold. The chain of superstition appeared to be broken, while many circumstances which would have been offensive in the highest degree to the natives, as connected with their peculiar superstitions, were wont to pass off without notice, as they were convinced of their folly in holding those opinions any longer.

Ripi, the chief of Mawhe, with his party, were steady in their attendance on Christian worship. The manner in which the Sabbath was kept by his tribe would have shamed many country parishes in England. It was really a day of rest; their firewood being prepared and their potatoes peeled on the preceding day. The chapel in which they met was soon too small for the congregation, and was replaced by a larger building. When Mr. Davis entered into conversation with Ripi on the subject of baptism, he said, "I am afraid to tell you my thoughts about it, lest you may think me a hypocrite. If I could write, you should know all about it. I have prayed to God to reveal to me the sinfulness of my heart, and he has done it; and now I want to be delivered from all sin." Inquiry being made into the state of his wife's mind, he said, "You and I cannot look into people's hearts, but the other day I spoke to her, and she told me that her heart was desponding and sorrowful, on account of her many sins."

When Ripi first went to the neighbouring village of Kaikohe to talk with his friends on religious subjects, he was well received by the chiefs, but afterwards, under the influence of the war party, who were preparing to go to Tauranga, notice was sent to him that he must discontinue his visits. Although there was some interruption in direct intercourse, yet there was a work going on. A few months afterwards the old chief Atuahaere went to see Mr. Davis at Waimate, accompanied by two young men. He said, " I am come to know what I must do with the rubbish that is about my place and in my house." Having caught his figure, Mr. Davis answered, " I have told you that you must pray for strength from on high to enable you to clear it away." " Yes," said he, " I wish to clear out my house, in order that the Holy Spirit may come and dwell within it." Mr. Davis told him that his desires were of the right kind, but that in ourselves we are weak and helpless, and that without strength from above we can do nothing. The old man listened with much earnestness while some of the invitations and promises of the Gospel were explained to him. It was, indeed, a pleasing sight, and the two young men who accompanied him, being some of those who had first come for instruction twelve months before, seemed to be filled with joy on account of their aged companion.

The number of Christian baptisms up to this period was confined for the most part to a few of the natives connected with the different mission stations; and with these it was the endeavour of the missionaries to use the greatest caution. We read of the' course pursued by Augustine, the first archbishop of Canterbury, that 10,000 of the men of Kent were baptized under his direction before he had lived twelve months in his new diocese. But in New Zealand, after nearly twenty years of labour, the native Christians did not exceed fifty. They were subjected to a lengthened period of instruction, during which there was opportunity given to obtain an insight into general character. "We are solicitous," it was stated, "to err rather on the side of caution in admitting persons into the Church, and the consequence has been that of the number baptized there is scarcely an instance in which there is cause for regret."

A few of the Christian natives were now also admitted to the Lord's Supper.

"Having conversed several times," wrote one of the missionaries, "with some of the candidates, I called them together preparatory to their admission on the morrow. I am satisfied with them all, but only two wish to partake at the present time, the rest preferring to wait for another occasion. One of the two remarked, 'This sacrament is a means of strengthening my faith, therefore I desire to partake of it. I do not wish to delay, because I know not how soon death may overtake me.'" It was no wonder that, amidst the repeated shocks which the kingdom of Satan was receiving, he should have employed his remaining strength in exciting to acts of bloodshed those who had not yet received the truth in the love of it.

The time seemed now to have arrived when steps might be taken for the extension of missionary labours to the more distant parts of the country. The natives of Tauranga and Rotorua had expressed their wish that missionaries should settle among them, but that part of the island was in too disturbed a state to admit of it. It was determined therefore that an exploring party should visit the tribes in the northern part of the island, with whom as yet no intercourse had been held. The party consisted of Messrs. Baker, Hamlin, Puckey, Matthews, and myself. Ripi also, who had been baptized by the name of Paratene, and a few of the Christian natives from the mission stations, were of the party. We set out from Kerikeri on the 26th of November, 1832. The narrative of the journey furnishes many particulars which throw light upon the state of the country and its inhabitants. Proceeding on the road to Whangaroa, there was little to interest except the recollection of former times. When we arrived in the neighbourhood of the old Wesleyan station, the ravages of war were but too apparent. Portions of very fine land, once in a good state of cultivation, were now lying desolate, while the few scattered inhabitants afforded a melancholy contrast to its former state. It was gratifying to hear a conversation which passed between Paratene Ripi and one of the chiefs. He was relating an interview which he had just had with some people in a neighbouring valley, from which it could be clearly gathered that he did not in the least shrink from declaring to others those good things of which he had himself tasted.

Proceeding a little further we came to a deserted fortification, the greater part of the fence still remaining. It had belonged to Hongi and his followers, but many of them had been killed within the last two years. At length we arrived at Papuke, the residence of Ururoa, where we pitched our tent. This Pa, when Hongi was lying here after he was wounded, was full of people, but it now partook in some measure of the general desolation. Ururoa and Paratene were relatives, and chiefs of equal standing, and it was truly gratifying to witness the boldness and the force with which the latter delivered his sentiments. Speaking of the general motives which influence the natives, which are power and reputation, he said, "The name which a native gains is like the hoar frost, which disappears as soon as the sun shines upon it; but if a man is brave in seeking after the things of Christ, his name lasts for ever." After speaking for a long time, he ran off in a hurry, and returned immediately from the tent with his native book. He then proceeded, "It has been said by the natives that the missionaries bewitch them, and cause them to die." He then read a few of the Scripture sentences at the commencement of the Liturgy. "Now," said he, "what does all this say? Where is there anything here which can harm us? No;

God does not harm you, and all that He wishes is, that you should not harm yourselves, but that you should listen to Him and be saved." He then continued, "Who made this land in which we live ?" They then gave some evasive answer, but he pushed them hard, repeating his question : when at last he told them, it was not Maui, but the God of the Europeans. They at last said, " You are right, Ripi : your ideas are correct and ours are wrong." He also said much about native food, which they think will not grow, unless their superstitious rites are observed. This subject he handled in a way which missionaries cannot reach, and therefore with more effect. He concluded by saying, " You do not laugh at what I say to you now, but I suppose, when we are gone, you will say it is all false."

Proceeding to the valley of Oruru, we came to the village of Whaare, the principal chief, where we expected an invitation for the night. We gave to the natives a general outline of our message ; and Paratene, who was also related to this chief, spoke plainly to him in reference to their former wars ; but so much unconcern was shown, that we were glad to pass on. We went about eight miles further, and brought up at dark, by the side of a river, in a most solitary part of the country, where there was neither cultivation nor dwelling of man, but we observed marks of many Pas which had been in occupation in former times.

The night was very stormy—the wind blew high,

with violent rain, thunder and lightning—but very little rain came through our tents. We were now in a country altogether new to us; but a strange native had discovered us, and in the morning we were conducted to a village. Two chiefs of the place made speeches of welcome, which were quickly followed by a cooked pig, smoking hot out of the oven, with fish and kumara. This afforded a pleasing contrast to the cold reception we met with at Oruru, and was received by us as an earnest of a good welcome among the Rarawa tribes, to which our hosts belonged. A little further on we came to the river Whakarake, where Panakareao, one of the leading men, resided. We hoped to gather from him the information we required, to show where it might be desirable to form a missionary station. But it was necessary to observe the utmost caution, as we did not feel ourselves at liberty to make any promises which might raise their expectations. There was evidently an opening for missionary labour in various parts of the district, but as this tribe was unacquainted with us, and we with them, we determined to be guided by the disposition which they might manifest towards us. Panakareao gave us some encouragement. Conversing with him upon the general subject of our message, he expressed a wish to have missionaries, saying, that Ngapuhi alone had been taught hitherto, and that if the Rarawa were instructed, they would give up their present mode of life.

December 2d being Sunday, our flag was hoisted at an early hour, and at nine o'clock we had service with our own party, being joined by about thirty strangers. After this we dispersed to the neighbouring villages, but we did not meet with many natives. There is one point which is worthy of remark—that, wherever we went, we found a general knowledge of our object prevailing. They well knew the difference between us and the Europeans living among them, who are connected with the flax trade. There was, also, some idea of the Sabbath, which they all profess to keep. Now, whether they observed it or not, their profession at least showed a good feeling. They mentioned that there was a large party living at Whangape, on the western coast, who kept the Sabbath, and that whenever they went on a journey, they offered up a prayer to our God. These particulars would not be worthy of notice, except that we know that no missionary had been in any direct intercourse with them, and that all the light they had derived was gained from natives who had had communication with us. So sure is it that a little leaven leaveneth the whole lump. Nor was the case of this tribe a solitary instance of the fields being white already to harvest. Panakareao was very inquisitive to know what we thought of the place, and whether this was to be the only visit they were to receive from us. As we did not give him a direct answer, he at length observed that he was anxious to have a missionary, and pointed out a wood of good timber, which he had set apart some time before for the use of missionaries, in the hope that, sooner or later, he might have one. We then told him that perhaps, if the other tribes were favourable, a settlement might be formed. His countenance at once brightened up, and he said, he knew they would all desire it. After a careful examination of the district a site was found at Kaitaea, which seemed calculated in every respect to answer our purpose; but we told Panakareao that we could not make any promises, and that they must not consider us guilty of breaking our word if nobody should come to reside among them.

In the course of this journey it became abundantly apparent how great is likely to be the value of native agency. An intelligent New Zealander, if only his thoughts are directed into a right channel, is much better able than a foreigner to adapt his language so as to arrest the attention of his countrymen. He is able to show them so much better the falsehood of their superstitions. It comes home with much force to say, " I have done all these things, and have learnt the evil of them." As we passed up the valley of Kaitaea, Ripi pointed out several places, to which he had been in former times to fight and pillage. On one occasion he was talking about his own case, and said, among other things, " Since I have believed, I never quarrel with my wife, as I used to do." To which a native replied, " It is because you have only one wife." Ripi answered, " I had three wives, who are now all alive : by one I had seven children, and by another three, who all died some time ago ; but when I began to think of the things of God, I said to myself, ' If I keep these three wives, they will always be a snare to me.' I therefore put aside two, and find myself much happier with one."

The subject of polygamy came under the consideration of the missionaries at an early period. It has been stated, by high authority, that the missionaries did wrong to interfere in those cases where a man having several wives came forward as a candidate for Christian baptism. It was felt, however, that some general rule must be adopted. It was quite evident that, under the Christian dispensation, the practice is not allowed, and that no Christian man having a wife can be allowed to take to himself another during her lifetime. The only difficulty was how to deal with those persons who had more wives than one before they came under the influence of Christian instruction. In looking into this subject, it was clear that the plurality of wives among the natives was a great injustice. The proportion of the sexes has been found to be painfully unequal. Throughout the country, there are about four males to three females. A chief was allowed to take as many wives as he pleased, but many a poor man had none. While, however, there was some hesitation as to what course should be followed in the case of converts to Christianity, the difficulty was disposed of by the natives themselves. The majority of those concerned acted as Ripi did. They were under the influence of higher principles, and, without hesitation, they put away all their wives but one. Such is the Christian rule, and we have followed it. There have been, indeed, some cases in which there seemed to be a degree of hardship. A native might be warmly attached to his wives, and they to him. But when the example had once been set by the majority, it would not have been right to have made exception in favour of a few, because they had rather not come under this rule. If it had been so, there are, doubtless, many others who would have said, "If my neighbour keeps his two or three wives as a Christian man, why may not I take a second wife without damaging my Christianity? Some years afterwards, a native of Waiapu came forward as a candidate for baptism, with his two wives, both young and interesting women. Upon the subject of general information in Christian truths there was no obstacle to their baptism. The question was then put to the husband, what he thought of doing about his two wives. Poor man! he cast a look, which could not be mistaken, first at one and then at the other, and said, "I cannot tell you." The two women were baptized at that time, as they had no power in this matter. The husband was recommended to take time for consideration. He subsequently made choice of one, and was then baptized.

There was now a fair prospect of advancing the labours of the missionaries to the northern extremity of the island. A large population had long been sitting in darkness, but the Sun of righteousness was about to shine upon them. In the south, however, there was all this darkness rendered the more gloomy by the desolating effects of war. There was little hope of a termination of this state of things until missionaries could be located among them. Still there was a work going on ; the words of Him who spake as never man spake were winning their almost silent and unseen way. Inquiry was abroad, but the question, Who will come over and help us ? had yet to be asked for some time longer.

After the return of Ngapuhi from the expedition against Tauranga, Titore appeared determined to carry on the war, though he had professed a desire for peace. No great deeds had been accomplished, and he wished to do what others had been unable to do. He had returned to the Bay of Islands in November, 1832, and in a short time he prepared to set out again, taking with him a large number of the Rarawa tribe. It was remarkable that this movement should have been made immediately after steps had been taken to send missionaries to the Rarawa. Satan was at hand to exert his power for evil, before the Gospel could be carried to them. The Rarawa had not the most distant connexion with the Tauranga quarrel, but they were still the slaves of Satan, and that was sufficient.

The Rev. Henry Williams determined to follow this party, and again try to effect a reconciliation He and Mr. Chapman therefore set out in two boats

on the 7th of February, following close after the
hostile armament. On the 11th they observed fires
at Whakatuwhenua, and they soon landed among the
Rarawa. The natives treated them with civility,
although they knew that their object was to thwart
them in their proceedings. From this point Mr.
Williams and Mr. Chapman went forward in their
boats, having had experience on former occasions of
the dilatory movements of the natives, and left the
Rarawa to follow at their leisure.

As they drew near to Maketu, which is the sea-
port of Rotorua, they observed a flag hoisted half-
mast high, and soon learnt that ten persons had been
killed the day before by the opposite party on the
road to Rotorua. It is necessary here to observe that,
in the former campaign of Ngapuhi against Tauranga,
they had been joined by the Rotorua tribes, and the
conflict between Rotorua and Tauranga was still
going on. The missionaries met with a very friendly
reception on shore, but the people seemed to be
determined to continue the contest, and little hope
appeared of leading them to peace.

After a week's detention the firing of musketry
was heard beyond the Tumu, a Pa of Ngatiawa at a
short distance from Maketu, and within sight, being
close to the beach and on the road to Tauranga. The
Maketu natives immediately prepared for action, and
crossed the river to attack the side of the Pa nearest
to them, under the idea that Titore and the Rarawa
were assaulting the opposite side. They disregarded

all remonstrance, and left only women and children behind, expressing their confidence that the Pa of the enemy would be taken. As they crossed the river they gathered around their priests, who stood in the water during the performance of a religious ceremony, sprinkling the people occasionally with water, at the conclusion of which they caught up handfuls of sand, and throwing it into the river they all ran off towards the enemy. As they approached the Pa they slackened their pace, and most of them were content to sit down under the cover of a rising ground ; but few were inclined to expose themselves to the enemy's fire. In about two hours they returned, bringing two wounded men, but none were killed. In the afternoon a party of those who had gone out in the morning returned in a frantic state, exclaiming that Tupaea, the chief of Ngatiawa, and twenty of his people were killed, and their bodies taken ; upon which all the women showed the strongest signs of exultation, tossing up their hands, and presenting a most frightful appearance. It was a relief to learn shortly afterwards that two only had been killed on each side.

Te Amohau, the father of a man who had been shot a few days before, after he had lamented over the corpse, addressed himself to the people, saying, that as he had now lost a son in the war, it was for him to decide what should be done, and that he should proceed with the missionaries, and make peace. He wished for no payment on account of his

THE OLD MISSION HOUSE AT TE NGAE, ROTORUA.

son, his only desire was that these proceedings might be stayed. When Mr. Williams met the old man, he proposed that a letter should be sent in the morning to some of the leading men of the enemy, and if they were willing, he would then accompany the missionaries in their boat to Tauranga to meet Titore and the Rarawa, and at once make peace. The poor man appeared to be much in earnest, but when at length news arrived that the Rarawa had entered the harbour of Tauranga, and Mr. Williams and Mr. Chapman prepared to depart for that place, Te Amohau was unwilling to go with them : perhaps he thought that now his allies were at hand in strong force, he had a better prospect of effecting the destruction of his enemies.

At Tauranga they found Titore, with Papahia the Rarawa chief, and Te Rohu, a chief from the Thames, who had joined them with about seventy of his people. Te Rohu seemed to be much surprised that any foreigner should come among them for the purpose of turning them from their ancient custom of killing each other. He spoke of the sufferings of his own people from war, and of their strong desire that missionaries should live among them to preserve peace. When Titore was asked what they proposed to do, he first said that they should fight, but after a private conversation with Papahia he requested Mr. Williams to go to Otumoetai and talk to Ngatiawa. He went therefore and told them what Titore had said. They appeared to be rejoiced in the prospect of peace, though doubtful of Titore's sincerity.

The next morning there was the sound of firing in the distance, and by the help of glasses it was observed that the Rarawa were making an attack on Otumoetai, though with much caution ; and that the people of the Pa were in their trenches, not returning the fire. It was now evident that there was nothing more to be done by delay. Here was a fresh body of natives just arrived from the north, come with the intention of fighting, and it was clear that they would fight, until they might be convinced by experience that nothing was to be gained by this course. The missionaries on their part, at great personal sacrifice, had followed them to the scene of warfare ; and after three weeks had been spent in fruitless expostulation, they were obliged to leave them to their own devices and return home to the Bay of Islands, which they reached on the 4th of April.

At this juncture a circumstance occurred which seemed to be of little consequence at the time, but which led to important results some years afterwards. A whale ship anchored in the Bay of Islands, having on board twelve natives from East Cape. They had boarded the vessel as she lay becalmed off the Cape, intending to return on shore in the morning ; but a breeze springing up, the captain stood out to sea, and bore up for the Bay of Islands. It was of little consequence to him where he landed them ; his only object was to get rid of his visitors, so he put them on shore at Rangihoua. The first idea which occurred to the Ngapuhi was to keep them as slaves, and they were at once divided among the chiefs. The missionaries interfered, and pleaded the great injustice of detaining people belonging to a tribe with which they were not at war, and who had come into their hands by an accident which was no fault of theirs, but rather that of the white man. They at length agreed to give them up, on condition that the mission schooner should be sent to take them home. At the end of April they were embarked from Paihia, and in three days, when just in sight of the place of anchorage at Hicks's Bay, a heavy gale came on from the eastward, which drove the vessel back to the Bay of Islands. It was then thought advisable that these natives should remain at Paihia until the following summer, and for the time they were located in the mission settlement, and received regular instruction. This continued for the next eight months.

CHAPTER IX.

1833, 1834.

THIRD BOOK OF TRANSLATIONS PRINTED—INDICATIONS OF CHANGE —DEATH OF TOHITAPU — WEHE—GOD WORKS BY HIS OWN INSTRUMENTS—VISITS TO THAMES AND MATAMATA—STATION AT PURIRI — EAST CAPE NATIVES RETURN—MEETING AT HICKS'S BAY—SUNDAY AT WAIAPU—MESSRS. BROWN AND HAMLIN VISIT WAIKATO — MURDER OF KAPA AND HIS WIFE — SUPERSTITIOUS PRACTICES.

THE work of translation had been steadily advancing, and in the early part of the year 1833 an edition of 1800 copies of another work was printed in New South Wales, containing a large portion of the services of the Prayer Book, and about half of the New Testament. This little book was much valued, and the number of those who were able to make a right use of it was rapidly increasing. A portion of this edition was shared with the Wesleyan missionaries, who were carrying on their labours with success on the banks of the river Hokianga.

While the warlike disposition of many of the Ngapuhi still continued, and the natives of the Bay of Plenty were all in arms, there was a great number of those who had gone to Tauranga the preceding year who would on no account have undertaken a similar expedition. The inhabitants of the villages within reach of the missionaries were for the most part anxious to have instruction, and regularly attended the services which were held. There was a striking difference in their general bearing, from what it had been a short time before. Visiting the Kawakawa in the usual course of duty, my boat's crew consisted of two Christians and four candidates for baptism. This happened without any particular arrangement, but because the majority of those who were in the mission settlement were of this class. Pulling up the river, many questions were put relative to passages in the new book, and I could not but notice that the copy which one of the crew had with him, had been well used since it came into his possession. On our arrival we found the people assembled, and I held service with about one hundred and twenty natives, having made arrangements for my companions to proceed to two villages about three miles distant for the same purpose. My congregation expressed a wish that one of the Christian natives should remain constantly with them, to give them daily instruction.

At Waimate and in the neighbouring villages the same change was perceptible. " It would cheer the hearts of Christians at home," wrote Mr. Clarke, " as well as shame those who only bear the name, to see how a Sabbath is now spent in New Zealand at our settlements. Long before service commences in the morning, you see the natives drawing together in little groups around the church. No sooner is the door opened than an effort is made to get a place within, and at times the building is completely filled in about five minutes, and many remain outside for want of room. In visiting the out-stations, there is much to encourage us to perseverance and diligence; although at the distance of from three to ten miles there is still the same order which is observed in the mission settlement. They lay aside all unnecessary labour, and have morning and evening services at the appointed time. Many read the Scriptures, and others have them read; they join in the responses of our excellent liturgy, and listen most attentively to the instruction afforded them."

The Gospel was bringing about a general outward change in that part of New Zealand, and in some of the natives an inward change also. Those who were under missionary influence and instruction had almost lost their ferocious appearance; and instead of rushing about with their muskets and spears to revenge every little insult, it was not unusual to see the old tattooed warrior coming to ask how best to settle the real insults and losses which they often sustained from an unprincipled neighbour. Those natives who still adhered to the old customs showed by the confusion which they manifested when met on a Sunday, that they were not ignorant of the untenable nature of their superstitions. They seemed to say, " Hast thou found me, O mine enemy ? " when they unexpectedly came in contact with a missionary, and were affectionately warned to flee from the wrath to come.

Upon the minds of some of the older natives there seemed to be a faint glimmering of light, but it was not sufficient to lead them to forsake the old path. Tohitapu was of this number. He was a man of great repute in his day as a priest, and was an object of terror to all who came under his displeasure. His naturally savage disposition was perhaps increased by his peculiar calling, and many of his countrymen had been butchered by him for violating the native rites. Living within a mile of Paihia, he had continued intercourse with the missionaries, and was much influenced by them during the latter part of his life. He laid aside many of his evil practices, and professed a strong desire to do what was right; and on many occasions he exerted himself to bring about a reconciliation between contending tribes. He listened also to religious instruction, but his heart was closed against a real reception of the truth. A few months after his return from Tauranga he became seriously ill; and, though he felt that he should not recover, he was as little disposed as ever to receive the light of the Gospel. He appreciated the attentions which were paid to him, and seemed to have a sincere regard for the missionaries, but he died as he had lived, his mind still enslaved by the superstitions of his fathers.

It is pleasing to turn from this notice to an account of a young woman who had benefited by Christian instruction. Piri, the younger of two sisters, had come to live at Paihia, at a period when there was much difficulty in keeping any girls, owing to the influence of the shipping. After a short period the elder sister Wehe, who was one of those who frequented the ships, came and removed Piri, in spite of all remonstrance, and nothing more was seen of them till about fifteen months before this time, when the younger sister applied to be received into the house, stating that she was weary of her depraved mode of life. She was taken upon trial, and then Wehe requested to be admitted also. She had been unwell for several months, and asked for permission to come and end her days with the missionaries, as she knew she should not recover. Her deportment was good, and her attention to school and general instruction was very decided. She would frequently reprove any impropriety she might observe in those around her. She always gave a good account of the sermons she heard, and showed that she did not listen in vain. While her strength would admit of it she was very industrious, and it was often necessary to require her to lay aside her work. Such is the outline of the character of this young woman, who had long been in the school of vice, and was now fast approaching the verge of the grave. Considering the great earnestness which she had manifested, and her apparent delight in the prospect of a blessed immortality, it was thought proper that she should be admitted into the Church of Christ by baptism. Accordingly, the little Christian band was assembled for this purpose, and the right hand of fellowship was given to her. The scene was most gratifying, and when her change of character was contrasted with her former life, there was indeed reason to praise God and exclaim, " Surely this is a brand plucked out of the fire ! "

There is something grand and wonderful in the change which is wrought by the Gospel ;—that those who are by nature the children of wrath should become the children of God ; and this transition becomes still more striking in the case of heathens—of savage heathens who are in the very lowest grade of human beings. Mr. Chapman remarks upon this subject :—" In seasons of native baptisms, the tide of ages, dark ages, bloody ages, ages of murder and treachery, cruelty and hatred, rolls, as it were, before me ; and yet here stand the children of murderers, accepting offered mercy, and desiring to wash all their guilty stains away ! Thoughts such as these force themselves upon me, and I must weep."

The manner in which God is often pleased to work his purposes, by instruments of his own choice, and such as man would not have reckoned upon, is shown in the good which has often been effected by natives who had received a little instruction, and then have been hastily removed from it to some distant quarter. Young people often came to the mission settlements, and were employed there and taught. Some, perhaps, were soon fetched away by their parents or masters ; others left from causes over which no one had any control ; and some, perhaps, behaved ill and were sent away ; but all carried away something, and there were few who had not some information to give which might benefit their distant friends. How many times has disappointment been felt because the labour which had been spent seemed to be lost, though it afterwards proved to be as the "bread cast upon the waters, to be found after many days." How good, then, is it to hope, and quietly wait for the salvation of the Lord !

In the month of October, 1833, a detachment of the missionary body, consisting of the Rev. Henry Williams, Rev. A. N. Brown, Mr. Fairburn, and Mr. Morgan, left the Bay of Islands in two boats, for the purpose of selecting a site for a missionary station at the Thames. After an examination of the western coast of the Frith, which they found without population, they passed over to the opposite side. The natives here were numerous, notwithstanding the fearful devastations committed by Ngapuhi some years previously. Te Totara was one of the Pas taken at that time. Ngapuhi had been encamped near the Pa several days, receiving presents and holding friendly intercourse with the inhabitants ; but having obtained their confidence, they rose upon them, and killed a very great number, and then took all whom they could seize as slaves. The most horrible cruelties were practised. Some of the posts of the Pa were still standing, and from the extent of ground it occupied, it must have contained a large number of people. Human bones lay scattered about in all directions, and some of the people pointed out the spots where their relatives had been killed and eaten. Pulling up the river Waihou they came to a small branch stream, which they entered and found a body of natives at their cultivations. They expressed great pleasure when they learnt who their visitors were. Having taken their evening meal, they assembled from 150 to 200 natives to evening prayers. It was a pleasing sight. They were confined for room in front, owing to a plantation of maize, and were consequently obliged to extend to the right and left. There were several fires in front of the tents, which, with some torches held by those in the distance, gave a striking effect to the scene. The missionaries commenced as usual by singing a hymn, but what was their surprise when they heard the whole assemblage join and sing correctly with them; and in the prayers also the responses were made by all as by the voice of one man. Nothing like this had been witnessed before, and they believed that the Lord had now led them to the spot where his altar should be erected. When addressed upon the Gospel message, the natives were very attentive. Many asked for books and slates; of slates there were none, but one of the new books was given to Tuma. These people had received instruction from three youths who had lived in the mission families at Paihia. Thus the work of God was carried on without the previous arrangement of man. They continued their course up the river, and on the 15th of November they reached Matamata, where Waharoa, the great chief of this tribe, resided. The old man was sitting in state, and gave them a hearty welcome. They pitched their tents in a clear spot, a goodly assemblage watching their movements with much interest. On the Sunday, the people congregated together beneath the trees in an adjoining wood, where the message of peace was listened to with apparent respect by a body of savage warriors. Old Waharoa asked many significant questions, and inquired what they were to do without a missionary to teach them. From this point they returned down the Waihou river to Puriri. The natives were all anxious to know what determination had been arrived at about the mission station, and after some consultation, the missionaries concluded that Puriri was the most eligible site. They accordingly took a survey of the ground, and gave orders for the erection of three raupo houses. This place, though deficient in some respects, possessed many advantages. It was central, lying between the contending tribes of Waikato and the Thames, and the establishment of a mission there might tend to restore a better feeling among the tribes.

The season of the year was now favourable for the return of the East Cape natives, who had been living at Paihia since the month of May. The schooner *Fortitude* was therefore chartered for the twofold purpose of conveying timber and stores for the new station at Puriri, and of taking these people back to their homes. Mr. Preece, Mr. Morgan, and myself, went as passengers; the two former proceeding to their station at Puriri, while I had charge of about sixty natives, thirty of whom belonged to the East Cape, some of the number being slaves, to whom their masters had given their freedom.

We left Paihia on the 19th of December, and on the 24th came to an anchor a few miles from the proposed settlement at Puriri. The next morning we proceeded up the river, calling at several villages on the way. Passing over the site of Te Totara, which has been already mentioned as the Pa destroyed by the Bay of Islanders, one of my natives, who had been present on that occasion, described the position held by the different parties, and detailed many particulars, which confirmed the accounts of the extreme barbarities exercised by the natives in their wars. It was late in the day when we reached Puriri, and after the tent was pitched we called the natives together. It was a beautiful evening, and the moon was so bright as to enable us to read without the help of any other light. The utmost attention pervaded the whole assembly, amounting to about one hundred; and every voice among the motley group seemed to join in concert, as though they had been accustomed to this service for a long season. The recollection, too, that this was the natal day of our blessed Saviour, added much to the solemnity of the occasion. We read that on the morning of this day, the multitude of the heavenly host appeared in concert with the angels, praising God, and saying, "Glory to God in the highest, on earth peace, good will toward men!" and the scene of this evening was doubtless looked upon with delight by the same blessed company, and by our glorified Saviour himself.

We resumed our voyage, and on the 8th of January, 1834, we anchored in Hicks's Bay. The natives on board began to enumerate the desolating battles which had been fought by their relatives in this quarter. "That hill," said they, "was inhabited by a tribe which was cut off by Hongi; and that on the opposite side was the site of a Pa taken by Pomare." In another part of the Bay was a village which had been destroyed, about three years before, by the natives of Whakatane, on which occasion an Englishman was killed. We saw smoke on the side of the Bay nearest Waiapu, whither our natives on board were bound, and in a little time two canoes pulled off to us. But as the Bay was not now inhabited, through fear of the Whakatane natives, our people were uncertain whether those approaching us were friends or foes. All our party, therefore, was sent below, leaving only two chiefs on deck to ascertain, as the canoes came near, to what tribe they belonged. I presently heard the sound of ramrods ringing in the muskets of the people in the hold, and now we first discovered that they had a large number of firearms, which had been taken to pieces and stowed away in their boxes; it having been made a condition of their coming on board, that they were to bring neither muskets nor powder with them. As soon as the canoes were alongside, our East Cape chief recognised two of his own brothers. It was not long before the whole party were on board, and joy was marked in the countenances of all, soon, however, giving way to copious floods of tears, which to the New Zealander are always the most sincere token of affection. We learnt that the party on shore was assembled for war, and was only awaiting the arrival of chiefs further south to go and attack their enemies living to the westward; but in some of the speeches made on deck, they said they should perhaps give up the expedition if the missionaries told them to do so. We now prepared to go on shore, conducted by the two canoes, and had some difficulty in landing, being nearly upset in the surf. Very few persons were visible on the beach; but as soon as we had landed, about three hundred men suddenly sprang up from among the bushes to welcome us. I had never before seen so wild looking a set, and they soon gathered around us to gaze upon their visitors. They were, however, exceedingly friendly, and did not attempt to press upon us. The party which had been living at Paihia soon began to relate their adventures; for their relatives had heard no tidings of them since the ship had carried them away. They told them some of the customs of the missionaries, carefully distinguishing between us and the foreigners they had hitherto had to do with. There was a full assemblage at evening prayers, and they used the same expressions as the people at the Thames : " Give us missionaries to instruct us, and we will leave off our wars. We like what you tell us ; but when you are gone, we shall have no one to teach us." I passed the night upon a most luxuriant bed, made of the tender branches of trees. In the morning, striking my tent as early as possible, we proceeded by land to Waiapu, accompanied by a large party of natives. It was near the close of the day when we came to Rangitukia, the outer Pa of Waiapu. It was situated in an extensive valley, was large, and well fortified in the native style, and, according to their report, mustered 560 fighting men. Many were absent ; but in the evening there were upwards of 500 men, women, and children at prayers, the largest assembly I had yet spoken to in the country. There were many old priests in the party, but they showed no disposition to cavil, nor any symptom of fear lest their craft should be endangered : on the contrary, they seemed ready to listen to any new thing which might be told them.

The next day I went up the valley to Whakawhitira, about ten miles distant. My companions pointed out several places on the way where Pas had stood, which had been destroyed by Ngapuhi, some years before, when numbers were killed, and many taken away as slaves. The present inhabitants consisted principally of those who had escaped to the woods. That desolating war was undertaken, so far as I could learn, without any aggression on the part of this people, but solely for the purpose of taking slaves. Whakawhitira contained, it was said, 2,000 fighting men. On assembling those who were at home, there were from 800 to 1,000 present, including at least 400 young children. The village was very large, and was well situated in the midst of extensive cultivations. Waiapu, as a place for a missionary station, surpassed any I had yet seen.

From a conviction that we must soon have a settlement in this quarter, I paid particular attention to the neighbourhood, and in my mind I fixed upon a site not far from the Pa. Returning to the tent, I fell into conversation with an old chief, who, about fifteen years before, had been taken prisoner to the Bay of Islands, but was returned again to this place by the conquering party. He seemed to be well versed in all the native superstitions, and had been talking much about the forefathers of the New Zealanders. He told my natives that he could make thunder, and that he would produce it that evening. He sat at the tent door, wishing me to talk with him about the creation of the world, and the formation of the first man. After hearing the old man's account of the origin of the New Zealanders, I gave him the history of the creation, the fall, the flood, and the confusion of tongues, when he repeatedly observed that our account was the most straightforward.

The Sunday following was the first Sabbath which had been observed at Waiapu; but it was kept, I believe, quite as a day of rest. I heard many speaking of it beforehand, and they seemed to know that they were not to work. At ten o'clock the natives were called together by the substitute for a bell, which was an iron hoe suspended, and struck with another piece of iron, and soon about 500 people came together. Among them were many hoary heads ; but their long familiarity with the superstitions of their forefathers did not seem to make them indifferent to the preparations for the worship of Jehovah. Rukuata, the chief we had brought back from the Bay of Islands, made all the arrangements to the best of his judgment. The largest compound in the Pa was chosen, and there the people were assembled, closely arranged upon the ground, and many were perched on the roofs of the surrounding huts. At those parts of the service where it is usual to stand, they all stood ; and they knelt during the prayers. The greatest order was observed, and the attention was marked. Rukuata also took pains to explain that at Paihia, after service, the men and boys had school, and that the females were instructed by the missionaries' wives. After partaking of a little refreshment, the dogs of the Pa having devoured the principal part of our store, I set out for Whakawhitira. A man of forbidding appearance, who had accompanied me on a previous day, had attached himself to my party ; but he improved much upon acquaintance, and turning round to me, as he was walking a little in advance, he said that he was in quest of something for himself; and, pointing to his own breast, and then to mine, he said he wished to hear more of what I had to say.* The conversation of the natives, on the way, turned upon the new doctrines which were now laid before them. My friend remarked to another, that their god is a killing god, but that ours is a saving God; and he then asked why there could not be a missionary at each of the two principal villages to instruct the people. When we arrived at Whakawhitira, we were told that all the people were absent: about 700, however, old and young, came together. And here again I was asked whether missionaries would not come and live with them. A piece of good advice, which was a little amusing, was given to the women by one of my companions, just before I addressed the people. " Sit quietly," said he, " and do not speak a word: if your children cry, feed them at the breast; and if that does not quiet them, walk away a short distance, and come back when they are still."

The primary object of this visit was now accomplished; the natives who had been carried away to the Bay of Islands were returned to their friends, accompanied, too, by many of their relatives, whom their master had liberated. There was as yet no prospect of forming a missionary station among these interesting tribes, for the simple reason that there

---

* This man was one of the first to embrace Christianity, and was for some years employed as a teacher. He was recently killed in a conflict with the Hauhau fanatics.

was no one to undertake the work ; but an important step had been taken, the district had been explored, and there was sufficient proof that it was a fine field for future occupation. We again embarked from Waiapu, and proceeded to Table Cape, which had been described as a place of some consequence. About sixteen years before this time, a body of Ngapuhi, after committing great devastation at Waiapu, went on as far as Table Cape, and after destroying many, carried away great numbers into slavery ; but shortly after Te Wera, the Ngapuhi chief, set most of his slaves free, and then went to live among the people he had conquered, and was received by them as their chief. This circumstance became of great advantage to all the tribes living south of that place, as far as Cook's Straits. From that part of the Island Te Rauparaha had expelled nearly all the inhabitants, and at one time the whole population of Wairarapa and Heretaunga were congregated at Table Cape, under the protection of Te Wera, and thus escaped destruction. In this visit, however, it was not possible to see enough of the people to allow of any plans being formed for the future.

A new station having been already formed at Puriri, there were many reasons which made it desirable that the neighbouring district of Waikato should be occupied at the same time, especially with a view to put an end to the continual strife which had been going on for generations between these contiguous tribes. One extreme part of Waikato, that which extends to Matamata, at the head of the Thames river, had been already explored, and it was now thought expedient to examine the district from another point. With this view the Rev. A. N. Brown and Mr. Hamlin left Waimate at the end of February, 1834, proceeding through the middle of the island by way of Mangakahia and Kaipara. The state of the country was very different at that period from what it afterwards became. Apprehension of a foreign enemy had obliged the tribes severally to withdraw into their own fastnesses. Hence all those connected with Ngapuhi retreated towards the north, while of the Waikato tribes there was not a single individual to be found further north than Ngaruawahia, at the confluence of the rivers Waipa and Horotiu. The greater part of Kaipara, with the whole of Manukau, Waitemata, Tamaki, and all lower Waikato, was a waste unoccupied country. The travellers, therefore, when they reached Kaipara, had to travel by compass through a broken and trackless region, often making their way with great difficulty through the high fern and bushes. A journey of between seventy and eighty miles, which occupied seven or eight days, at length brought them to Waikato river. But as there were no inhabitants, there were no canoes, and it became necessary to construct a kind of float, made of flags tied fast together in the form of a small canoe, sufficiently buoyant to support two persons, which is called "moki." On ten of these moki they paddled across, and found them to answer so well, that they proceeded some miles in them down the river. The natives were cautioned when they started not to pull ahead of one another, lest they should fall in with any people, who might suppose they were Ngapuhi who had come again to fight. Notwithstanding this caution, two of them pulled on, when they came all at once upon a boat pulling towards them, full of people, among whom were a younger brother of Te Wherowhero, the principal chief of Waikato, and an Englishman. When they saw the foremost moki, they called out to the two men, " Where are you from ? " " From Ngapuhi," they replied. Seeing the rest of the moki astern, he said, " You are a fighting party." He then told his men to load their muskets and fire. The two men called out, " We are not a fighting party, but are come with some missionaries, who are close behind." He did not believe them, but told the Englishman to turn the boat round, and wait till they came up. One of them then cried out in English, " Halloo ! " which the Englishman recognised, and said, " There are some Englishmen behind." The boat then pulled onward, and when they saw who the party were, they gave a hearty welcome, and entered freely into conversation. They said the missionaries had remained so long at the Bay of Islands that surely their children must be old enough to become missionaries too. The chief added, " If you had come among us some time ago, Taranaki would have been alive, but now we have cut them nearly all off." They were very friendly, offered the missionaries a passage in the boat to Waipa; and what was still better to famished travellers, they gave them nearly all the potatoes they had.

That some new principle was needed to put an end to their interminable acts of treachery and bloodshed was painfully manifest. Any wicked man had it in his power to commit an act of murder, but the New Zealand customs did not visit the murderer as among civilized nations, but his tribe, and most generally vengeance fell upon the innocent. The station at Puriri was scarcely formed, and preparatory steps were being taken for the adoption of a similar course at Waikato, when a barbarous murder was committed, at the very time when the wives of the missionaries had just landed from the Bay of Islands. Kapa and his wife, natives of Waikato, went to Puriri to see a relative, and had been there some days, when a young chief from another party, whose name was Koinaki, who lived thirty miles lower down the river, and between whom and the Waikato party a deadly feud existed, came to the valley, under the cloak of friendship, to see these natives, professing a desire that all past animosity should cease. After remaining three days eating and sleeping in the same house, he succeeded in persuading them to accompany him down the river. They had not gone more than twelve miles before the vulture landed with his prey, killed them both with his hatchet, and then conveyed the bodies to his village, where they were afterwards eaten. All this was done in revenge for the death of a relative who had been killed about seven years before.

The following instance of superstition and want of natural affection occurred about the same time. Mr. Fairburn, having heard that Kohirangatira was very ill, prepared some medicine for him, and accompanied by Mr. Morgan, started early in the morning for Taruru, a distance of eighteen miles. They reached the place at midday, and found a dozen people sitting around two others who were playing at draughts. They inquired where the sick man was, and were told he was tapued. Mr. Fairburn said he had heard he was ill, and was come to see him. Hearing that he was under the charge of a priest, he told one of the players, son of the sick man, to inform Kohirangatira that they wished to see him. He reluctantly rose from his game to convey the message, and soon returned, saying that his tapu was so great that he could not be seen. It is worthy of remark that when persons of distinction were taken ill, and their friends imagined they would die, they conveyed them to an open shed, and prohibited every kind of food from being given to them, water only being allowed. Thus the poor sufferer was literally starved to death. The young man coolly resumed his place at the draught-board. Mr. Fairburn told him they had come a long distance, in the hope of affording his father some relief, but "Whiro," their great enemy, wished him to die, that he might go to his place, and he supposed that he must take the medicine back again. He then turned to the two natives who had accompanied them, and said, " Come, let us go, we are not wanted here." " Wait a little," said the young chief. He then paid another visit to his father, and shortly after they were invited to advance towards the place where the sick man was lying, with the priest close to his elbow. He eyed them very suspiciously, and no doubt imagined that contamination was drawing near. Still, however, they found that they were not to approach the invalid nearer than six yards, a line being marked off by branches of karaka stuck in the ground around his shed. Mr. Fairburn then called to the sick man, and told him he was sorry he could not benefit him by the medicine which he had brought on purpose to ease his pain. The sick man said something in a low tone to the priest, and then requested them to advance. Mr. Fairburn offered him his hand, which he did not take till he had first placed a leaf of the karaka in his own hand. When this ceremony was over, he was allowed to sit on the ground beside him, the old priest in the meantime watching every motion. Having ascertained that his complaint was rheumatism, he was prevailed upon to allow an old woman of the tapued party to rub his ancle with some liniment. The priest wishing to know what the liquid in the bottle was, it was handed to him. He applied it to his nose, and being strong, it brought the tears to his eyes in abundance. An electric shock could hardly have surprised him more, while the sick chief and the bystanders laughed

heartily.   Mr. Fairburn gave him also a little medicine, which he took in his hand, with a leaf placed in
the palm as before ; then putting his hand behind
him, he repeated some words in a low voice, and
swallowed the dose.   Superstition seemed to be as
deeply rooted as ever in this part of the country.

CHAPTER X.

1834

MESSRS. BROWN AND WILLIAMS VISIT WAIKATO—PERILOUS POSITION AT WHAKATIWAI — PASS ON TO MARAMARUA — NGARUAWAHIA — MATAKITAKI — TE RORE — STATION FIXED AT MANGAPOURI — VISIT TO MATAMATA—WAHAROA PLEADS EARNESTLY TO HAVE A MISSIONARY—TAURANGA—STATION AT TE PAPA—PROGRESS OF CHRISTIANITY IN THE BAY OF ISLANDS—DEATH OF MARY—TAPAPA—BLIND KURI — EDUCATION OF A NATIVE PRIEST—JOURNEY TO NORTH CAPE—TE REINGA.

AFTER the favourable report given by those who had recently visited Waikato, it was determined by the Committee of Missionaries that a station should be formed in some part of that district, and Messrs. Morgan and Slack, together with myself, were appointed to this post. Some years previously, when peace had been made between Ngapuhi and Waikato, the daughter of Rewa, a Ngapuhi chief, had been given in marriage to Kati, the brother of Te Wherowhero; and it happened most opportunely that Kati, with his wife and several of his people, were at that time on a visit at the Bay of Islands. This gave an opportunity for acquiring much useful information, and also for cultivating a friendly feeling with a party of great influence. The barque *Bolina* called at the Bay of Islands on her way to the Thames, and the Rev. A. N. Brown and myself took passage in her, together with

Kati and his people. Our intention was to land at Whakatiwai, on the western side of the frith of the Thames, not many miles from which there is a small tributary stream, Maramarua, running into Waikato, which would afford a convenient approach to the district. Preliminary steps were to be taken towards forming a station at Waikato, and then we were to continue our journey to Tauranga, with a view to the adoption of a similar course in that quarter.

We sailed from the Bay of Islands on the 19th of July, and in four days we anchored in the harbour of Mahurangi, as a gale was coming on from the eastward. A canoe presently came off, and reported that only the week before, a large party from Waikato had made an attack upon a village near Whakatiwai, and had killed twenty natives, five of whom were persons of consequence. Our Waikato friends were greatly disconcerted. This was the very place we wished to land at ; but now, according to all New Zealand practices, it would have been an act of madness for Kati to venture. I went on shore to ascertain the state of feeling. There were several natives just come from Whakatiwai, and they appeared to be under great excitement. They spoke of the ground being drenched with blood, which was still lying upon its surface, and it seemed as if nothing would give them greater satisfaction than to get our party into their power. However, Wharekawa, a leading chief, went with me on board to see Kati, and gave him assurance of safety, saying that it was clear he had had no concern

in this attack, and that he need be under no apprehension. Kati and his party then landed, and were
well received, considering that Kati's relations were
among the late assailants. They were told also that
they might proceed home by way of Whakatiwai
without molestation. Still I felt no confidence in
these assurances, and proposed to Kati to purchase
for him a whale boat from a vessel lying in the harbour, in which he and his people might pull up the
river Tamaki, and then drag their boat over the
portage into Manukau, from whence they would have
an uninterrupted course into Waikato. But Kati had
with him a very large quantity of property, which
had been given to him by his wife's relations, and he
was unwilling to leave this, as I proposed, in the store
of Mr. Gordon Brown, at Mahurangi. He had rather
that, under the most imminent risk, all should go
where he went. In the course of a few days we
moved up the Thames in our vessel, and anchored
off Whakatiwai. There was a large gathering of
natives there, for they were expecting that the
Waikato people would return again to the attack.
They were therefore assembling from all quarters, and
increasing the defences of their Pa, and it was no time
for Kati to make his appearance. There was one
chief only to whom we could look, Patuone, a
Ngapuhi, the brother of Waka Nene, and a near
relation to Kati's wife, who was living with this
tribe, having married the sister of their chief, Te
Kupenga ; but he gave me little encouragement, say-

ing he had no influence, being only a stranger. I then spoke to Te Kupenga, but he said little, and all the people looked sad and sullen, thirsting for vengeance. There was, moreover, present in the Pa, Koinaki, who had but a few months before murdered the two Waikatos near Puriri, whose heads I had seen him hold up as he pulled down the river. What was more likely, therefore, than that he would be the first to imbrue his hands in the blood of these natives. The chiefs we had brought with us from Mahurangi were most disposed to befriend us, and went off to fetch Kati from the vessel. As the canoe was returning, I felt that the critical moment had arrived, and Mr. Brown and I went down to the beach to walk up with them, being determined that if they were to be killed it should be done in our presence. All, however, was quiet, and we were conducted safely to the house of Te Kupenga; but I was a little uneasy that neither this chief nor any other person of consequence made their appearance. In the course of an hour there was a great hue and cry on the beach, and all the people rushed out of the Pa to see what was the matter. We soon ascertained that the property of Kati and his people had arrived, having followed them from the ship in another canoe. There was a large amount of muskets, powder, blankets, and clothing of all kinds. This was considered lawful spoil, and in a few minutes there was not a vestige of it to be seen. It was well for Kati that there was this peace-offering to put before them ; and it seemed to have a good effect. After quiet was restored, several of the chiefs came to see Kati, and the speeches were for the most part favourable. The next morning there was another meeting, when one man in particular made use of very offensive language, and some objected to our proceeding in company with Kati. They felt no doubt that our presence might interfere with the fulfilment of their wishes.

After a delay of two days we were told we might proceed on our way, and we set out from the Pa accompanied by several armed men, who went with us about two miles. They had left us but a little while when one of them returned to call us back, stating that four canoes had come from the opposite side of the Thames in the night, and that the people were gone upon the road by which we had to travel, to destroy canoes belonging to the Waikato natives. The party was headed by the man who had made use of the threatening language, so that we were thankful to return as speedily as possible. Our friends wished to know whether I had no book by which I could tell whether there was danger or no. I replied that I had prayed to God for protection in the morning, and that I believed the messenger who came to tell us of our danger was sent by him.

We had to remain quietly in the Pa for another week, until it was deemed prudent for us to move, and during the whole of this time there were frequent alarms of an approaching enemy. One night in particular there was great confusion. At midnight the report of a musket was heard near at hand, when all instantly flew to arms, crying out that the enemy had arrived. There was a quick succession of musket balls flying in every direction. We supposed for some time that the enemy was come, and we began to consider that our safest position was that which we then occupied—in our beds. The firing, however, soon ceased, and we were glad to learn it was a false alarm.

At length we set out on our journey with Kati and his party, and walked about twelve miles towards Waikato, taking up our quarters upon a potato culti- vation belonging to the people who had been lately killed. The Waikatos had burnt the potato stores, and there were then lying exposed to destruction little short of a thousand bushels of this food.

The next morning, after a walk of four miles, we came to the banks of Maramarua, where we found three canoes, in which all embarked. Mr. Brown and I were in the hindermost canoe, and as the river was very tortuous in its course, our companions were often out of sight. Presently we heard a long report, as of a musket, and then another, and another, and we thought of Koinaki and his threats, and that the work of slaughter might be going on. We pulled on however, and presently we opened upon a long reach of the river, where we saw Kati striking furiously upon the sides of a new canoe with his axe, and he did not leave off until he had smashed it to pieces.

It appeared that it was the property of the Waikatos, and he was only pouring out his anger because of the peril in which he had been placed. Truly thankful were we to find that our fears were groundless, and that we were quickly out of the reach of further danger from Koinaki.

After pulling for two days against the rapid current of the Waikato, we encamped on the future site of the Rev. B. Ashwell's station, not knowing that we were within a short distance of Ngaruawahia. Before starting the next morning one of our natives discharged his musket, which sounded loudly among the hills, and presently it was remarked that natives were coming down the river. We asked how they knew it. "Don't you see that flight of ducks," they answered, "which is come from that quarter? they have been startled this way by canoes." Presently nine canoes, full of natives, came in sight; and before they were within reach Kati, still under the influence of vexation, began to fire upon them with ball cartridge. I called out again and again to him to desist, for if any one had been hit we could only have expected a return fire. It was a relief to see his balls fall short of the approaching party, who, having ascertained that it was Kati who had arrived, returned to the Pa to carry the tidings. When near the Pa we remained in our canoes some time on the opposite bank of the river, when an old priest, all besmeared with oil and red ochre, paddled over to us, and, having landed, he called Kati and his companions on shore, to have a religious ceremony performed, on account of their narrow escape at Whakatiwai. They threw off all their garments, even divesting themselves of the ornaments in their ears, and remained seated for some minutes before him, while he repeated his karakia. This concluded, we passed over to the Pa, when the usual ceremony of crying was gone through, which was followed by an ample repast.

Continuing our course up the river, we passed two places which are memorable in the history of the New Zealanders. The one was Matakitaki, a Pa which is said to have contained 5,000 natives, and which was taken by Hongi when this people had no fire-arms. They fell an easy prey, not being able to make resistance. Great numbers were slaughtered, and many carried away into slavery. The other was Te Rore, where Pomare, a Ngapuhi chief, who went to Waikato soon after Hongi had made peace, met with his death. He had committed many depredations, killing numbers and destroying much property, when at length a large body of people waylaid him on either side of the river, and succeeded in killing him and most of his followers.

The place fixed upon for a mission station was Mangapouri, and we sent for the inhabitants, who were absent. Awarahi, the principal chief, was a young man, with much vivacity in his manner. He said that if I liked to remain I should have a house erected immediately, but that, with respect to himself, he was a man of war, and to war he must go at present. " Perhaps you may have one little boy to believe on your preaching now, and by and by we may possibly all believe. Ngapuhi did not listen till the missionaries had been long with them, neither can we." On telling him I had made up my mind to remain, he directly got up and asked me to point out the spot for my house, and in about five minutes forty men were employed clearing the ground upon which it was to stand, and the dimensions were at once marked out.

Our next object was to proceed to Matamata, and from thence to Tauranga, with a view to the selection of another mission station. On the 2d of September we reached the former place, and found old Waharoa seated outside the Pa to receive us. This man was one of the finest specimens of a native I had yet seen. He was of middle stature, with small features, well formed ; his beard was grey, and his hair, which was partially so, was exceedingly neat, while his dress and general deportment marked him out among the multitude as a superior chief. He had long been celebrated as a warrior, but his manners were mild, and the expression of his countenance pleasing. I had expected to find a surly old man, not very well pleased that other places were being supplied with missionaries while he was passed by. He soon began to talk upon the subject, but it was in a very quiet way. He said that he had heard of Jesus Christ, and that, in consequence of what the missionaries had said to him, he had refrained from

fighting, though he had had much provocation to do
so. " But," said he, "how can I believe ? I have no
one to teach me ; no one to tell me when it is the
Sabbath-day, no one to direct me what to do ; and
the people around me begin to jeer, and to say I am
remaining quiet in vain, for that no missionary will
come." I explained to him our plans for Waikato
and Tauranga, and said that when a mission was
established at the latter place, we hoped to do something for him. Our settlement in the Thames and
those projected at Waikato and Tauranga formed a
triangle, Matamata being in the middle of the three.

The next morning we followed Waharoa to his
potato-field. On this occasion all the people of the
place were come together, and the young men, upwards of 100 in number, were planting the seed for
him. At the conclusion of the work an abundant
supply of food was served up, which was the only
return made for the work. We counted on the
ground 550 men, women, and children. On our
return to the village, the old man renewed his application for a missionary. " It is a very good thing,"
he said, " that missionaries should live at Waikato
and at Tauranga, but you will want to pass from
one settlement to the other, and your road will lie
through this place, and you will be much ashamed,
when you pass, if there is no missionary here.
When I turn towards the Thames I shall see a white
man coming, and they will tell me that it is a missionary going to Waikato. I look towards Waikato,

and see a white man, and learn that it is a missionary going to see his friend at Tauranga." He wished to know why Mr. Morgan could not stay with him, and said that if none of those missionaries who were moving southward could come we must send for some one. I believe that Waharoa was sincerely desirous of having instruction, and, taking into account the number of people in connexion with him, I could not but hope that something might be done in his behalf.

We arrived at Otumoetai, the principal Pa of Tauranga, on the 6th of September; and the next day being Sunday, Hikareia and Tupaea came to see us, when I explained the object of our visit. We received scarcely a word in reply, and it seemed to be a matter of indifference to them whether we formed a settlement or no. We proposed to assemble the natives, and about 500 came together, who showed more interest in what was said than their leading chiefs had done. The next day we went to Te Papa, which had been previously recommended as the site for a mission station. We found the situation exceedingly advantageous, and gave directions that two raupo houses should be put up for the missionaries who might be appointed to the place.

On our return, when we arrived within two miles of Matamata, the rain came down heavily, and we were glad to take refuge in a small village, where we pitched our tent, and sent to Waharoa for food. The food came, and was soon followed by the old man, who wished us to have proceeded to his Pa; but, finding we were in a comfortable position, he stayed with us. He soon resumed the subject which was uppermost in his thoughts,—that of having a missionary. "The Thames will believe," he said, "and Tauranga will believe, and Waikato, but what am I to do?" In the evening we had prayers, when I spoke of the happiness of heaven, and said it was God's wish that they should all go there, and that, to this end, He had sent His Son to die for us. The old man looked deeply interested, and exclaimed, "This is the reason I wish for a missionary, in order that I may be instructed." How different were the expressions of feeling here, from what we had witnessed at Tauranga!

Having proceeded thus far with the account of opening prospects at the south, we return again to the mission in the Bay of Islands, where, after years of anxious trial, was now making a steady progress. Many were coming forward and desiring to be admitted into the Christian Church by baptism, and much care was used to keep them for some time under probation. When the catechumens were really in earnest, it was a great pleasure to hold converse with them. Their manner was sufficient to show that there was a reality in their professions. One of these men said to Mr. Clarke, " I have long heard that there is a heaven and a hell; I want to go to heaven, and I am come to ask you the way, and how I shall get there." Mr. Clarke read to him the following words, " I am the way, the truth, and the life :. no man cometh unto the Father, but by Me." Another said, that his feet had a long time dragged his heart to attend to instruction, but he was not satisfied, because the heart did not agree with the feet in going to the house of God; how was he to act so as to make them agree? He recommended him to look by earnest prayer to Him who alone can make our duty our delight. A third said he was sensible that the great storm would overtake him, if he continued to live in sin; and he felt himself without excuse, because he had heard of Jesus Christ as a shelter from the storm; but he felt he was so tied to the devil and his works, that he did not know how to get away from him. He was told that one grand object of Christ's coming into the world was to set the captive free, and to destroy the works of the devil; that it was Christ alone who could liberate him. Another was struck with the conversation between our Lord and Nicodemus, upon the subject of being born again, before he could go to heaven: he wanted, he said, to go to heaven, but did not know whether he was born again. Mr. Clarke endeavoured to point out to him something of the nature of the new birth, and directed him to Christ that he might be renewed in the spirit of his mind.

There was a fervour in some of these early Christians which did not admit of doubt respecting their sincerity. Mary, a young woman of Waimate, naturally weak and timid, was often greatly afflicted, and seemed to shrink from death. But in her last illness a great difference was observed in this respect. She said, Jesus had made this difference :—that she was once greatly afraid of dying, but, since she had known Him, she was not only not afraid to die, but was waiting with desire for her great change. Her language was, "When will He come to fetch me?" A few minutes before she died, she spoke in a clear voice to all the natives around her, and especially to her husband, entreating them to lose no time, but immediately to flee to Jesus for salvation, and then in a lower tone she said, "Farewell, wicked world! farewell, sin and sorrow! for ever farewell, all of you!" and expired.

The influence of Paratene Ripi at Mawhe continued to produce great benefit to his people, and much of the good which was done by him was not generally known. Mr. Davis had been holding service at Mawhe, and was asked to visit Tapapa, a sick man with whom he had had no previous intercourse. He was lying in the verandah of his house, covered with a dirty garment. He was an old man, fully tattooed, and his countenance had been remarkably fine, but it was now fixed in death. "I knelt over him," said Mr. Davis, "with feelings of sorrow and regret. Surely, thought I, this poor man's glass is run out, and his spirit is about to appear in the presence of his Maker, but what can be done for him now?" He hung over the dying man and spoke to him. He tried to reply, but his pale blue lips refused to perform their office. After a weak hollow cough, the power of speech returned, and his countenance brightened up as he said, "My mind is fixed upon Christ as my Saviour." "How long have you been seeking Christ?" "From the first," he replied; "Christ is in my heart, and my soul is joyful." He was told to keep a firm hold of Christ, and to beware of the tempter. He replied, "I have no fear, Christ is with me." After prayer, he said that he blessed God for sending His servants to him with the message of salvation. He said he was dying, and that he longed to be with Christ. It was a relief to hear this simple expression of faith. To outward observation he appeared to be a poor ignorant savage, but he bore the mark of one of God's children. His views of the Saviour were uttered with clearness, and his countenance beamed with joy. In short, the savour of the name of Jesus seemed, as it were, to bring him back for a few minutes into life, in order that he might leave a dying testimony behind him.

The history of poor Tapapa is by no means without interest. He was originally a chief of some note at Taranaki, but, during the incursions of Waikato in that quarter, he was taken prisoner, with his wife and daughter. He had been brought, with many other Taranaki slaves from Waikato, to be sold to Ngapuhi for muskets and powder. Not being disposed of at the Bay of Islands, their master had intended to carry them to Hokianga, and sell them there: but, calling at Mawhe on their way, they were recognised by some of their relatives, and persuaded to run away at night into the woods, and to hide themselves until their master had left the district. This advice they took, and on the return of the Waikato natives they put themselves under the protection of Paratene's tribe, and soon after came under religious instruction.

Kuri, a near relative of Temorenga, had been for several months quite blind. He had, nevertheless, paid great attention to school, in order that he might learn the Catechism, and the services of the Prayer Book, and such portions of the Scripture as were in print. He had requested the Rev. Henry Williams to give him a book, saying, that though he could not see he could hear, and, if he possessed one, he could let others read to him, until he could see with his heart. His request was complied with, and some time after Mr. Williams witnessed a gratifying sight. The blind man was lying on the ground with his book before him, as though he was pondering over its contents. Being asked what he was doing, he observed that he was reading the fourth chapter of St. Matthew, and then he repeated it verse by verse with great correctness.

The New Zealanders had no settled form of religion, no deities to whom regular worship was paid; nevertheless there were priests, whose services were called for on particular occasions, especially in times of war or sickness. They were supposed to possess the power of bewitching whom they pleased, and hence they were much feared by the whole community. Their art was properly the black art, and, in the education given to a person who was afterwards to hold the

office, pains were taken to increase the natural disposition for evil. A remarkable account was given to
Mr. Davis by a young man, the son of a noted priest,
who became a convert to Christianity. "Before I was
yet born," said this young man, "my father devoted
me to the powers of darkness. As soon as I was able
to struggle for my mother's breast, I was often teased
by my father, and kept from it, in order that angry
passions might be deeply rooted in me. The stronger
I grew, the more I was teased by my father, and the
harder I had to fight for nourishment. All this was
done before I was old enough to notice the plants
which are produced by the earth. When I could run
about, the work of preparation went on more rigidly,
and my father kept me without food that I might
learn to thieve, not forgetting, at the same time, to
stir up the spirit of anger and revenge which he had
so assiduously endeavoured to implant in my breast.
My father then taught me how to bewitch and destroy
people at my pleasure ; and he told me that to be a
great man, I must be a bold murderer, a desperate
and expert thief, and able to do all kinds of wickedness effectually.

"I recollect while I was a child, my father went to
kill pigs. I tried to get a portion for myself, but my
father beat me away, because I had not been active
in killing them. When the tribe went to war, and I
was able to go with them, I endeavoured to fulfil my
father's wishes by committing acts of violence ; and
when I succeeded in catching slaves for myself, my

father was pleased, and said, 'Now I will feed you, because you deserve it; now you shall not be in want of good things.'

"I followed this course, firmly believing I was doing right, until Paratene Ripi came to visit us at Kaikohe. He told us we must not work on the Sabbath-day, but pray to God and think of Him. Missionary visits now became frequent, but I still followed my own course. After a time I began to question whether it was right or not to proceed as I had begun under my father's tuition, and it was not long before I saw how exceedingly wicked I was, and I soon felt a hatred of my past life. My father, finding how matters were going on, separated himself from me, and is now living at a distance from Kaikohe, in order that he may be out of the way of instruction."

The New Zealanders believed in a future state, and the place to which the spirits of the departed went was the Reinga, the road to which lay over the extreme point of the North Cape, from which the spirits plunged into the sea, and there found their way to this abode of happiness, where all earthly enjoyments were to be allowed to them in their fullest extent. Mr. Puckey, who was now stationed at Kaitaea, was about to visit a small tribe living near the cape, who were a vanquished remnant of Te Aupouri tribe. He took with him six natives, and Paerata, an old chief, as guide. This once bloodthirsty warrior, who was partly the means of annihilating this tribe, was now in the way to become as bold and useful in the cause

of the Redeemer as he had been desperate in the
service of Satan. Whiti, a very aged chief, hearing
that the party was intending to explore the Reinga,
communicated the fact to another chief, who said to
Paerata, " I am come to send you and your white
companion back again; for if you cut away the
' aka '* of the Reinga, the whole island will be destroyed." Finding that they were bent on proceeding,
he said, " Don't suffer your friend to cut away the
ladder by which the souls of our forefathers were
conveyed to the other world." The whole body of
the New Zealanders, although composed of many
tribes, who for the most part were living in malice,
hateful and hating one another, yet firmly believed
that the Reinga was the one only place for departed
spirits. They supposed that as soon as the soul left
the body it made its way with all speed to the
western coast; the spirit of a person who had lived
in the interior took with it a small bundle of the
branches of the palm tree, as a token of its place of
abode; if of one who lived on the coast, the spirit
carried a kind of grass which grows by the sea-side,
and left it at different resting-places on its road to the
Reinga.

When within a few hours' walk of the Reinga the
party came to one of the resting-places of the spirits,
where they were told they should know if any native

* The aka was the root of a tree projecting out of the rock at the
extreme promontory of the North Cape, by the help of which the
spirits made their descent into the Reinga.

had lately died, as there would be a bundle of the green leaves as a token of the spirit having rested there on its way; but they found none. The next day they proceeded to explore the sacred spot. The last resting-place of the spirits was on a hill, called Haumu, from whence they could look back on the country where their friends were still living, and the thought of this caused them to cry and cut themselves. Here they saw many of these dry bundles of leaves, which a native said had been left by the spirits. Mr. Puckey asked if it were not possible for strangers, who passed that way, to do as they were then doing, namely, twist green branches, and deposit them there, as a sign that they had stopped at that notable place; a general custom of the natives whenever they pass any remarkable spot for the first time. They then passed over sandy hills and sandy beaches till they came to a river, where they took breakfast, and then ascended a craggy steep, covered with patches of slippery grass, upon which it was very difficult to walk. From the summit of this hill they gradually descended by a much better road till they came to the water's edge. Here was a hole through the rock, into which the spirits were said to pass, and after this they climbed again, and then descended by the " aka," a part of which had been severed by the violence of the wind; but was said to have been broken off by a number of spirits, which went down to the Reinga after a great multitude had been killed in battle. Having gazed a while at the "aka," the guide took them about one hundred yards further on, where he directed their attention to a large mass of seaweed, washed to and fro by the waves, which he said was the door which closed in the spirits of the Reinga. The name of this is Motatau; where, the guide remarked, fish are caught, which are always quite red, from the red ochre with which the natives smeared their bodies and mats. The scenery around this place was most wild, while the screaming of the sea fowl and the roaring of the waves dashing against the dismal black rocks suggested, to the reflecting mind, that it must have been the dreary aspect of the place that led the New Zealanders to choose such a situation as this for their Hades.

During Mr. Puckey's absence, rumours were spread among the tribes that he had gone to cut away the "aka" of the Reinga. Many angry speeches were made, and some said they would waylay the travellers on their return. All their superstitious feelings were aroused; while those who began to feel a little enlightened, said, "And what if the ladder be cut away? It is a false tradition, the spirits never went there." On being asked, "What, are you afraid of having no place to go to?" some of the old men said, "It is very well for you to go to the 'rangi' (heaven): but leave us our old road to the Reinga, and let us have something to hold on by as we descend, or we shall break our necks over the precipice." Many threatened a quarrel with Paerata, as they laid all the blame on him; and accordingly, on their return, a body of forty men went a distance of ten miles to inquire into the truth of the report. After two old chiefs had spoken, and declared that it was a very wicked thing to cut away the ladder to the Reinga, and only right that Paerata's property should be taken as a payment, Paerata rose up, and made an animated speech in defence of his new faith, which lasted two hours. He related all the incidents of the journey, and also spoke of the absurdity of their believing in such a place as their Reinga being the abode of departed spirits, and he added, with much feeling, " There is another Reinga, which I am afraid of; the one which burns with fire and brimstone;" and with regard to the spirits walking along the beach, and leaving tokens at the different resting-places, he asked sarcastically which way the soul of the man went who died while they were on the road, as they had seen nothing of the marks he had left behind. They replied, " He must have gone some other road," that is, to heaven. " No," said one, " how could that be? for the man was not a believer." Paerata then satisfied the people by assuring them that their old Reinga had not been disturbed by him, and that the road still lay straight before them.

CHAPTER XI.

1835.

DEATH OF PARATENE RIPI—CANDIDATES FOR BAPTISM—INDIFFER-
ENCE OF MANY—FEAST ON OCCASION OF REMOVAL OF BONES—
KOINAKI'S PLOT FRUSTRATED — MR. HAMLIN GOES TO MANGA-
POURI—CHARACTER OF AWARAHI—·BARBAROUS MURDERS.

PARATENE RIPI, the chief of Mawhe, was the first
person of high rank who had ventured to stand forth
on the side of Christianity.   His example had been
followed by many of his people, and his influence
was felt by others over whom he had no control. He
was in the prime of life, and a man of great natural
energy.   But, at a time when his presence seemed to
be of great consequence, it pleased God to lay His
hand upon him.   His Christian character had become clearly developed, and he was prepared as a
vessel meet for his Master's use.   In January, 1835,
he was seized with an attack of erysipelas in the
head, which was so severe that it prevented the possibility of much communication with him, and in a
few days he was taken away to a better world.   To
our short-sighted view, his continuance among his
people would have been an advantage.   It is natural
that the Christian should look with sorrow and regret
upon the removal of those who are doing much good ;

but Paratene had finished his appointed work, and, in the short course which he had run as a Christian man, he had become a blessing to many. And the same God who had raised him up as an instrument, was preparing many others to supply his place.

The number of persons anxious for instruction was now very much on the increase; indeed, so much was this the case, that the missionaries felt the necessity of using extreme caution in receiving their professions; fearing that they might often proceed from a desire to conform to the views of their neighbours, now that an avowal of their principles no longer drew upon them shame or reproach. It was clear, however, that a decided change had taken place; which was indicated by a total cessation from war, and by a discontinuance of those petty quarrels which were formerly of very frequent occurrence. The change of conduct on the part of those who were admitted to baptism gave us sufficient reason to believe that most of them had become the subjects of true repentance. There was among them a harmony of feeling which had not been seen aforetime, and a desire to promote the best interests of those around them. "How different," it was remarked, "our work is now from what it was a few years ago, when we were obliged to go from house to house, entreating the people to assemble together for instruction."

During the examination of candidates for baptism there was often a striking display of character. A native named Taki gave the following account of himself:—"When the station was first formed at Waimate, some of the Christian natives used to come and visit us. When they told me that I should be cast into the fire if I remained in sin, I professed my disbelief of a heaven or a hell, and told them I would put them into hell, if there were such a place. At length a portion of an old native book came into my hands, in which there were three hymns; and, without any regular instruction, I began to learn to read. After this I obtained another book, in which was the Lord's Prayer. I read, 'Our Father, which art in heaven.' What, thought I, is there a God in heaven, and is He a Father to us? and is His will to be done on earth, as it is in heaven? And then I thought, This is the God against whom I have so often spoken. From that time I began to inquire after Him." This man subsequently became a valuable teacher in the southern part of the island.

Korora was an old man, whose back was bowed down with age. He had frequently visited Mr. Davis for instruction, walking the distance of eight miles with as much regularity as the youngest and most healthy. He had a pleasing countenance, and spoke with much animation on religious subjects. Some of his children and grandchildren had been already admitted into the Church. "I have many sins," he said, "but Christ will take them all away. He died upon the cross for me, and then told His disciples to go and teach all nations." When asked what he thought of the love of Christ, he said, " His love is not on this side, nor on that side, but it is right in the middle of my heart." This old man soon realized the full enjoyment of that love in heaven; and was a glorious instance of what the grace of God can do at the eleventh hour. The name of Simeon was given to him, for he could truly utter the exclamation of that servant of God, " Now lettest Thou Thy servant depart in peace."

Akitu was an elderly lady of great respectability, formerly noted for her violent temper, and her activity in works of darkness : she became a simple-minded Christian, clear in her views of the Gospel.

Tama and Poti, chiefs of Kaikohe, had been desperate characters, always forward in mischief. They now gave reason to believe that they would become as active in the service of Christ as they had been in that of Satan.

Toi was a chief of Olaua; a place distant twenty miles from Waimate, and seldom visited. He had but little opportunity of instruction, but he obtained a clear insight into the truths of the Gospel. His wife was like-minded with himself; and his daughter, who was quite a child, seemed to have read her Bible to good purpose. Indeed, the whole party from that place, eight in number, were among the most intelligent of the candidates, showing the power of the grace of God; while many who enjoyed much greater advantages remained in total ignorance.

As one and another were separated from among

the heathen party, there was often a reaction produced in the minds of those who had no wish to
become Christians. The idea would occur to them,
"We are being left behind ; but perhaps after all our
friends are in the right." There was a large proportion of elderly chiefs present at a baptism held at
Waimate, who paid much attention. At the conclusion of the service some of them made remarks
on passing events. One spoke to the following
effect :—" Let us listen to all that the missionaries
tell us, for we shall derive benefit from them. Here
am I, a noted thief, who never spared your pigs or
your potatoes ; but I am now as one buried, I am
not heard of. I have a great regard for our relatives
who have been selected from among us this day.
Let us all attend to the instruction which they have
listened to. Our fathers did not believe these things
because they had none to teach them ; but when
foreigners came and brought guns and axes, they
were glad to obtain them : and if they had been told
of Jesus Christ they would also have received Him."

There was still a great number, however, who
withstood all overtures which were made to them.
Hihi was a dignified-looking chief, who had taken an
active part in the conflict which occurred at Kororareka, in 1830. It was he who killed Hongi, on account of whose death the raid was made by his sons
upon Tauranga, which led to so much bloodshed.
He was living as a respected chief near Waimate ;
but he held out against instruction, and his people

followed his example. He had no reason to allege against the truth, but, like the multitude in Christian countries, he was indifferent about it. In one respect he was obliged to acknowledge that a change for the better had been effected through the Gospel. In former days, the season at which the principal crop of food is taken up was always the time for settling differences, because there was then plenty of food which could be plundered. Hihi said that he used to cultivate kumara for Hongi and Te Koikoi, for they generally found some excuse for carrying off his crop; but he added, "I have been visited by no party during the last three years." This was evidence which might be depended upon, and was the more valuable because it was given by one who rejected the truth, while he securely enjoyed the benefit resulting from it.

The New Zealanders had a practice of holding a feast every two or three years, on occasion of taking up the bones of all the members of the tribe who had died during the interval. At these times their lamentations were repeated with as much bitterness as had been manifested when their relatives had died. There was a gathering of all the people, and it was usual to invite some other tribes to be present with them, and a great preparation of food was made for the entertainment of their guests. After the feasting was at an end, the bones were carried to their final resting-place, which was generally a cavern at some distance from the abode of man. All affairs of state were reserved for discussion at these times, and many of their warlike expeditions were then determined on, to be carried out as soon as convenient. There was some advantage in bringing the people together, and it often tended to keep up a good understanding between neighbouring tribes. But there was much more of evil which had its origin at these times, than was counterbalanced by any attendant good; and the enormous consumption of food caused a scarcity which was felt, more especially by the poorer people, during the whole remainder of the season.

These feasts had continued to be held up to this period without intermission, and one upon a large scale was now about to take place at Waimate, having been prepared by all the people in that neighbourhood. The guests on this occasion were the natives of Hokianga, and, according to the custom of the country, the compliment would have been returned by that tribe the following year. But the natives were now beginning to see the folly of these things; and, while the chiefs who had embraced Christianity had silently given up the practice, its continuance had now become a state question among those who were not under the influence of Christian principles. Persons of this character were weary of the practice, because it was attended with much trouble and expense; and they were glad to avail themselves of the assistance of the missionaries to get them out of the difficulty.

Rewa, the principal man on this occasion, requested

them to come forward, and state publicly that this
feast was to be the last, and that no return was to be
made for it by the people of Hokianga. The two
parties were quartered about a mile from the settlement. The provision of food consisted of two
thousand bushel baskets of kumara, and fifty or
sixty cooked pigs, which formed a heap three
hundred yards in length. At the extremities and
in the centre of the heap of food, three small flags
were hoisted, appended to which were placards, desiring the natives of Hokianga not to make any
return for this entertainment, and informing them
that from that time the removal of bones was to
cease. No bones were exhibited to view on this
occasion, but the different families collected their
own respectively, and committed them to their final
resting-place.

In a former chapter an account was given of the
murder of two Waikato natives by Koinaki, not far
from the mission station at Puriri. This deed was
followed by an attack from Waikato, in which twenty
natives were killed near Whakatiwai. A few months
had passed away, when tidings were brought to Puriri
that a party of natives was going across the frith the
next day, for the purpose of cutting off a Waikato
party who were then at Manawhenua, about twenty
miles from Whakatiwai, on their way to visit the
Ngatipaoa tribe. A neutral chief was with them,
for the purpose of making up past differences between themselves and that tribe. Koinaki was at

this time preparing his canoe at Kaweranga, intending to precede the rest of his party in the night, in order that he might have the first opportunity to glut his revenge without restraint. Mr. Fairburn determined at once to launch his boat, and proceed to Manawhenua, and, if possible, to intercept Koinaki and his party, so as to give the poor creatures timely notice of their danger. He started under cover of the evening, in company with Mr. Wilson. They pulled leisurely across the frith, and, as the little creek which they had to enter could only be approached at high water, they anchored the boat, and lay down till daylight. Having ascended the first hill, they took a survey of the frith, and at once saw Koinaki's canoe pulling right in the direction of the little harbour they had chosen. They had a native guide to conduct them by the nearest road, and it appeared that Koinaki had chosen the same route. They now quickened their pace, and, as they passed over each succeeding hill, they could observe the canoe fast approaching, and at length they saw the people land. Up to this time Koinaki had no knowledge of this movement, but at the landing-place he would find the boat and the tent in charge of two natives, from whom he would learn who were before him. The missionaries now quickened their pace, till they were within about two miles of the spot where they expected to find the Waikato party. They were compelled to rest for a while before they could proceed further. They then examined several places without success, but observed recent footmarks in the sand. Mr. Fairburn immediately despatched the guide to the landing-place at Maramarua, with directions, should he find the natives, to tell them of their danger. After an absence of an hour he returned, saying that all the men, except three, who had remained with the canoes, had arrived safely the day before at Whakatiwai, and were then with their friends ; but the women, forty in number, had been left behind with three canoes, which, on the arrival of the messenger, they launched, and pulled down the stream. The missionaries had not proceeded far when they heard the report of a musket in the direction of the canoes. It was a time of anxious suspense, for it was probable that Koinaki or some of his party had slipped past through the bushes, and had come up with the poor women. On reaching a rising ground, they saw a man, who proved to be Koinaki, loading his double-barrelled gun. Shortly after, several others made their appearance, like a pack of bloodhounds scenting their prey. Mr. Wilson now passed on with the guide in the direction of the canoes, while Mr. Fairburn turned about to face Koinaki and his party, at the same time doubtful as to the issue of this interference with his design. Koinaki, however, put on an air of civility, and asked whether it was supposed he was come there to kill anybody. But he was restless and impatient, and inquiring whether any natives had been seen there, he turned off in search of the poor women, with all his party, twenty-three in number. Mr. Fairburn followed close after him, and in about ten minutes they came in sight of a newly-built shed. The foremost of the men made a rush towards it, hatchet in hand, while those in the rear were close after him. This was to be the crisis of their fate, but Mr. Wilson came up at the moment and said, "All is right; they have just passed out of sight down the creek." Thus was this diabolical scheme frustrated. The missionaries had at least two hours' start of Koinaki, but, if he had been an hour earlier, it is probable the whole of this party would have been murdered. Koinaki, finding they were still within hail, called out to them in a friendly manner to return, but in vain; they knew well that their only safety was in flight.

The sun was now below the horizon, the rain was falling in torrents, and the clothes of the missionaries were drenched with travelling through swamps and underwood. Their tent, and blankets, and provision were fifteen miles distant, and the only hut near was in an unfinished state, the roof being covered only on one side. But Koinaki, notwithstanding the failure of his project, invited them to share the hut with him and his party, and gave directions to cover the end they were to occupy, that they might be sheltered from the rain. By the help of fire they managed to get their clothes tolerably dry. The next difficulty was the want of provisions. They had depended for supply upon the natives whom they went to rescue, but they were gone, and here again Koinaki

stood their friend. Two of his party carried provisions for the rest, and, as soon as he found that Mr.
Fairburn had none, he shared his supply with him.

The next morning the whole party were returning
again in the direction of the boat, when Koinaki,
holding up his double-barrelled gun, observed, with a
significant smile, "I should have tried this gun yes-
terday if I had been in time." Mr. Fairburn told
him that it was persons like himself who had brought
whole tribes into trouble; that most of the chiefs of
his own party were disposed for peace, but so long as
such men as he were thirsting for blood, peace could
never be established. He assented to all that was
said, and promised that this should be the last time
he would come on such an errand.

I was about to occupy the station at Mangapouri,
on the banks of the river Waipa, according to the
arrangements which had been already made; but, on
my return to the Bay of Islands to remove my family,
it was settled by the Committee that I should go to
Waimate, to take charge of the school for the missionaries' children, and that Mr. Hamlin should supply
my place at Mangapouri, joining Messrs. Stack and
Morgan, who were already there. It soon appeared
that the desire expressed by the Waikatos to have
missionaries living with them was of an interested
character. It was not the new instruction that they
wanted: of that it could not be expected they should
form a right estimate; they rather looked to the
worldly advantage which the residence of mission-

aries might bring to them. With this feeling predominant in their minds, they were prepared oftentimes to act in such a manner as to cause much
annoyance. Exorbitant demands were made by the
natives who had conveyed the supplies to the station.
Then there was great dissatisfaction when the payment agreed upon for the erection of the raupo house
was given. This was a trial of strength, which had
often been met with elsewhere, and required to be
treated with firmness at first, when afterwards a
good understanding generally followed between the
parties.

Awarahi, the chief, had spoken honestly when he
said that he was not going to believe in the new
teaching; and many circumstances soon made it
apparent that he was a man of violent temper, which
was kept in check by no good principle. In a conversation one day with Mr. Stack, he gave an account
of an event which had taken place four years before.
Horeta, a native from the Thames, visited Tamarere's
brother, who, during the time of his visit, was taken
ill. It was recollected that a child of the sick man
had, in foolish simplicity, talked of eating Horeta's
head. It was therefore immediately suspected that
he had been practising incantation against the child's
father, and some advised that he should be killed.
His death, however, was deferred, that the result of
the witchcraft might be seen. Tamarere's brother,
finding himself getting worse, sent for Awarahi, and
asked him to kill Horeta, who, he positively asserted,

had bewitched him, and added that his only chance
of life was to have the wizard killed. Horeta, considering himself among friends, had no suspicion ;
and the knowledge of this fact operated upon the
feelings of Tamarere so much, that he would not
consent to kill a man who was confiding to his
honour and friendship, and who was also in some
way related to him. The sick brother's importunity,
however, prevailed over all natural sense of right and
wrong, and Awarahi was fixed upon as the execu-
tioner. He at once sharpened his hatchet, and prayed
to the native god for success in his intended design.
Tamarere, who was of a less cruel disposition, deferred
the deed, till at last the sick man lost all patience ;
when, by a previously-concerted signal between Awarahi and Tamarere, the former rushed into the hut,
seized Horeta by the hair of the head, and dragged
him outside. His voice was soon lost in death.

Three days after hearing this account, Mr. Stack
being at a neighbouring village with Mr. Morgan, the
subject of witchcraft was referred to, when a young
man who was present, and was said to be bewitched,
begged him not to allow Awarahi to hurt any one on
his account. But acts of cruelty such as these were
very common. The bystanders related that a woman
had been murdered, two days before, not far from the
spot where they then stood—the slave wife of one of
their tribe, a young woman of comely person, who
had borne him one child, the only charge against her
being that of witchcraft. After declaring their ab-

horrence of such conduct, the missionaries wished to ascertain the fact, and took a lad as guide to show them the remains of the unfortunate deceased, which they found in a secluded place, near a beautiful stream of water, about a mile from the village. The spot on which she had slept the night before her death was shaded by an overhanging tree. A few feet from this lay a heap of white ashes, w th several portions of human bones, burnt almost to powder. The by-standers, who were chiefly female slaves from Tara-naki, the birthplace of this unfortunate young woman, told Mr. Stack that the murder had been committed by a native of Kawhia, at the request of her master, because he supposed she had bewitched another of his wives, who was sick. While their hearts mourned over this victim of cruelty and superstition, they could do no more for her than cover her ashes with large stones, to mark the infamy of him who had violently cut off, in the prime of life, one who had claimed his protection and safeguard.

There was nothing as yet to encourage those servants of God who had undertaken this post of labour but the assurance that the final triumph of the Gospel is certain. As yet the ground was hard and the soil barren, and it required much faith to believe that the seed would grow.

CHAPTER XII.

1835, 1836.

STATION AT MATAMATA — ANNOYANCES — WAHAROA QUARRELS
WITH NGATIKOROKI — DEATH OF PARINGARINGA — MR. CHAP-
MAN BEGINS A STATION AT ROTORUA — MURDER OF HUNGA
—WAHAROA TAKES MAKETU — HORRIBLE SCENES ON THEIR
RETURN — RETALIATION EXPECTED — TUMU TAKEN—WAHAROA
MAKES GREAT SLAUGHTER AT ROTORUA—MISSION-HOUSE PLUN-
DERED—PROPERTY SENT FROM MATAMATA PLUNDERED—TARA-
PIPIPI—NGAKUKUS'S CHILD KILLED.—WAHAROA'S DEATH.

AFTER the Committee of Missionaries had well considered the relative claims of Matamata and Tauranga,
it was decided to give the preference to the former
place ; and the Rev. A. N. Brown undertook the formation of this station, in which he was to be assisted
by Mr. Morgan, who for this purpose was to leave
Mangapouri. Mr. Brown arrived at Matamata in
April, 1835. There were many difficulties to be
encountered here also ; but it was found that a quiet
and firm course of treatment generally sufficed to
remove them.

These troubles often arose out of the every-day
occurrences of life. Mr. Brown having purchased a
large supply of potatoes for a winter stock of provision, Paharakeke, the principal chief engaged about
the erection of the house, was angry because the
potatoes were not all purchased from his tribe, and,

perceiving a heavy rain coming on, he tapued the house, in order that the potatoes might not be put under shelter. Mr. Brown felt that if this conduct were not checked, he might some day or other take it into his head to tapu him also. He therefore went to the old man, and told him that though the missionaries would not violate their sacred places, they could not allow the natives to tapu theirs. He then went into the house, and, much to the astonishment of the natives who were collected around, he took down the dirty mats which Paharakeke had tied up to the posts of the house as a sign of its being sacred, and took them outside; after which the natives, who had before refused to carry in the potatoes, went in without hesitation.

A few days afterwards, Paharakeke tried to have his potatoes purchased at a different price from that agreed for with other natives; but as he found begging and scolding equally unavailing, he at last good-humouredly gave up the point.

As there were no natives at work at the house the next day, Mr. Brown inquired the reason, and found that Paharakeke had desired them all to leave off work. On this he told the chiefs present that he could not bring his family till a house had been built for their reception; and as Paharakeke had, without any reason, refused to allow the men to continue their work, he should return to Puriri, and remain there till they sent him word that the house was finished. This intention was at once communicated to the old chief, who very soon made his appearance, and requested to make peace, promising that the house should be proceeded with immediately. He stated also that he had not been angry with him, but with one of the natives who had sold the potatoes. Mr. Brown, therefore, recommended him to be reconciled with the person who had given him this annoyance. To this he consented, and, in English fashion, they shook hands, instead of rubbing noses.

Matamata was quite in the interior, and communication with friends at other places was dependent wholly on the will of the natives. One day Mr. Brown had the mortification of hearing that messengers from Puriri, with letters, had been detained on the road, in consequence of a tapu, a usual custom at the commencement of the eel-catching season. The natives, however, promised that the tapu should be taken off, and the road re-opened in two days. At the time fixed, the lads from Puriri arrived; but they had been plundered, and the box containing the supplies and letters taken from them. This conduct was trying, for the natives had broken their promise. Mr. Brown sent, therefore, for Waharoa, and complained that he had been deceived respecting the tapu, and stated also that it was absolutely necessary for him to go over the sacred ground. The old man said that, if he persisted in passing, the people would perhaps be very troublesome, as the eels would not go into the nets if the tapu were violated. Mr. Brown thought, however, that it was desirable to go

to the confines of the sacred spot, and have an interview with the chief who had the box. He therefore
left Matamata, and parted on excellent terms with
the natives ; and with no one more so than with his
troublesome friend Paharakeke, who urged him to
make haste and return with Mrs. Brown, and he
would become a believer as soon as he went back
again. In a few hours he reached the sacred spot,
and the box was soon placed at the tent door, without
any observation. The chief who had plundered the
lads then made his appearance, and took to himself
very great merit for not having kept anything belonging to Mr. Brown, and asked if he would not
make peace with him. To give him some idea of the
rights of property, Mr. Brown told him that the
white man's property was not more sacred than that
of the natives', a doctrine which he seemed quite
incapable of comprehending. Mr. Brown promised,
at his request, not to proceed on his journey till the
morning, as he wished to take off the tapu during
the night ; and he then went on to argue, in a way
most convincing to himself, that as they sat still on
Sunday, because they were told to do so, it was the
duty of the missionaries, in return, not to pass over
tapued ground which had been made sacred for a
season only.

One morning after Mr. Brown's return from Puriri,
there was a disturbance made by three natives scaling
the fence, one of whom commenced chopping the end
of the house with his hatchet. It turned out that

this man was one of those who had been engaged in the erection of the house, and having left his work unfinished, Ngakuku, who had completed it, proposed that the payment should be given to him; and they took this mode of showing their annoyance. The aggressors received a good scolding for their conduct; and at last the ringleader, feeling ashamed of himself, jumped back over the fence, and ran off to his home. The next day the work was paid for without any expression of dissatisfaction, and the native who had made the assault on the preceding day sent a letter of apology, and requested that he might be allowed to bring a pig as a peace-offering.

In this unsettled country, there was frequent occasion to feel how true is the declaration, " Thou knowest not what a day may bring forth." While Mr. Brown was at breakfast one morning, Te Waharoa entered the house, his countenance betraying the anger which was working within. He said that the natives of Maungatautari were on their way to Tauranga, with flax for a trader who had engaged to place a white man with them, and that he was determined to fire upon them, if they attempted to pass through Matamata. This was evidently a political movement on his part to prevent guns and ammunition passing into the hands of those who, though nominally his friends, might perhaps at a future time turn their force against him. Mr. Brown could not enter into the cause of their present quarrel, but earnestly urged him not to go to war with a tribe so

nearly related to him as Ngatikoroki. In the evening
a messenger, who had been sent by Waharoa to tell
them that if they persisted in coming on he would
fire upon them, returned with the tidings that Ngatikoroki would not regard his threat, and had sent
back to Maungatautari for their guns. Looking to
the Prince of Peace for a blessing, Mr. Brown determined to visit Ngatikoroki in the morning, and
endeavour to prevail upon them to return to their
homes, and Ngakuku consented to accompany him.
This chief was nephew to Waharoa, and had formerly
been, according to his own account, a very desperate
character; but he was now making an open profession of religion before his countrymen.

Ngatihaua, the tribe of Waharoa, now left off scrap-
ing flax in order to make ball cartridge; Waharoa,
however, gave his consent that Mr. Brown should go
to Ngatikoroki. On the road they met a second
messenger who had been charged by Ngatikoroki to
tell Ngatihaua, that they had thrown away their flax,
and had armed themselves, intending to proceed to
Matamata. Some distance from the encampment of
Ngatikoroki they met a few scouts, who ran back with
the intelligence that a white man was coming. On
reaching the spot they found about one hundred
armed men, and about the same number of women
and children. Mr. Brown took up a position about
twenty yards from them, and, according to native
custom, sat for some time in silence. At length one
of the chiefs got up and made a speech; which he

commenced by saying that he supposed the missionary was come to send them back to their homes; but they were too brave to listen to him. He was followed by others, some of whom were very much inclined to be insolent, but the older men spoke more reasonably; one of them observing, that it was not right to be angry, till they had heard what Mr. Brown had to say. He told them he was not a messenger from Waharoa, but a messenger from Jesus Christ, who commanded all men to love one another. They listened with a good deal of attention, and finally consented to go back in the morning. Wishing to show how very brave they should have been, had they proceeded to Matamata, they commenced their hideous war dance. After a time the principal chiefs adjourned to Mr. Brown's tent, of which they took quiet possession, and kept on talking till after midnight, often requesting him to leave Waharoa's tribe, which they designated as a very bad one, and to go and reside with their tribe, which was composed altogether of men with "very good hearts and very quiet spirits."

Although Waharoa had allowed Mr. Brown to try and effect a reconciliation, he started off with his people by another road in pursuit of Ngatikoroki, and the next day they returned in a very sullen mood, because they had been deprived of the pleasure of shooting some of their relatives, Ngatikoroki having gone home.

Paringaringa, a chief of some note, died about this

time. When his relatives found that he was near his end, they wished to remove him from the settlement, but he objected, and desired his wife not to dispose of his corpse according to the native custom. As soon as he was dead they made the house tapu, and nailed it up. They refused to allow him to be buried in a coffin as being contrary to their practice, but afterwards they so far overcame their prejudices that the body was placed in a large box, which they buried in a grave. When the earth was being pressed down, the widow said, "Let it rest lightly on him, that he may be able to rise again." Paringaringa's friends entertained the idea that he had died a believer, and had gone to heaven; but so blind were they to everything of a spiritual nature that they took two small loaves of bread, and placed them in the box, in order that he might have something to eat on his way to heaven.

While Mr. Brown was commencing his work at Matamata, Mr. Chapman was preparing to take some steps at Rotorua, and for this purpose he left Paihia in the month of February, in an open boat, proceeding first to Puriri in the Thames, and from thence overland to Rotorua, which he reached on the 19th of March, accompanied by a carpenter. A beginning was also made at Tauranga, and it was hoped that now all the principal tribes in this part of the country would be at once brought under Christian instruction, and that an end might be put to those feuds which had for generations back torn their people asunder. But whereas these operations had been long deferred by intestine wars, so now, as soon as an entrance had been effected into this part of Satan's dominions, he again stirred up evil, for the purpose of delaying that conquest which he knew would be certain in the end. The missionaries had but just taken possession of their new habitations, and the well-disposed natives were beginning to gather around them, and were listening to instruction which they had not yet made up their minds to receive, when a native of high rank belonging to Matamata was murdered at Rotorua. Retaliation was the necessary consequence, while the incipient station at Tauranga, the natives of which place were in alliance with those of Matamata, was bound to share with them all the evils of war. The treacherous act which led to this state of confusion is thus related by Mr. Chapman :—

"We were just beginning to feel some little ease from the burdens which for four months had pressed heavily upon us, when on Christmas morning of 1835, just as I was preparing to assemble the natives for service, intelligence was brought me that a chief, named Huka, had that morning murdered, in a most barbarous manner, Hunga, a near relative of Waharoa, and that the body had been taken to Huka's Pa, on the other side of the lake, to be eaten. I immediately had the boat launched, and, favoured with a fair wind, landed in little more than an hour. The natives received me in sullen silence, no doubt guessing my

errand. They made no answer to my inquiries, and
Huka himself, I found, was then at the great Pa,
having gone there, as I afterwards learnt, to hang up
the poor man's heart in a sacred place, in order to
avert any danger from himself. I called upon them
to give up to me the body of the murdered man;
upon which a young man rose, and said that they had
not the body, but that it had been quartered, and
sent away in different directions;—that they had the
head, which they were willing to give me, but were
afraid of Huka's anger. I told them that I would
take the responsibility upon myself. He then walked
a short distance, and with the utmost unconcern
brought me the head, wrapped up in a bloody mat.
Placing it in the boat I brought it away, and on the
following morning delivered it to some of the poor
man's relations."

As soon as the tidings were carried to Matamata,
it was apparent that Waharoa would not rest until
ample revenge had been taken. This chief was a
consummate warrior, possessing much military tact,
and, like Hongi in the north, he was extremely
cautious in disclosing his plans, lest information
should be carried to the enemy.

The murderer of Waharoa's relative lived at a
village on the banks of Rotorua lake, in the interior,
and the Rotorua people naturally supposed that his
vengeance would be directed against that quarter;
but the crafty chief preferred a different course.
According to native custom, Huka's relatives might

be attacked with as much propriety as Huka himself. He decided therefore upon a movement against Maketu,* a Pa on the sea-coast, fifteen miles beyond Tauranga.   At the same time, the more effectually to throw the natives off their guard, he refused to allow Mr. Brown to go to Rotorua to hold communication with Mr. Chapman, but directed him to go to Maketu and send for Mr. Chapman from thence, stating also that most of the Rotorua natives had consented to leave that place and reside at Maketu, so that he might have only the tribe of the murderer to engage with.   After waiting about two months he assembled his forces at Matamata, with the avowed object of going to Rotorua, and then, making a rapid movement to Tauranga, where he was joined by the natives of that place, came unexpectedly upon Maketu.

The Rev. Messrs. Brown and Maunsell, the latter having lately joined the mission, had wished to go over from Matamata to Tauranga, but were not allowed to move until the army had taken its departure, but they followed quickly after, and on the night of their arrival they were aroused by a report that the army was close at hand on its return from Maketu.   Among the foremost of the party was Waharoa; and as the great body of the natives purposed sleeping in the neighbourhood of the mission station, he came and lay down before Mr. Wilson's house, as a guard for the property.   The number of natives killed in the

* Maketu, Matamata, and Rotorua are situated at the angles of a triangle.

Pa was about sixty-five. They brought away one hundred and fifty as slaves, and entirely destroyed the Pa. The premises of Mr. Tapsell, a flax trader, were burnt to the ground, and all his property either destroyed or carried away. So completely indeed was the place ransacked that the natives dug up the body of Mr. Tapsell's child, which had been deeply buried in his garden, in the hope of finding treasure in the coffin. This body of natives was made up from various tribes, many of them from the distant parts of Waikato; and being flushed with victory, and having tasted the sweets of plunder, there was reason for apprehension lest they should be turbulent towards the missionaries. They were, however, restrained from mischief, but the horrors of the scene were dreadful. Dead to all feeling, they shook the heads of their vanquished foes in the view of the missionaries, and displayed the hands and feet from the baskets of flesh which they were carrying on their backs. A young child was seen dandling upon his knees and making faces at the head of a Rotorua chief who had been slain, showing how readily human nature is reconciled to these scenes of cruelty. Moreover, the feeling of horror excited in the minds of the missionaries was much enhanced by the fact, that it was the anniversary of the day on which the blessed Saviour agonized on the cross for wretched fallen man, that he might save him from sin and the dominion of the prince of darkness.

It was in company with these natives, about 1,000

in number, that Mr. Brown and Mr. Maunsell had
to return to Matamata, while the smell of their garments, and the baskets of human flesh, which some
were carrying as presents to chiefs at a distance, quite
tainted the atmosphere. One of the natives told Mr.
Brown that he only went to fight in order to seize
some female slaves for Mrs. Brown; while Waharoa
asked, in bravado, if he would not have some flesh
to eat. And on replying to him that he would
find that eternal death is the wages of iniquity,
he said, " If you are angry with me for what we
have been doing, I will kill and eat you and all the
missionaries."

The work at the mission station at Matamata was
now brought to a stand. It was expected that the
natives of Rotorua would make reprisals upon
Waharoa's stronghold, so the schoolboys always left
their houses at night, and either went to the Pa to
sleep or secreted themselves in the bush. Waharoa,
too, advised that the wives of the missionaries should
be removed to a place of safety, before an attack
should be made. It was an anxious time, spent
within the sound of savage yells, the firing of guns
and all the signals of war. An alarm being given
that the enemy was approaching, all was immediately
in commotion. The school lads and the girls fled to
the Pa; the women, carrying provisions, crowded the
paths, and the men seized their guns and prepared for
fight. That night was passed in no small anxiety.
The patrols that hitherto had traversed the woods,

crying, "Whakaara" (rise up), were now silent, not a gun was heard, and the "pahu," the native alarm bell, had ceased to be sounded. The very silence, which had of late been unusual, was alarming.

The Sabbath dawned without any further tidings, and it was considered expedient to remove the wives of the missionaries to Puriri. The school natives were accordingly summoned, and twenty gave their names as willing to convey them. The distance to the boat was only a few miles, but the deep swamps made the road heavy. Provisions were hastily prepared, clothes were packed up, and litters for the females were got ready. Suddenly, however, a report was raised that the enemy was near at hand, and had fired guns just in the path by which they were to travel. No alternative was now left, and the movement was suspended. The report had its origin in a great measure from the prediction of a priest on the night previous. He said that Whiro had told him that the enemy would divide their forces; that one party of two hundred would advance to the Pa on the Thames side; and that the Pa forces having been drawn out to meet them, another party of three hundred would rush forward from their ambush, and take possession of the Pa, the women and children being left without protection.

But the Rotorua natives had no intention of coming to Matamata at this time. There was a weak point which promised them success with much less difficulty. On the road to Tauranga, about two miles

from Maketu, was the village of Tumu, occupied by
a portion of the Tauranga natives. The position of
this village was most insecure,—built upon a sandhill
which rose from the sea-beach. It had no natural
advantages on any side, and the irregular nature of
the ground afforded abundant shelter to an attacking
party. The only reason for occupying this place was,
that it had the advantage of an extensive flax swamp
at the back, from which large quantities of this
material had been prepared for sale to the traders.
As timber of every kind was at a great distance, the
artificial fences of the Pa were unusually weak. The
Rotorua natives planned the destruction of this place
immediately after Maketu was taken; and it was a
singular infatuation on the part of Ngatiawa that they
should continue to occupy a post which was far in
advance of their remaining strongholds. All the
country at the back of Tumu was in the hands of
their enemies, and was in the direct road to Rotorua.
A little before daylight on the 5th of May, the Rotorua
natives, mustering about 800 men, attacked the place
from two points in the rear, having made their approach through the swampy land unperceived, while,
as soon as the firing commenced, a division from
Maketu rushed by the beach, and came upon the Pa
on the eastern side. A brave resistance was made for
some time, but the force within was not sufficient to
keep off superior numbers coming upon them from
different points of attack. Many were killed on both
sides during the assault, but at length the outer fence

was gained, and then the only safety that remained was in flight. The women and children all fell into the hands of the victors, and were either killed or retained as slaves, and of the men but a small proportion escaped to carry the tidings to Tauranga.

Waharoa at once set out to take counsel with the chiefs at Tauranga respecting their future movements against Rotorua, and he gave out that he would leave Matamata with all his people, and live at Tumu until he had destroyed the Rotorua tribes. It was an empty threat to be made by an old man, standing on the borders of eternity ; and he ought to have known from past experience, that while it was in his power to inflict a heavy blow upon his enemies, he must reckon, from the nature of native warfare, upon suffering as severely in return.

Affairs continued in a state of uncertainty until July, when Waharoa began to assemble a force at Patetere, a village lying far up on the banks of the Thames, half way between Matamata and Rotorua, and in the early part of August he appeared before Ohinemutu, the principal Pa on the lake Rotorua, adjoining which was the mission station. Mr. Chapman was absent at Matamata, but had left the premises in charge of his assistants, Knight and Pilley. Waharoa's forces were not numerous, but he was a good general, and placing a strong division of his men in a sheltered position, he sent a smaller force towards the Pa, which soon retreated, and drew the enemy forward, until they were assailed on all sides by the concealed party, and put to the rout. Unfortunately they fled by the mission premises, and thus the enemy was brought within reach of a temptation they were unable to resist. It was to little purpose that the house was locked. The doors and windows quickly yielded to a moderate force, and all the moveables in a moment disappeared, and were distributed among the assailants. Others again flew upon the two young men, and deprived them of nearly everything that was upon them; and one of them making a vigorous resistance, was very roughly treated, and threatened with the loss of his life. It was the time of war, and according to the native usage, the white man might have lost his life in common with the natives who had fallen into their hands. The usual horrors of a New Zealand conflict were all enacted over again, and they had a strong motive to influence them; they felt that they were taking revenge for their friends who had fallen at Te Tumu. As Waharoa had said a little before, "How sweet will the flesh of the Rotorua natives taste along with their new kumara!"

It was now clear that no mission property in these disturbed districts could be considered safe. It was expedient, therefore, to save what remained, and with this design that which was most valuable at Matamata was put together in convenient packages, in order that it might be carried to the banks of the river Waihou, and conveyed by canoe to Puriri. Waharoa and most of the people of influence were

still absent, but there were some ill-disposed persons
not brave enough to meet their enemies in open fight,
but ready to commit acts of depredation upon those
whom they ought to have protected. As soon as the
property had been sent away, they followed the
bearers to the place of embarkation, and blacking
their faces for the purpose of concealment, they
carried off the whole. Some young men, headed by
Tarapipipi, the son of Waharoa, at once set off in
pursuit, followed by Mr. Morgan and Mr. Knight
from the station. The latter had reached the neighbourhood of Waiharakeke, when they heard the voices
of some of the school girls calling them to return,
as a party was coming through the wood dressed in
English clothes. They accordingly retraced their
steps, and soon came in sight of these people. They
had a most novel appearance as seen issuing from the
wood, dressed principally in white shirts, and armed
some with axes and others with muskets. There was
also something ludicrous in the scene, for one man
was marching before the rest, with the utmost consequence, his head and olive-coloured face being en-
veloped in a black silk bonnet belonging to Mrs.
Chapman, while a strip of cotton print, tied round his
neck, formed the remainder of his apparel, he having
left his own clothes at home, in order to his being
lighter for fighting, or anything else he might have
to do. It was found, however, that they were not the
robbers, but the party under Tarapipipi, who had
fallen in with the robbers, and had stripped them of

the things they had just stolen. On the way to the Pa, a young man was seen in a white shirt proceeding thither also. In an instant Tarapipipi and his brother rushed upon him, and the shirt changed owners in a moment.

The work of evangelization among the natives of Matamata was only in its infancy. Satan, indeed, had been but too successful in distracting the attention of the people from all that was good. But there were a few, principally sons of leading chiefs, who had refused, from motives of conscience, to join the party which went to Rotorua, and among them was Ngakuku, nephew to Waharoa. The line of communication between Matamata and Tauranga had been always open, and frequent intercourse was kept up between the two places. In the middle of October a party consisting of twenty-one natives and one Englishman set out for Tauranga. Ngakuku was the head of the party, having with him his two children, a boy and a girl. They brought up for the night in a romantic spot at the foot of the steep ascent of Wairere, where a magnificent cascade, falling from the high forest land above, gives the name to the place. The Englishman pitched his tent, and the natives occupied a small temporary house which was often the resting-place of travelling parties. They cooked their evening meal, and then, under the guidance of Ngakuku, they commended themselves to the protection of that God whom he was now beginning to know. But the glimmering light of their evening

TE WAIRERE, NEAR THE WAIHO RIVER.

fire had been noticed by a Rotorua party far up the valley, and they naturally concluded that there were natives resting there for the night, belonging either to Tauranga or Matamata. Under cover of the darkness, they crept stealthily along the mountain's side, and came upon the encampment a little before break of day. Happily they were attracted first by the Englishman's tent. They thought it would contain something worth having, and at once rushed upon it, each eager to secure some article of clothing for himself. They left the poor man but a vestige of what he had had the night before, but they did him no bodily injury. This momentary interruption was the preservation of nearly the whole party. The noise which was made, together with the barking of a dog, aroused those who were in the hut, and they rushed out towards the rising ground, and were soon in a position of safety. Ngakuku snatched up his boy by one arm, and swung him upon his back, and tried to arouse little Tarore his daughter, but she was heavy with sleep, and the enemy were already rushing in at one end of the hut, so the poor child was left behind. As the daylight came on, Ngakuku, who was hovering on the higher ground in dreadful anxiety for his child, called out to the natives below, telling them who he was, and inquiring after the child. They told him she was safe, and that if he would go down to them they would give her up. But Ngakuku was too well practised in native treachery to trust them. He waited, therefore, in his lurking place until he saw the enemy depart; then, descending to the hut, he found the mangled corpse of his little child, and returned to Matamata to carry the sad tidings to his friends. The Rev. A. N. Brown wrote :—" While talking to poor Ngakuku this afternoon, and endeavouring to administer consolation to him, he remarked, ' The only reason why my heart is sad, is, that I do not know whether my child has gone to heaven, or to the Reinga. She has heard the Gospel with her ears and read it to Mrs. Brown, but I do not know whether she has received it into her heart.' After evening prayers at the chapel, Ngakuku arose and spoke to the natives from John xiv. 1."

The next day poor Tarore was buried. Those who had so narrowly escaped a like death, followed the corpse to the grave, around which were arranged various groups, from the different native residences. After Mr. Brown had addressed the assembled party, Ngakuku expressed a wish to speak a few words, and said with deep solemnity of feeling, " There lies my child; she has been murdered as a payment for your bad conduct. But do not you rise up to obtain satisfaction for her. God will do that. Let this be the conclusion of the war with Rotorua. Let peace be now made. My heart is not sad for Tarore, but for you. You wished for teachers to come to you; they came, and now you are driving them away. You are weeping for my daughter, but I am weeping for you—for myself—for all of us. Perhaps this murder is a sign of God's anger towards us for our sins. Turn to Him; believe, or you will all perish."

It is a remarkable circumstance in connexion with the murder of this child, that in an attack made upon Matamata some weeks afterwards, out of five Rotorua natives who were killed, four were concerned in this sad tragedy; and that after the lapse of a few years, Uita, the man who led the attack, having a desire to embrace Christianity, first sought for reconciliation with Ngakuku.

This destructive war continued until the year 1840, without much actual fighting, but the adverse tribes were in continual fear of each other, and always watchful of opportunities to cut off any stragglers who might fall in their way. The missionaries were advised to remove with their families for a time to the Bay of Islands, but in the year 1839 Tauranga and Rotorua were again occupied, the head-quarters of the latter being on the island Mokoia, in the middle of Rotorua lake, out of the reach of hostile attacks. Like the walls of Jerusalem which were built in troublous times, but still were not the less firmly built, so was a church being raised up in the midst of conflicts; and the little band being often sorely tried by the taunts and opposition of the heathen party, were the more likely to cling with faith to that better master whom they had chosen to serve. The leaven was working, and the sons of some of the leading chiefs were at the head of the movement. Waharoa complained that his sons would

not accompany him to fight, and he was annoyed
because they urged a reconciliation with his enemies.
But the old man's race was run. Long before the
conclusion of the war he was smitten by sickness,
the effects of which he tried in vain to ward off by
resorting to his old superstitions. He retained the
reputation of a great warrior, but he died without
one ray of light from that Gospel which had been
placed before him. His favourite son Tarapipipi was
soon after admitted into the Church by baptism, receiving the name of Wiremu Tamihana.

Soon after Waharoa's death the tribe was urgent
with Tamihana to forsake his profession and join
them, in order, as they said, that the spirit of
Waharoa might be appeased, and his name kept
alive ; but he firmly resisted their overtures. He
was naturally brave, but there was another influence
at work within him, which led him to adopt a course
that many of his people could not understand. An
instance of this soon occurred. A party of 400 had
passed Tauranga, with the intention of making
another attack upon Maketu. They encamped at
Mangamana and remained quiet during the Sunday,
when the missionaries from Tauranga went to remonstrate with them. In the evening they held a
council of war, and many recommended a vigorous
course. Tamihana Tarapipipi at length rose with
his Testament in his hand, and in a bold yet pleasing manner witnessed a good confession before his
countrymen, whom with Christian courage he re-

proved, rebuked, exhorted. Only one man attempted a reply, and that was done with so much rage, and withal so much foolishness, that not one of his companions in fight took part with him. Indeed, the next speaker, a venerable old man, said that Tarapipipi's speech was very good, and recommended that they should listen to him and return.

Tamihana continued to pursue a steady course, and encouraged to the utmost of his power the extension of Christianity among his people ; but meeting with much annoyance from the heathen part of his tribe, he determined to build a separate Pa for the Christian community, at a little distance from his heathen relatives, and when it was completed there were nearly four hundred, including children, to inhabit it ; who all, nominally at least, forsook heathenism, and joined in worshipping the true God. He drew up a simple code of laws for their guidance, and a paper was attached to one of the posts of the chapel in Tamihana's handwriting, to indicate that any persons who wilfully transgressed these regulations should no longer continue an inmate of the Pa.

CHAPTER XIII.

1836—1839.

NEW TESTAMENT PRINTED AT PAIHIA — PROGRESS OF CHRIS-
TIANITY—NATIVE WAR IN THE BAY OF ISLANDS — MR. MARS-
DEN'S LAST VISIT AND DEATH—ARRIVAL OF ROMISH BISHOP—
STATION REMOVED FROM MANGAPOURI TO MANUKAU — WORK
OF EVANGELIZATION ON EAST COAST—INFLUENZA—VISIT FROM
BISHOP BROUGHTON — OPINION OF THE BISHOP — INCREASE OF
CHRISTIAN PROFESSORS—GREAT DEMAND FOR BOOKS—MISSION-
ARIES SPREAD MORE WIDELY OVER THE COUNTRY — DEATH
OF EDWARD NGATARU.

AT the northern part of the island Christianity was
working its way with a steady course. Many of the
old chiefs, men who had become inured to deeds of
cruelty in the desolating wars of Hongi, continued
to resist the overtures made to them. They were
hardened in superstition and sin; but great numbers
of the young people had embraced Christianity, and
their influence was gaining ground. Many hundreds
had been received into the Church by baptism, and
of this number there were upwards of two hundred
communicants. The translation of the New Testament was now completed, and an edition of 5,000
copies was speedily put into circulation. This became an important instrument, under God's blessing,
in the extension of the good work ; for a knowledge
of reading now prevailed in every village, so that

wherever the book was carried there was at once within reach the grand source of information, and God vouchsafed His blessing upon it.

But again the quiet progress of the Gospel was to be interrupted by civil war. The same tribes which had been engaged in conflict seven years before, headed respectively by Titore and Pomare, entered upon a deadly feud, for the sake of what turned out to be only an imaginary grievance. A woman belonging to Pomare's people had disappeared from Kororareka, and no account could be given of her. It was at once supposed that she had been killed, and retaliation was made. The conflict extended over many weeks, but happily there was a large expanse of water between the combatants, and they did not often come to close quarters. Altogether about fifty persons were killed, and many of these were principal chiefs. One of them, a Waimate native, who had long kept aloof from the Christian party, having been again invited to come over to them, replied, "I am going to-morrow to join our people at Otuihu, and as soon as I come back I will become a believer." Three days afterwards his lifeless corpse was carried home to be buried. There was, however, an important difference in this contest from those which had gone before. The Christian natives, now amounting to a large body, refused to take part in it; and this circumstance, perhaps, tended in some measure to hasten the settlement of peace. Some months afterwards the woman, on whose account the quarrel had been undertaken, made her appearance. She had been on board a vessel which had sailed to the southern part of the island.

It was during the continuance of this contest that the Rev. Samuel Marsden paid his seventh and last visit to New Zealand. He landed at Hokianga in the month of February, 1837, accompanied by his youngest daughter. He was now in his seventy-third year, and though still retaining much mental vigour, he was no longer able to travel, as in former times, on foot, making his way through swamps and rivers. Neither was it necessary. The natives, whether Christians or heathens, all recognised in the good old man a father and a friend. After spending a few days at the house of the Rev. N. Turner, the Wesleyan missionary, he set out for Waimate and the Bay of Islands, attended by a large company of natives, who insisted on carrying him in a litter the whole distance.* He went round to all the mission stations in the Bay of Islands, and then visited Kaitaea, farther north. He had travelled many a weary mile in former days, traversing a large part of the country. He had seen the natives in their most savage state, and had witnessed the desolating effects of their wars. Again and again had he reasoned with them on the evil of their course, and had

* They would not allow him to mount a horse which was sent for his use, Te Waka Nene saying that he would at once leave him if he did so.

endeavoured to point out the advantages they would gain from Christianity and civilization; but they used to answer him that they must continue to follow the customs of their forefathers. After his fourth visit, in 1823, there was a little glimmering light, but it burnt very dimly, and served only to reveal the surrounding darkness more strongly. On occasion of his sixth visit, in 1830, when the natives had been fighting fiercely in the Bay of Islands, there was also a hard conflict between light and darkness, and some of the outposts of the enemy had been carried. But now this veteran soldier of Christ was permitted to see a large body of Christians in every locality he came to, while the New Testament was coming into circulation, and accomplishing that sure and certain work which God had appointed. It was about the year 1807 that the hope seems first to have entered Mr. Marsden's mind that Christianity would be introduced into New Zealand, and now, after waiting for thirty years, he comes to take a last survey of what was going on. He did not look for that degree of success which we are not warranted to expect in the present condition of the Church, but he saw that the cause which he had so earnestly endeavoured to promote was in a fair way to prosper. He returned to New South Wales, and in a few short months he was called to his eternal reward.

The seed of the Gospel was now vegetating far and wide, and God was preparing the Church for further trials which were to come upon it. Such have been

God's dealings from the beginning. The Church has thriven best in the midst of trials, which seem to conduce to a more healthy and vigorous growth. It is not in the days of quiet prosperity and of ease that the Christian's armour is kept bright. God therefore wisely permits, in the counsel of His will, that events shall happen which short-sighted man would not have ordered. But withal He prepares His people for whatever trials He may direct. It was at this time, when Christianity was assuming a substantial form, that the attempt was made by the emissaries of the Romish superstition to establish themselves in New Zealand. The spirit of inquiry after truth was becoming stronger every day, and many had learnt to value the word of life, but still the larger portion of the community was in a state of heathenism. A French bishop and two priests landed at Hokianga, giving out that they expected shortly to be strengthened by the addition of nine other priests. The Bishop was a man of dignified bearing and engaging manners, literally ready to become all things to all men, and the course he pursued was characterised by an artfulness which was worthy of the cause he supported. He told the natives that he had no wish to interfere with the disciples of the missionaries : " Let them continue quietly to follow the teaching in which they have been instructed ; the heathen only are my flock, and they all belong to me." The progress of Christianity had already begun to make divisions among the tribes and families, and there was often a strong feeling on the part of the heathen against their relatives who had renounced the religion of their forefathers. They were annoyed because they could no longer carry out their heathenish practices with the same zest as formerly. They believed that a change might be to their advantage, and they gladly availed themselves of the more easy discipline of the Papists, which allowed them to retain much that the missionaries had told them was to be given up. These new teachers gave their sanction to polygamy and to the practise of tattooing; and they allowed their followers to do various kinds of work on the Sabbath day, and to continue also their old heathenish dances. The consequence was, that numbers rallied to their standard, and their praises were loud in the mouths of all the more worthless part of the community. Soon after this an account was printed in the *Annales de la Foi*, which represented that the number of converts they had made in New Zealand was thirty thousand, but this statement, it appears, was without foundation. The Christian natives, with the Scriptures in their hands, boldly confronted the priests, showing that they taught many things for which there is no authority in the Bible. When they replied that our translations were incorrect, their own followers requested to be supplied with a correct version, in order that they might meet the arguments of their countrymen. They were told they should have one, but that Europe was a long way off, and

that it would be five years before the books could
arrive. The novelty soon wore off, and the majority
of those who had taken up with the new superstition,
not from any principle, but because they wished for
a change, gradually joined the Protestant community,
so that at the present time there is a very small
remnant of Papists either at Hokianga or in the Bay
of Islands. This diversion, however, was productive
of ultimate good to the Church ; it quickened the
diligence of the appointed instructors of the natives,
and it led the latter to a careful investigation of the
grounds of that faith which was placed before them.

When the first attempt was made to hold intercourse with the tribes of Waikato, there were no
inhabitants north of Ngaruawahia. The rightful
occupants of Manukau and Lower Waikato had all
congregated in the Upper Waikato, that they might
protect one another against the frequent inroads of
Ngapuhi. Hence the first mission station was fixed
at Mangapouri, not far from Otawhao. But as soon
as the natives found that Christianity was exercising
its influence upon the Bay of Islanders, and that
they would now be safe from attacks from that
quarter, they began to spread over the country, and
returned to their own homes. It then became necessary to remove the station from Mangapouri to
Manukau, and it continued to be occupied for some
years by the Rev. R. Maunsell and Mr. Hamlin.

Native agency was now beginning to tell upon the
country to a remarkable degree, so that while the

enemy was busily scattering erroneous doctrines
abroad, God was working in His own way by such
agents as He chose to honour. A Ngapuhi chief
called at my house at Waimate, who had lately
returned from the neighbourhood of East Cape, where
he had accompanied a large armament, which included
most of the natives from Table Cape to Hicks's Bay.
They had been to attack a strong Pa near Cape Runaway, having had as their allies several tribes living
on the shores of the Bay of Plenty, the object being
to obtain satisfaction for a previous raid which had
been made by the opposite party upon Waiapu. He
related various particulars of the expedition, and then
asked how it was that no missionary went to East
Cape, saying that they would pay much more attention to instruction than Ngapuhi did : that at Waiapu
they refrained from work on the Sunday, and assembled regularly for Christian worship. I asked, how
it came about that they turned their attention to
these subjects ? who there was to instruct them ?
" Do you not remember Taumatakura," he said,
" whom you left at Waiapu three years ago ? He is
their teacher, and the natives all pay the greatest
attention to him." Now this Taumatakura was formerly a slave, and had attended school at Waimate,
but had never given any reason to suppose that he
took an interest in Christian instruction. He was
not even a candidate for baptism, but he had learnt
to read ; and when the party of East Cape natives
were taken home in January, 1834, his master gave

him liberty to go to his friends. The occasion of the return of these natives was deeply interesting, but it was hardly thought that any good result would follow. Taumatakura, however, began to teach and to preach according to the little light which he possessed, and he gave instruction to a small extent in reading and writing, and some short prayers, and hymns, and texts of Scripture were written upon scraps of paper, and were valued with a superstitious regard. When the expedition to Cape Runaway was proposed, Taumatakura was requested to go with them. " I will," he said, " if you will attend to what I say to you. When we come to the enemy's Pa, if we kill any people you are not to eat them; neither must you wantonly break up canoes which you do not care to carry away, nor destroy food which you do not wish to eat." When the Pa was at length assaulted, Taumatakura led the attack, with his book in one hand and his musket in the other; and though the balls flew thickly around him, he was not hit. The natives at once ascribed this circumstance to the protection of the God of Taumatakura, and his influence was consequently very much increased. Here then was a mixture of truth and error, of superstition and of Gospel light; but God was pleased to make use of this man to prepare the way, and the people were now earnestly desirous of further instruction. It was an opening which was not to be lost, but there was no missionary at liberty to undertake the post as yet. It was determined, therefore, to look for help among the Christian natives, and soon there were six volunteers, men of good character, five of whom were connected with that part of the island. Towards the end of October, 1838, these men were conducted to the East Coast by the Rev. Henry Williams, and three of them were placed at Waiapu, and three at Turanga. At every place the natives seemed ready for instruction, and the demand for books was general ; a proof in itself that a knowledge of reading was beginning to prevail.

In the month of December of this year the northern part of the island was visited with influenza in its most virulent form. Every person seemed to be affected by it, both old and young, and many for a time were laid quite prostrate. Great numbers were carried off, particularly the aged and infirm, and persons who had been weakened by previous disease. It was in the midst of this calamity that Bishop Broughton arrived from New South Wales on a pastoral visit to the native Church. So great was the prevalence of the epidemic, that it was not possible to assemble the natives to any extent ; but the visit was of much importance, and seemed to give a new impulse to the work, by removing the Church from that seemingly isolated position it had heretofore occupied. About twenty members of the Mission families received the rite of confirmation, and about forty natives, the sickness preventing a larger number from coming together. At the same time, also, the Rev. O. Hadfield, who had recently arrived from

England, was admitted to priest's orders. The visit
of the Bishop followed very shortly after the departure of the Rev. Samuel Marsden to his rest;
and it is remarkable that he preached at Paihia on
Christmas-day, exactly twenty-four years after the
establishment of the mission, Mr. Marsden having
landed on the 24th of December, 1814, and preached
his first sermon on the beach at Rangihona on the
following day. A striking impression was produced
on the mind of the Bishop as to the religious condition of the natives. He was the most competent
person to take an unprejudiced view, and, in a letter
to the Church Missionary Society, he wrote:—" At
every station which I personally visited, the converts
were so numerous as to bear a very visible and con-
derable proportion to the entire population; and I
had sufficient testimony to convince me that the
same state of things prevailed at other places which
it was not in my power to reach. As the result of
my inspection, I should state, that in most of the
native villages, called Pas, in which the missionaries
have a footing, there is a building, containing one
room, superior in fabric and dimensions to the native
residences, which appears to be set apart as their
place of assembling for religious worship, or to read
the scriptures, or to receive the exhortations of the
missionaries. In these buildings generally, but sometimes in the open air, the Christian classes were
assembled before me. The grey-haired man and the
aged woman took their places, to read and undergo

examination, among their descendants of the second and third generations. The chief and the slave stood side-by-side, with the same holy volume in their hands, and used their endeavours each to surpass the other in returning proper answers to the questions put to them concerning what they had been reading. These assemblages I encouraged on all occasions, not only from the pleasure which the exhibition itself afforded, but because I was thus enabled, in the most certain and satisfactory way, to probe the extent of their attainments and improvement. The experience thus acquired has induced me to adopt the habit of applying the term 'converts' to those alone; for many such I found there were, who, in the apparent sincerity of their convictions, and in the sufficiency of their information, compared with their opportunities of acquiring it, may be considered Christians indeed."

The progress of Christianity had been hitherto slow but certain. It was like the field of wheat, which in the early part of the season shows signs of life, and the husbandman lives in prospect of seeing the fruit of his labours in due time, but during the inclement weather of early spring the chilling blasts prevent the development of the plant. Then a genial warmth succeeds, and the whole aspect is changed, the blade shoots up with vigour, the seed-stalk follows, and soon the fields become white unto the harvest. It was at this period, during the year 1839, that this was realized in the gospel-fields of New

Zealand. God had poured out his Holy Spirit, and had inclined great numbers to listen to the invitation given to them. At all the old mission stations in the north there was a great increase in the congregations, and in six months two hundred and twenty-nine persons were received into the Church. Those natives who had embraced Christianity gave this proof of the sincerity of their profession, that they endeavoured to bring in their relatives also who continued in heathenism. The chief of the Rarawa tribe, Nopera Panakareao, distinguished himself in this way. He often went, for a week at a time, to the surrounding villages, with his Testament in his hand, bearing testimony to the benefit he had received, and inviting his countrymen to partake of it, and was thus the means of inducing many tribes to join the Christian band, who before had kept quite aloof. At the Thames also, at Waikato, and at Tauranga, the movement was of the same character, though perhaps less general; while the desire for books was so great, that it was impossible for some time to meet the demand. The 5,000 copies of the New Testament which had been printed at the mission press were quickly dispersed, and it became necessary to ask for 10,000 copies to be printed forthwith in England, the mission press being occupied in printing the Prayer-book and portions of the Old Testament. We may form an opinion of the rate of demand by the course which was followed with the Prayer-book. An edition was commenced of 3,000 copies of the entire book; but when it was advanced to the end of the Evening Service, it was deemed expedient to put into immediate circulation this small portion, with the addition of the hymns, and to strike off 4,000 more for the entire work; but the 4,000 were required as soon as printed. Then 6,000 copies of the entire work were commenced; but before the type of the first three half-sheets was distributed, 20,000 more of the smaller book were ordered: thus making a total of 33,000.

Another feature is observed in the mission at this period. The wide extent of the field to be occupied, and the limited number of the missionaries, obliged them to separate as much as possible. Mr. Hamlin, therefore, was left in occupation at the heads of Manukau, and Messrs. Maunsell and Ashwell moved to the mouth of Waikato, and eventually Mr. Ashwell proceeded far up the river to Taupiri.

True Christianity requires a change which is designated as a new nature; the evil and corrupt heart being removed, and another heart of a totally different character being given in the stead of it. When the work is of God, this is the manner of it. But it was to be expected that when Christianity came to be received on an extensive scale, there would often be an incongruous mixture of the good and the bad. The new doctrines were frequently ingrafted upon a stock which yet retained much of the old superstition, and there were many in whom the change was little more than external. This is sufficient to account for those numerous cases of painful inconsistency which are frequently to be met with where a Christian Church has been newly established. But, happily, the missionary had frequent cause to rejoice over those who were Christians indeed. At an early period of his labours in Waikato, the Rev. R. Maunsell had a brilliant instance of that mighty change which is wrought by the grace of God, and it was received as an earnest of that blessing which was to follow. Ngataru, a young chief, had been for some time afflicted with consumption, and seemed to be not far from death. It was expected that, with a man of his rank, everything around would be sacred, and that none would be allowed to approach but the person whose business it was to feed him. When Mr. Maunsell, however, visited him, he invited him to draw near, and entered readily into conversation on religious subjects. His wife, also, seemed to be a superior woman. She produced their copy of the Testament, which bore marks of frequent use. She had kept it tied up in a neat little bag, and, lamenting that it was so much worn, asked if it could not be repaired. Shortly after this, Ngataru left his native village, and went to a house on the mission station. This was taking a decided step. His relations felt it to be a degradation that he should go to the land of another tribe, and his grandfather, Kukutai, the head chief, and a very proud old heathen, did not approve of the step. Mr. Maunsell hastened, therefore, to see him, and asked plainly what his soul rested on for salvation. " The cross," was his only reply. "But what good thing is there of yours to bring you near to God?" "Nothing," he said, "but the death of Christ." "But do you not think that the native 'tapu' will restore you to health?" "Ah!" said he, "it is all horihori, unmeaning nonsense." On a subsequent visit, it was thought well to propose to him that he should be baptized. "How can I," said he, "as I have got no garment?" "What garment do you mean?" "I have no garment for my soul," he said; "it is naked. My ideas are very limited." "Yes; but Christ will be a garment for it." "But who knows," he rejoined, "that I have got hold of Christ?" It came out afterwards that there was a further meaning in his remarks. His clothes were sacred, according to native usage, and he had written to his relations for their consent to his baptism. His grandfather, Kukutai, had sent word that he would not consent to this so long as he retained those garments. Their custom was that the clothing and the whole person, and the head particularly, of a chief, should be sacred; and if he suffered any desecration, the tribe would often deem it due to his rank to come and strip him of all the property they might find about him, as a proof of their regard.

This was the obstacle with Ngataru. If he presumed to divest himself of his tapu while he retained his former garments, his relations would most likely deprive him of all his little property. It was pointed out to him that this difficulty might soon be met, by following the course of those that used curious arts, who, when they believed Paul's preaching gathered together their books, and burnt them in the presence of all. This plan pleased him, and he asked to have the passage pointed out. After further conversation, Mr. Maunsell considered that both Ngataru and his wife were fit subjects for baptism. The consent of some of the near relatives had been obtained, but it was suggested that it would be better to wait for Ngapaka, the eldest son of Kukutai. He was asked, "If Ngapaka object, how will you proceed? will you then decline baptism?" "No," he replied; "Ngapaka's word shall sink, and mine shall float." The subject of the garment was again talked of. A good pair of blankets and a comfortable mat, together with his wife's clothing, which was also tapu, all these articles being of far greater value to a native than a European can well imagine, were consigned to the flames. That same day, Ngataru and his family were admitted into the fold of Christ, before a crowded congregation, he and his wife receiving the names of Edward and Mary. Kukutai came to see him on the day of his baptism, and wept over him; and on his return from the chapel he said to him, "That pakeha can have but little love for you, otherwise he would never have directed you to destroy your clothes." "Do not say that," replied Edward; "it is quite right that the clothes should have been destroyed; neither is what you say about his having little love for me true." "Well," replied the old man, "take care of yourself, and don't go near the fire where food is cooked, nor associate with slaves." "Indeed," replied Edward, "I shall do no such thing, for I have now left off all the old practices, which are all nonsense." Ngapaka, taking up the subject, observed that, Ngataru having joined the Church, it was very improper that this language should be addressed to him. The subject was therefore given up for the present.

The subsequent history of Edward is brief. Shortly after his baptism, he was induced to go inland to superintend the cultivation of his kumara grounds ; and in compliance with the wishes of his friends, he remained with them. There was some reason to fear lest their influence should shake his faith, and induce him to turn back to the refuge of lies, the tapu, as a means of restoring his health. His mind, however, rested firmly upon his Saviour. After a time, however, as he seemed to be at the point of death, the chief men came to his hut to weep over him, and standing around, burst into loud wailings. Kukutai also came among them, having his hatchet in his hand, chanting a dirge as he approached—" When wilt thou leave ? When wilt thou depart ? When wilt thou fly to thine abode in heaven ? When wilt thou go to Jesus Christ !" After standing for a short time among the band of mourners, he was observed to move backwards, with his hatchet firmly grasped, as if intending to inflict a blow upon a female slave of Edward's, who was sitting near. His object was to carry out the horrible practice of killing a slave to be the attendant upon the departing spirit of his grandson, but his two elder sons, perceiving his intention in time, sprang forward and rescued the unfortunate woman from an untimely death, and thus baffled the malice of the wicked one, who would gladly have spread so dark a cloud over poor Edward, as he sank tranquilly into rest.

CHAPTER XIV.

1839, 1840.

PROGRESS AT WAIAPU—GOSPEL CARRIED TO COOK'S STRAITS BY
RIPAHAU—RAUPARAHA APPLIES FOR A MISSIONARY—ARRIVAL
OF FIRST SETTLERS AT WELLINGTON—THEY FIND THE NATIVES
PROFESSING CHRISTIANITY—REV. O. HADFIELD GOES TO OTAKI
— RECONCILIATION BETWEEN THE TRIBES — COLONIZATION —
TREATY OF WAITANGI—INFLUENCE UPON THE NATIVES—SIMUL-
TANEOUS PROGRESS OF CHRISTIANITY—ZEALOUS EFFORTS OF THE
ROMANISTS.

THE native teachers who had been left at Waiapu and
Tauranga by the Rev. Henry Williams, in November,
1838, had been actively employed at their posts; and
when I visited them, in company with the Rev. R.
Taylor, in the following April, we found that the
attention paid to them by the people was truly
astonishing. At Whakawhitira, a large village of
Waiapu, a chapel had been erected, sixty feet by
twenty-eight, one of the best buildings of the kind in
the country. The congregation on the Sunday was
about 500, and schools attended by women and girls
were in active operation. Along the coast also to
Tauranga there was the same opening for missionary
labour. Indeed, from the centre of the Bay of Plenty
to Table Cape, the natives were generally ready to
lay aside their old superstitions, and to listen without reserve to instruction. A letter from one of the

teachers, written soon afterwards, mentioned that 200 natives attended their classes for more direct instruction, and the names of several leading chiefs were given, and among them that of Kawhia, now the Rev. Raniera Kawhia.

The inhabitants of the southern parts of the island had often said to the missionaries, "Why did you not come to us sooner? We should then have left off fighting, and our tribes would not have been cut down so much; but you remained with Ngapuhi while they came from year to year to destroy us." It is easy to understand the difficulties which lay in the way of a more rapid extension of operations, besides which the caution had been frequently given by the parent society, that the heavy demands from other parts of the world forbade them to add to the number of their missionaries already in the country. But these restrictions were to be overruled. God had designed that the whole country should receive the boon which had been given only to a part, and the Gospel was to work its way without waiting for the regular arrangements of a missionary society. Although communication between the distant tribes was then much restricted, information had reached the natives as far as Cook's Straits, that changes of an extraordinary character were going on at the north, the effects of which were productive of good to the people. Old Rauparaha formerly resided at Maunga-tautari, but in consequence of some quarrel with the neighbouring tribes at Waikato, he had moved to the

south, and gained a footing for himself by conquest
at Otaki and its neighbourhood. He was a bold
warrior and a great savage, but having now some
flax traders located among his people, he thought that
it would be well to have a missionary also ; and about
the year 1836 he sent a letter to the Rev. H. Williams
to ask for one, but it was not then possible to enter-
tain his request. It was a period when all the efforts
of the missionaries were necessarily expended upon
the new stations in the centre of the island. In the
meantime there was a slave at the Bay of Islands
whose master had been killed in a quarrel, and his
headless body was carried by Tohitapu to be buried
near Paihia. The slave Ripahau was then at large,
and went to live at the mission station, where he
received the regular instruction of the place. This
was before much movement had been made in favour
of Christianity ; and though Ripahau behaved well,
there was no reason to think that he had become a
Christian. It was at the time when the tribes of the
Bay of Islands, in league with the natives of Rotorua,
were fighting with those of Tauranga. After the war
had continued some time, Ripahau requested permission to accompany a fighting party which was
just leaving the Bay of Islands, in order that he might
go and see his relatives, who were living partly
at Rotorua, and partly in Cook's Straits with Rauparaha. Nothing more was heard of him for two
years, when at length a letter reached Mr. Chapman
at Rotorua, in which Ripahau applied for some books,

saying that he was living in Cook's Straits, and that there were numbers of people there wishing for instruction. The letter was forwarded to Paihia, and not long afterwards it was followed by a deputation consisting of the son and nephew of Te Rauparaha, who had taken passage in a trading vessel from Entry Island, and had come for the sole object of obtaining a missionary to live with them. The account they gave was most remarkable : that Ripahau first went to live at Otaki among his own relations, and talked to them from time to time about the teaching of the missionaries, and read to them from his own book various passages in confirmation of what he told them. A few of the people paid attention to him, and this encouraged him to take up the work in a more systematic manner. He taught some to read a little and to write, but having only one book and no slates, the process was a tedious one. They obtained a little paper from the whaling stations which were near, and upon small slips of this Ripahau copied texts of Scripture, and selections from the prayers, every syllable of which was soon spelled over and committed to memory. At length there came a party from Rotorua, bringing with them a few fragments of books, which were at once caught up as a great prize. Among them was a part of the Gospel of St. Luke, printed at Paihia, having in it the name of Ngakuku, whose little girl had been killed at the foot of the hill at Wairere. The party which made that attack carried it off among the spoil, and part of it had been torn up for cartridges. The remainder now found its way to Otaki, and was the book from which these two young men had learnt to read. Ripahau then went to Waikanae, the Pa, of which Te Rangitaake* was at that time chief; and there he met with a much more cordial reception than at Otaki, and remained there for some time until Rauparaha's son induced him to return to him by a present of a shirt and some tobacco. The Rev. Henry Williams listened to this account with intense interest, and at once said that if there were no other person to undertake the mission, he would go himself. This, however, was objected to, because the Ngapuhi had long been accustomed to look up to him as their adviser in their often-recurring quarrels, and his presence among them seemed to be necessary. The two young chiefs were sent to tell their story at Waimate, and the question was asked, what was to be done. The Rev. O. Hadfield was then staying there, and was giving assistance in the school for the sons of the missionaries. He had only been a few months in the country, and was in a very precarious state of health. He had been ordered by his medical attendant to give up his residence in Oxford, because he was subject there to frequent attacks of asthma. When the story given by the two natives was related to him, he at once started up, saying, " I will go. I know I shall not live long, and I may as well die there as

* Wiremu Kingi Te Rangitaake, of whom so much has been heard in connexion with Taranaki.

here." It was at first thought that it would be im-
prudent for him to take this step, but the desire grew
upon him, and there was reason to think that it had
proceeded from Him who imparteth strength also for
the fulfilment of those desires which he has implanted. He went off to Paihia, and it was soon
arranged that the Rev. Henry Williams should accompany him to Otaki, and introduce him to this
field of labour.

The character of missionary work was now much
changed. Instead of that indifference and opposition
which the first missionaries had encountered, here was
a people all ready to receive instruction. God had
prepared them by sending his own instruments
first, and He had granted so large a measure of
success, that a change was perceptible, even by the
casual observer. It was at the very period when the
first settlers were brought out by the New Zealand
Company; and Colonel Wakefield remarks in his
journal at the time, that a change of this character
had recently taken place among the natives. It was
stated also by one of the early settlers—"The whole
of the native population of this place profess the
Christian religion, and though there are no missionaries among them, they are strict in the performance
of their religious exercises. As is to be expected,
however, they are but imperfectly acquainted with the
doctrines of Christianity, and are superstitious in many
of their observances. Compared with what they must
have been before the introduction of these doctrines

among them,—and this is obviously the true standard
of comparison,—the improvement effected by their
conversion to Christianity is most striking."

The Rev. O. Hadfield, accompanied by the Rev.
Henry Williams, left the Bay of Islands in October,
1839, and in the following month arrived in Cook's
Straits. The two powerful tribes under Te Rauparaha
and Te Rangitaake were then engaged in a deadly
feud, arising out of the division of the payment given
by the New Zealand Company for Port Nicholson,
and Rauparaha had attacked his opponents with the
loss of seventy of his men. He was therefore bent
upon revenge, and it was a providential circumstance
that the messengers of peace were at hand to mediate
between the combatants. Both were no doubt glad
to have the intervention of a third party, which
opened the way for reconciliation, without a compromise of their native dignity. Rauparaha, although
the loser in this contest, was expecting to have the
sole advantage, whatever it might be, which was to be
gained from the missionary, whom his own son had
conducted thither. But then it appeared that the
tribe at Waikanae had shown much more willingness
to attend to the instructions of Ripahau, while the
leading men of Rauparaha's party had been very
indifferent. However, the adverse tribes were soon
brought together, and it was at length amicably
arranged that Mr. Hadfield should have a house at
Waikanae and another at Otaki, and that his time
should be divided equally between the two places.

The congregations assembling at this time amounted to 500 and 200 at the two principle Pas, and there was a general willingness to receive instruction. The Rev. Henry Williams returned homewards through the country, by way of Whanganui and Taupo, and at the former place Christianity was already working its way. The natives pressed earnestly to have a missionary sent to them; and they proposed that he should take his wife with him, thinking that he would be more likely to remain.

So far back as Captain Cook's early visit to New Zealand, it had occurred to that enterprising navigator that at some future period this country might become an English colony. The long wars, however, at the end of the last century, and in the early part of the present, prevented the growth of any desire in that direction. But when England had settled down into quietness and peace, and there was no longer the outlet for the enterprising and the restless which the long war had afforded, there were many who began to look around for some new field of exertion. Great numbers emigrated every year to Canada or the United States, and soon the attention of the public was turned to New Zealand. A company was formed with this object so far back as the year 1825; and two vessels were sent out with a number of emigrants, who made an ill-concerted attempt to establish a colony in the Thames. After a short trial, the leaders of the expedition took fright at the appearance of the natives, and abandoned the scheme. The attempt was renewed in 1838 by the New Zealand Company, and in the following year the first settlement was formed at Port Nicholson. It does not belong to the present work to speak of the subject of colonization, except so far as it bears upon the progress of Christianity, and perhaps also to notice the opposition which was given by the Church Missionary Society to the proposal for making New Zealand a British colony. It is impossible to explain away the fact that the general consequence of colonization by a civilized race among a barbarous people has been, that the latter have gradually dwindled away, until they have almost disappeared from the face of the earth. In proof of this it is hardly necessary to mention the West Indies, North America and New Holland. For twenty-five years a mission had been carried on among the New Zealanders, for the purpose of instructing them in the principles of Christianity, which was now beginning to bear fruit, and there was much reason to fear that this new scheme might hinder a work which was happily progressing. Besides which, although the most liberal professions were made by the company in favour of religion, and the welfare of the native race, the first and only object aimed at was the interests of those who took up this matter as a speculation, while the company was wholly irresponsible even to the English government for the course it might pursue. On the other hand, it may be justly argued that it was unreasonable that a country, as extensive as the whole of the British Isles, should be reserved for the sole occupation of a race of people, who numbered no more inhabitants than are to be found in a moderate-sized English town. When the Divine command was given to our first parents, that they should replenish the earth and subdue it, without doubt it was intended that the earth should be occupied by their descendants as it might be required, and that its wild wastes should be subdued by cultivation, and made serviceable for the human race. It soon became apparent that colonization would proceed, and the English government felt it necessary to interfere. A large body of colonists were going to a new country without any reference to the government, and it became necessary that they as British subjects should be kept under the authority of the state. Captain Hobson therefore was appointed to negotiate a treaty with the natives for the cession of the sovereignty of the country, in order that colonization might be conducted in immediate connexion with the state. He arrived in New Zealand in January, 1840, and the Treaty of Waitangi was signed on the 30th day of that month. In carrying out these measures, which were attended with some difficulty, the governor received every assistance from the missionaries, who obtained the signatures of the native chiefs to the treaty, and thus secured the quiet settlement of the government. This was afterwards most handsomely acknowledged by the governor.

The colonists began now to crowd rapidly into the country, and it must in all fairness be acknowledged that the body of settlers introduced by the company were as unexceptionable as could have been chosen. Many gentlemen of the highest respectability were the leaders of the undertaking, and the mechanics and labourers who accompanied them were, as a whole, a well-selected and respectable class of people A large proportion of them were from the agricultural districts of England, and were ready at once to fall into those occupations which they had followed at home.

The New Zealander will work hard at certain times, when he has a sufficient object before him ; but it was an advantage to him to have the example of steady industry, such as the English labourer is accustomed to from his childhood—always at work because he is used to it. Then, too, there were many improvements in agriculture which the natives have not been backward to adopt, as the use of the plough, the cart, and the threshing machine. There was also a good market for their produce, and the settler has never yet felt that the Maori crops have interfered with his own, but rather it has been spoken of as an advantage that there should be a division of labour, and that the native should contribute his proportion to the general stock. It has followed, as a consequence, that the possession of money has enabled the New Zealander to follow the example of civilized man with regard to dress, so that to a great extent the Maori clothing has been entirely superseded. What was at first adopted as a luxury has since by use become a necessity ; and the supply of these necessaries was an additional incentive to industry, which they have had an abundant opportunity of exercising as labourers in the agricultural and sheep-farming districts.

This intercourse however became a dangerous snare to many. In all English towns, unhappily, there is a great amount of drunkenness. And although a stringent law has been made for the protection of the native race, it has not been put in force as it might have been. Drunkenness, therefore, with all its attendant evils, prevails more or less with those natives who frequent the towns, and they carry back with them to their distant homes the evil habits they have acquired, and sow them broadcast over the country. But these remarks will not apply to that part of the community which can justly claim the name of Christian. If right principles have been implanted, and that real change has taken place which belongs to the Christian character, there is then a safeguard against the temptations which are everywhere to be met with in this wide world. It is a grand mistake to think that safety is to be found in withdrawing from the world. The hermits of old retired to the seclusion of the desert with the idea that they would avoid evil. But human nature is the same everywhere, and in every tribe of the human family, and the only security is in a change of character which inclines the heart to reject the evil and to choose the good. It is a striking fact that before this great change took place in the country, which was to bring the native race into direct contact with temptations which might overpower them, the general diffusion of Christianity had to a great extent prepared them for it. A large proportion of the natives were at once ready to recognise Christian principles, in those who acted under their influence, and where there was an absence of those principles they were not slow to discern it.

During the first year of the establishment of the government, the spirit of inquiry after Christianity was greatly on the increase. In many it proceeded from a clear conviction of the evil of their former system, and of the blessings which Christianity offered to them. In others this change would be merely the effect of example. It was so in the early days of Christianity, and we are therefore prepared to expect a reaction, when any strong influence is brought to bear upon them, which might test a profession that is not based upon absolute conviction. The people now flocked in large numbers to attend the classes of candidates for baptism. This was particularly the case in the old stations in the Bay of Islands, and also at Waikato and the Thames; and in almost every part of the country the profession of Christianity became so general, that the total number of attendants at public worship was estimated at not less than 30,000, besides those in connexion with the Wesleyan mission.

Much that was really good was going on, and it was a time for Satan to stir up increased opposition.

Accordingly we find that the popish priests were now working with redoubled vigour. They received a great accession to their numbers, and thus they were able to plant their teachers in most of those localities where the missionaries were labouring, and by plausible arguments, supported by liberal presents of clothing, they obtained many followers. Nuka, the chief of Maungatapu at Tauranga, acknowledged that he had sent an invitation to the Romish bishop to establish a mission at Tauranga. He did not however disguise his motives. "We have heard," he said, "that the Bishop gives blankets to all who receive his doctrine, and we want some of them." But a noble grant of ten thousand copies of the New Zealand New Testament had been lately made by the British and Foreign Bible Society, and there were many among the natives who were able to wield this sword of the Spirit most effectively. Not only did they endeavour to arrest the effects of evil doctrines among their countrymen, but there were numerous cases in which they confronted the priests with that freedom of speech for which the New Zealanders are noted, not entering upon any abstruse questions, which they might have found it difficult to handle, but keeping to simple points, which required no subtlety of argument. One of these teachers met with a priest at Tauranga, and opening his book he called his attention to the second commandment, and said, "Our teachers tell us that these are the commandments of God; now this tells me that I must not bow down to idols, which you evidently do; and I find, moreover, that you have not got the second commandment among the others, but that it is altogether omitted. I do not therefore believe that your religion is true, and I do not like it. You say also that our missionaries are adulterers, because they are married and are living with their wives; but if you can call them adulterers you must call Peter an adulterer, for it says here in my Testament, that Peter's wife's mother was sick of a fever." On another occasion the Romish bishop said to a native at Waimate, "The missionaries have houses, and wives, and children; all their love is for them; but we have none, therefore all our love is for you." The native replied, "Is it then wicked for a missionary to have a wife and children?" He said, "I am an apostle and bishop of Christ, and I tell you it is." The native answered, "St. Paul was also an apostle, and he said, a bishop ought to be the husband of one wife." It is not a matter of surprise, therefore, to hear that numbers of those who had professed an adherence to the Romish Church were soon ready to leave it; that on one occasion twenty persons at Waimate, and on another sixty persons at Kaitaea, came forward publicly to join the Protestant Church.

At the time the Treaty of Waitangi was signed, there had been much hesitation on the part of some of the chiefs in accepting the proposals of government. The missionaries, from a conviction that it was the only safe course for the natives to follow, did their utmost to induce them to sign that treaty; but there was another influence at work instilling suspicion into their minds, which, though not successful at the time, was afterwards to become a fruitful source of trouble. And now, after the lapse of a few months, several of the chiefs betrayed symptoms of uneasiness on account of the cession of the sovereignty of the islands, and the assistance which the missionaries had afforded the government in that transaction. They had been told that the whole was a scheme to deprive them of their country, and the embers of discontent were smouldering for a time and gathering strength. In the meanwhile the gospel was to work its way in other quarters.

CHAPTER XV.

1840—1842.

STATION FORMED AT TURANGA—TEACHERS AT WAIROA — FIRST
BAPTISM AT WAIAPU—DESIRE FOR BOOKS—BAPTISMS—GENERAL
RECEPTION OF CHRISTIANITY ALONG THE EAST COAST—ROMISH
PRIEST TRIES TO ESTABLISH HIMSELF AT TABLE CAPE—MATIU'S
CONVERSATION WITH A PRIEST—LARGE SUPPLY OF TESTAMENTS
— SOME PROFESSORS DRAW BACK—ARRIVAL OF BISHOP SELWYN
—TESTIMONY OF DR. SINCLAIR — AUCKLAND — TRIAL OF PRIN-
CIPLES — RAUPARAHA'S SON CARRIES THE GOSPEL TO BANKS'S
PENINSULA— TRIAL TO A CHRISTIAN PARTY AT TAURANGA.

THE line of coast which runs from East Cape to the
middle of Hawks's Bay is peopled by three powerful
tribes, concentrated severally at Waiapu, Turanga,
and Wairoa. The native teachers who were conducted to this district towards the close of 1838 had
been actively employed in preaching the gospel for
more than twelve months, and God's blessing had
rested upon their work. In January, 1840, the
writer, who had been appointed to the general charge
of that part of the country, removed with his family
to Tauranga, where the Christian religion was nominally professed, and the numbers meeting together for
religious worship at the different villages were not
less than 1,500. Schools had been established at
every village, but under great disadvantages for want
of more competent instructors. The supply of books
and slates was very limited ; but notwithstanding

these drawbacks there was much elementary knowledge communicated, and numbers had learnt to read and write. The wish to possess books was intense, and the few already in their possession only tended to sharpen the desire of those who had none. Novelty, doubtless, would in many cases account for this revolution in the native mind; but a more unequivocal proof of good was found in the fact that there were many serious inquirers after truth, who, by their steady attention to instruction, and by their progress in knowledge, showed that in their case it was not a transient excitement, but the work of God's Holy Spirit in their hearts.

In anticipation of the first Sunday after our arrival, many strangers had come together the preceding evening, and at service the next day there was a congregation of at least 1,000 persons. We assembled in the open air, but the weather was fine, and the extreme attention of this large body was a grateful commencement of missionary labour. At noon the natives again met for school, when there were five classes of men, two numbering seventy each, one fifty, one a hundred and ten, one a hundred and fifty, besides the boys, who were fifty in number. The women were in two classes, one of a hundred and fifty, and one of twelve. The last, with one of the men's classes of seventy, read in the Testament; the rest, not being able to read, were instructed in the catechisms, the whole class repeating together the answer after the teacher. This was a very imper-

fect arrangement ; but still the mere repetition could
not fail to impart a good amount of Christian
knowledge.

To the Wairoa and Table Cape, the gospel had
been carried by three natives, who had found their
way thither in quest of their relatives, one of them
being from the Bay of Islands, and two from
Rotorua—natives who themselves needed much instruction, but whom God had made use of to impart
the first rudiments of knowledge to their benighted
countrymen. At one place a substantial proof of
this was afforded in the existence of a regular congregation of 500. The consequence was, that
throughout that neighbourhood the desire for books,
slates, and persons to give instruction was intense.
All that was possessed by many who were able to
read was a few manuscript prayers and hymns
copied from our printed books. They were beginning
to see that there were temporal advantages to be
gained. A chief at Table Cape, who had fled from
Wairarapa with his tribe some years before, through
fear of Te Rauparaha, said, " Bring your treasure for
the young and for the old, for the women and for the
children. It is by receiving the word of God that I
shall go back to my own place, for it turns enemies
into friends, and makes people live in peace."

At Waiapu there was still greater progress. The
native teachers had used much diligence, and congregations were then assembling to the number of
upwards of 3,000, generally in neatly-built chapels.

The schools, too, in the principal villages were carried on with regularity. From among the many inquirers, thirty-nine were selected after due examination, and admitted by baptism into the Church of Christ, the first-fruits of an abundant harvest which was to follow. In this number were several leading chiefs, three being heads of their respective tribes.

In a little while it might be said that almost the whole population in this district from north to south were seeking for instruction. Three chiefs came to Tauranga from Ahuriri for this purpose; two of them sent by their fathers the distance of a hundred miles overland: the third a candidate for baptism. The want of books was now being seriously felt, the grant from the British and Foreign Bible Society not having yet been heard of. Nine Testaments had been received from the press at the Bay of Islands, and if they could have been divided like the five loaves among five thousand, so that all should be filled, it would have been well; but it was necessary to conceal them until more should arrive, because so many were waiting to whom promises had been made, that these few could not be given without causing great dissatisfaction, and yet it was feared that this was the last issue of those printed in the country. This desire to possess the Scriptures was the same in every part of the country. A case occurred at Taupo, the most inaccessible and secluded part of the island. Captain Symonds, R.N. was travelling through the country with a party, and wished to ascend the

snowy mountain of Tongariro; but the natives opposed it, on the ground of its having been made
sacred by their forefathers ; and because if the tapu
were violated some evil would befal them. " They
offered us gold," remarked the old chief; " had they
brought us some Testaments we would have consented to their going up the mountain. Tell the
strangers that if they return in the summer, and
bring Testaments with them, the tapu shall be removed."

There was sufficient reason to believe that the
profession of Christianity was made in sincerity ; for
while the deeply-rooted superstitions of their forefathers had been with one consent relinquished, there
was nothing to set in the opposite balance save the
advantages which Christianity bestows. Human
nature is ever impatient of restraint, and it was no
easy thing to submit to the yoke of Christianity, so
opposed as it was in every point to their former
habits. When this change is met with, where a disposition to restless warfare has given way to peace,
and a murderous treachery to Christian simplicity—
where quarrels are settled by arbitration, and a power
to resent injury gives way to amicable adjustment—
where restitution is made for an injury done, and
where heathenish rites give place to Christian
worship : it is clear that something more than a
transient alteration has taken place—that the " strong
man," who had long kept " his goods in peace," has
been cast out by One who is " stronger than he."

This change continued in the case of those who were first the subjects of it, and a progressive advancement in other quarters showed that the Divine blessing was resting upon the work.

In the year 1841, the number of natives attending Christian worship was about 8,600, being 3,200 at Waiapu and Tokomaru, 2,500 at Uawa and Tauranga, and 2,900 at Table Cape, Wairoa, and Ahuriri. The services were conducted for the most part by native teachers, whose earnestness in their work was evidenced by the fact, not only that the congregations formed were kept together, but that so much progress was made in the attainment of Christian knowledge, as to warrant the admission of a large number of candidates to the rite of baptism. The candidates at this time amounted to 2,115, of whom 588 men and 251 women were baptized, together with 339 of their young children, making a total of 1,178. This large body of natives, baptized at various places, were not received to this ordinance until they had undergone long and patient examination. It has been thought by some, that in the prosecution of missionary labours, the young present the most hopeful element, their minds being supposed to be more open to conviction ; but in this case the old men, including the leading chiefs, were among the foremost to embrace the gospel—not only giving up with one consent their former practices, but submitting with wonderful simplicity to the course of instruction required by their teachers. When they came forward as candidates for baptism, the practice was to keep them back as much as possible, to allow time for proof to appear that the profession made was not merely that of the lips. None were passed, not even the sire of three generations, who did not appear to possess a clear understanding of the grand truths of salvation. The seed had been sown, and being watered by the showers of heavenly grace, the fields had become white. Who, then, could forbid water that these should not be baptized? The sincerity of the profession made had yet to be seen in the future lives of the new converts; but at this period it might be said that their idols had been cast to the moles and to the bats, their swords were beaten into ploughshares, and their spears into pruning hooks; that is, the whole fabric of native superstitions was gone, whether relating to the living or the dead, the old priests being as forward to take this step as any others. Their weapons of warfare were laid by, their animosities with distant tribes were given up, and their petty quarrels were being settled by arbitration. The change was apparent to the casual visitor of the natives. In the absence of more decisive testimony from persons unconnected with the mission, may be given the copy of a paper found at Waiapu, which had been left by the master of a vessel.

"Waiapu.

"These are to certify that John Brown, of the brig *Martha*, seaman, was unfortunately drowned on the beach, and was buried by the kind assistance of the

chiefs and missionaries (native), who paid every attention by having the rites performed in a proper manner,
and with good order.   Given under my hand at the
Pa, this 21st day of July, 1840.

" GEORGE POWELL,
" Master."

A great change was being accomplished, in which
the hand of God was signally manifest.   It was not
by might, nor by power, but by the Spirit of the Lord
of Hosts.   It was not through the labours of the
missionaries, for the Word had only been preached
by native teachers.   The missionaries literally stood
"still to see the salvation of God."

It was not likely that such a work as this should
go on without interruption.   Satan is too skilful in
his tactics to allow of this.   He steps forward, therefore, as an adversary in the way, to stay the progress
of that which is good.   The Gospel of Christ was
winning its silent way, and a Romish priest was sent
from the Bay of Islands to preach another gospel.   In
the month of October, 1841, he arrived at Table Cape,
and was favourably received by a party of some
influence, who had avoided all intercourse with the
Christian natives, in expectation of his arrival, and
an opportunity was very soon given to the writer to
discuss with him some of the leading points at issue
before a large body of natives.

The priest began by drawing on the ground a diagram of the Roman empire, and then explained that

Christ, having been crucified at Jerusalem, he afterwards sent his disciples to various countries to preach
the Gospel; that among all the apostles he declared
Peter to be the foundation upon which his Church
should be built; that Peter and Paul went to Rome,
which was the chief city of the world, and that Peter
being the first bishop of that city, the Church of
Rome was the head of all the Churches, and that
those who differ from them have departed from the
truth.

The diagram which he had drawn was a convenient
starting point for me; for according to his statement
the Gospel went forth from Jerusalem, which was,
therefore, the foundation from which the truth issued,
while Rome was only in the same position as other
Churches which rose up in different parts of the world.
As to Peter being the head of the Church of Rome,
there is no testimony from history to show that Peter
ever visited Rome. I stated that the Scriptures have
been given as our guide, and that all doctrines must
be tried by them, for that nothing is to be required of
any Christian man to be believed which is not written
in them, or may be proved by them. The priest had
much to say about councils, which had been assembled
at different periods, and enlarged upon the great numbers of bishops who had been gathered together at
these times, and that their decisions were all in favour
of the Church of Rome; but as this was a subject in
which the native mind could feel no interest, it was
not worth while to notice it. It was much more easy

for our audience to comprehend that the Scriptures which they had in their hands, and which the priest allowed to be the Word of God, are a rule which may be safely trusted. The priest then tried to throw discredit upon our translation, saying that the Scriptures had been committed to the Church of Rome, and that we had stolen our book from them. This it was easy to explain by a familiar illustration. A rivulet flows from the mountain side, and winds its course towards the sea. Those who are in quest of water resort to the stream, and each one takes for himself that which he requires. If among the number of those who frequent the rivulet any one may have collected a supply in his own vessels, no other person has a right to help himself from them. The Bible which the priest then held in his hand (a copy of the Vulgate) was a translation only ; it was water which the Church of Rome had taken up in their own vessel, and we had not interfered with it ; but our translation was taken from the originals ; we had gone with our vessel to the stream, and had taken up the water for ourselves. This discussion lasted more than four hours, and was attended with a happy result, for a good number of the priest's followers came over to the Protestant party, and became candidates for baptism. The priest made a strong effort to establish himself in different parts of Wairoa, but before nine months had expired he withdrew from the district altogether.

It was a great blessing to the natives that they had

the New Testament in their possession, and the skill
with which some of those who had carefully read the
book were able to meet the teachers of false doctrine
was truly wonderful. Their Christianity, as yet, was
only in its infancy, and it is the more remarkable that
educated men, who have been brought up under all
the advantages of scriptural instruction, should be en-
snared by the transparent subtleties of a system which
the illiterate New Zealander was proof against. The
secret is that the one has the teaching of God's Holy
Spirit, the other has not.

At the time when Bishop Pompallier was at Tauranga, in the year 1840, Matiu, a Christian native,*
who was afterwards appointed a teacher, had a contro-
versy with one of the priests, which is thus related :—
The priest said, " There is one God, the Father, the Son,
and the Holy Ghost." "That is true," replied Matiu.
The priest then, holding his crucifix in his hand, remarked, " We do not worship this, but it is to make
us remember Christ." " That," replied Matiu, " is
what you say ; but what says the book ? ' Thou shalt
not make to thyself any graven image.' Your image
is the work of man, and to make an image like that
is breaking God's commandment." Matiu then read

* In his early life Matiu had been a celebrated priest, and was
skilled in all the arts of native witchcraft. He was full of life and
energy, and when he became a Christian he at once took a prominent part in favour of that which is good. He continued to be
a valuable helper to Archdeacon Brown until his death, which
occurred just before the troubles which came upon Tauranga in the
year 1864.

Revelations xiv. 9, 10, 11, and asked the priest the meaning of the passage. The priest replied that he did not know enough of the native language to understand him, and was walking away. "Stop," said Matiu; "you sought this conversation with me, and if you cannot understand what I say, your disciple Haki Tara can. I will tell him what these verses mean, and he can explain it to you. "Haki," continued Matiu, "this receiving the mark of the beast means, among other things, carrying those medals of the Virgin in your ears, and those crosses round your necks; and now, Haki, tell me what this expression means, "If the blind lead the blind, both shall fall into the ditch." "I do not know," replied Haki. "Then," said Matiu, "I will tell you. That man (pointing to the priest) is the leader of the blind; and those who listen to his preaching, and receive his doctrines, and bow down to his images, are blind also; and the ditch means hell, into which both parties, unless they repent, will at last fall." The priest would not remain any longer, but turned angrily away, probably more firmly convinced than ever, that the Church of Rome is right in withholding from the common people that Word which God designed as a lamp to lead us into all truth.

On another occasion, a Christian native at Rotorua, who had encountered the Romish Bishop at Auckland, said that the Bishop justified their making carved images from the example of the carved cherubim and seraphim. The plain, common-sense, scriptural reply of the native to the Bishop was striking : " God," he said, " commanded the cherubim and seraphim to be made ; God *forbids* you to make carved images. God *spake* from the cherubim and seraphim ; did He ever speak from your images ? "

When the liberal grant of ten thousand Testaments from the Bible Society reached New Zealand, they were quickly put into circulation, and another supply was written for, the larger number of them being at once paid for at the full price. The first case which reached Tauranga, containing 490 copies, was disposed of in eight days. It follows, therefore, that there were many who were able to read, or if they could not read, there was an inducement for them to learn as soon as they possessed the book. The number of candidates, too, for baptism was greatly increased after a large body had been admitted to this ordinance. Many leading chiefs were in favour of Christianity, and the multitude soon followed, not, perhaps, from any conviction of its suitableness to their present comfort, or its importance to their future well-being, but because it was becoming the general religion of the country. There were certain advantages which could not fail to strike them, such as the quiet possession of their property, and a freedom from the hostile incursions of their neighbours ; but then there were restraints which could not be submitted to without feelings of dissatisfaction. Hence it not unfrequently happened that when a solitary individual has wished to cast off the Christian yoke, many others have been ready to follow the example. Such, without doubt, has been the course of Christianity from its commencement, and our Divine Master has taught us to expect no less. It is only a portion of the seed which falls upon good ground, and brings forth a fruitful increase. In the case of others, the word which was at first gladly received, is, after a time, choked by the cares of this world, and by the deceitfulness of riches, and by the lust of other things, and it becometh unfruitful. It is sufficient to know that the purposes of God's mercy are fulfilled in the case of many, while we look forward in prayerful expectation to the time when the Kingdom of Christ shall be fully established, and all shall know the Lord, from the least unto the greatest.

On the 30th of May, 1842, the Bishop of New Zealand arrived in Auckland. The appointment of a bishop had long been desired by the members of the mission. The Christian Church had now grown to an extent which made it inexpedient that it should be left under the management of local committees. It needed a presiding authority, to which all could look with confidence, together with the exercise within it of those ecclesiastical functions which are essential to its complete efficiency. The Bishop came all ready harnessed for the work. He had acquired during the voyage out a sufficient knowledge of the language to enable him to communicate freely with the natives on his arrival. He paid an early visit to the Bay of Islands, and then sailed to Wellington,

Nelson, and Whanganui, travelling thence through the heart of the country to Ahuriri, along the eastern coast to Tauranga and Waiapu, and thence along the coast of the Bay of Plenty back to Auckland. He was thus able to form a correct estimate of the condition of the natives, and the general wants of the country. The reality of the change which had taken place among the natives made a strong impression upon his mind.

The late Dr. Sinclair, who was afterwards Colonial Secretary for some years, was travelling in New Zealand at this period for scientific purposes, and gives the result of his own observations, which those who knew his character will receive as strictly impartial. Writing from Glasgow, on his return to Scotland, in November, 1842, he says :—" By means of the well-directed labours of the missionaries, the natives have become exemplary Christians, and show an intellectual capacity which strikes with surprise every one who goes among them. I might mention many circumstances to prove how sincere they are, and how well they seem to be instructed in religion ; but I will state only one, which made a deep impression upon me at the time. While staying for a few days in the hut of an Englishman, at a part of the coast very little frequented, where about thirty natives live, I heard, morning after morning, about daybreak, when, as Captain Cook beautifully observes, the warbling of the small birds in New Zealand appears like the tinkling of little bells, the sound of a person striking an iron bolt. On inquiry, I found this to be the call to morning prayer, and that on a small spot of ground, cleared for the purpose, all the little village assembled beneath the canopy of heaven, to offer up, in unaffected piety, their grateful thanks and prayers to their Great Creator. Their avidity to learn reading and writing, and to possess books, as well as to engage in discussion on religion and other subjects, is very remarkable. From what I have seen of those still unconverted, the state of the whole people, before the arrival of the missionaries, must have been more degraded and abject than that of any nation I have seen, whether on the coasts of Africa, on the north-west coast of America, the Sandwich Islands, or any other country which I have visited. I have observed myself, as well as heard it remarked by others, the great contrast between the modesty and good sense shown in the conversation of those who have been converted, and the ribaldry and indecency of those who still remain in darkness. Frequently have I heard a Christian native, when asked to buy or sell on the Sunday, or break any other commandment, make the decided answer, ' No, me missionar;' and that in circumstances when the temptation was great, and the means of keeping the transaction secret not difficult."

The progress of Christianity had hitherto gone on in an even course. Many had received it from a sincere conviction of its truth, others under the excitement of novelty; but the time of trial was at hand which was to test their sincerity. In the vicinity of Waikato and the Thames there sprang up the town of Auckland, in a locality which just before had been an unoccupied waste. No natives were living within many miles, for their mutual quarrels had separated the tribes, and driven them far away into their own fastnesses for security. The novelty of a civilized community, where the houses, the mode of living, and everything belonging to them was strange, could not fail to draw together all who could go and witness the sight. Then, too, it was found that the white man had many wants which the natives could supply. Their agricultural produce, pork, fish, firewood, and even bundles of grass, all commanded a good price, which was soon exchanged for such commodities as would conduce to the natives' comfort. Manual labour was also much in demand, and thus many located themselves in the neighbourhood of the town, until they had earned enough to secure for themselves some much-desired treasure. In many respects all this was an advantage to them, but there were many attendant evils. The change produced a sort of moral intoxication. The impression which religious teaching had made upon them not being deep in its character, was in danger of being soon effaced. It was the young, for the most part, who frequented the towns—those whose minds were ready to receive an impress from whatever was last brought to bear upon them. They looked upon the works of the white man with admiration. He was their superior in knowledge and in skill, and his example might be followed in all things alike. In the chief towns in New Zealand there is happily much attention paid to religious duties, and the quiet observance of the Christian sabbath is equal to that of any well-ordered town in England; but there are also hundreds of professing Christians, who give no visible sign of their fear or love of God. It is this part of the community to which the native of no fixed principles is most likely to attach himself, and hence many were too glad to throw off those restraints which are contrary to our nature, and when they returned again to their homes they carried with them a laxity of principles, and justified themselves by the example of the white man. On the establishment of the mission stations the old and the young attended school in the early part of the day, and hence the rapid progress which was made in the knowledge of reading. It was needful too that the little knowledge they possessed should be fostered, that it might increase and grow, but sometimes it was said by those who had visited Auckland, "We have been to the white man's church, but we do not see that the congregation remains after service to be taught in the Sunday school, and why should we?"

The alternations of light and shade, of discouragements followed by changes, which tend to cheer the Christian, have frequently appeared in the course of this narrative. Events have often arisen which seemed most fatal to the prosperity of the Christian

cause, but, on the other hand, adverse circumstances
have been overruled, or the hearts of wicked men
changed, so that they have been made to work out
God's purposes. Paul became a zealous preacher
of the faith which he once destroyed. After this
manner, too, the gospel was conveyed to the inhabitants of the middle island, who were living
at Banks' Peninsula. The natives now living at
Otaki and its neighbourhood migrated many years
ago from Maungatautari under Te Rauparaha, in
consequence of quarrels they had with the rest of
Waikato. Finding a weaker people where they
went, they easily brought them under subjection ;
and as fighting was their occupation and their delight, they attacked in succession every tribe within
reach. In the year 1824 Te Pehi, one of Rauparaha's relatives, went on board a whaling vessel off
Entry Island, and immediately directed his people
to pull back to the shore. His object was to go to
the white man's country. The captain waited in vain
for the return of the canoe, and Te Pehi thus secured
his passage to England. He gratified his curiosity,
and above all he obtained that which was his chief
object, a supply of muskets, and on his return to
New Zealand these were made use of against his
enemies. An expedition was undertaken to the
middle island, and at Banks' Peninsula Te Pehi lost
his life. This filled Te Rauparaha with the desire of
revenge ; and about the year 1830 he induced the
master of the schooner *Elizabeth,* under the promise

of receiving a cargo of flax, to take him on board with a large number of his followers. They steered for Banks' Peninsula, and Mauharanui, the chief, coming on board without any suspicion of treachery, was cruelly butchered and cooked in the ship's coppers; and then an attack was made upon the people on shore, and great havoc was committed among the inhabitants. After a lapse of eighteen years, Christianity having introduced a better state of things, Tamihana, the son of Te Rauparaha, with his cousin Matina Te Whiwhi, were anxious to make some reparation for the evils of former days. They went with a body of their Christian friends under the sanction of Archdeacon Hadfield, and carried the gospel to the survivors. When Bishop Selwyn some-time afterwards travelled down the coast he found the effects of this work. There was at least the profession of Christianity, and many natives had been taught to read, and were acting up to the light they possessed. Another party of teachers from the same tribe went to instruct the natives of the Chatham Islands.

It is often found that Christianity flourishes most in times of adversity. The Church is then driven to seek help from God, and does not rely upon its own resources. The trials which come upon it produce this effect, that the true Christian becomes more earnest, while nominal professors are weeded out from the flock. There was a small party of Tauranga natives under the chief Whanaake who had taken up their abode at Katikati, on the side nearest to the Thames. They were living in peace upon their own land, and suspected no evil from others. But old Taraia, a heathen chief at the Thames, was not at a loss for some pretext when he wished to indulge his old propensities. He came down suddenly upon them, killed six, including Whanaake, and carried away thirteen as slaves. Others escaped, though some were severely wounded. This was professedly a Christian party, and it was a great blow to their friends. Many were ready to say it was a judgment upon them for leaving the customs of their fathers, and some declared they would have nothing more to do with Christianity. Old Matiu, speaking of some of the baptized natives who had forsaken their profession, said to Archdeacon Brown, " Let not your heart be cast down on that account ; do not think that the Church of Christ has fallen because eight boys have gone outside the fence. We could not see the wheat from the chaff before ; but now the wind of Satan has blown away the chaff, we can better discern the wheat—the true believers." This trouble was soon followed by a large accession to the Christian flock. More than 500 natives were shortly after admitted to the Church by baptism at Tauranga, two-thirds of whom were adults.

CHAPTER XVI.

1844—1846.

SIGNS OF DISQUIET AMONG THE NATIVES — CHARACTER OF HEKE
— CUTS DOWN THE FLAGSTAFF — EFFECTS OF THE WAR UPON
THE CHRISTIAN CHURCH — MANY RELAPSE INTO INDIFFERENCE
—NUMEROUS BAPTISMS—RULE OBSERVED IN THE ADMISSION OF
CANDIDATES—CLEAR PROOF OF CONVERSION — QUARREL ABOUT
BOUNDARIES — CONFIRMATIONS — BLIGHTING INFLUENCE OF
HEKE'S WAR—WIDOW OF TE KOKI—HAPPY DEATHS—QUARREL
AT ROTORUA.

SOON after the signing of the Treaty of Waitangi
there were indications of uneasiness among some of
the natives   In the intercourse between a well-
ordered government, and a race of people who had
been acquainted with no order but that which was
regulated by their own customs, circumstances were
continually arising which tended to disturb the
native mind.   They saw before them a power which
possessed the elements of strength, and when any
serious difference arose there was no middle course
between quiet submission to the law, or open rupture.   In the case of a horrible murder which
had been committed in the Bay of Islands, Maketu
the murderer had been given up to justice, but it was
said afterwards that they would not give up another
of their countrymen in the same manner.   The
English population, too, was steadily on the increase,
and would soon outnumber the Maoris, and they felt

that if some check were not given speedily, the opportunity would be gone. A feeling of dissatisfaction was rankling in the breasts of many, but it was kept under for a time. A pretext only was wanting, and soon there was one at hand. A young chief, named Heke, was living at Kaikohe. He was a near relative to Hongi, of bold and impetuous disposition, one of those whom Hongi was always glad to associate with himself. He was with that chief when he attacked Whangaroa, and destroyed nearly all the inhabitants of that place, and thus he became inured to acts of daring and bravery. Five years afterwards he accompanied the Ngapuhi tribe in their attack upon Tauranga, and, though they did not succeed in their expedition, Heke showed himself to be one of the boldest of the party, and received a ball through his neck in an attack upon Maungatapu. On his return to the Bay of Islands he seemed to partake of that better feeling which began to prevail, and was quite disarmed of his ferocity. He went to live at the mission station at Paihia, and became a candidate for baptism, and for a time the lion was turned into a lamb. On the arrival of Governor Hobson he was at first opposed to the establishment of the government, but at length, after much discussion had taken place, he was the first to sign the Treaty of Waitangi. But soon another influence began to work. The natives were told by foreigners, who had no liking for the English Government, that this treaty made them slaves of the

English, and that the flag, which was flying upon the hill Maiki, overlooking the town of Kororareka, was the sign of their slavery. From this time Heke became more suspicious. He talked with the disaffected, and they endeavoured to add fuel to the fire. There was soon an opportunity for the trial of his strength. The native wife of an Englishman, living at Kororareka, made use of some offensive language respecting Heke's brother. Heke at once collected a party of about seventy men, and went to demand payment. He asked for a boat, which was valued at five pounds, and the police magistrate recommended that the boat should be given, but the woman's husband refused to make any compensation. This was on Saturday, and Heke declared that, if his demand was not complied with, he would cut down the flagstaff. He remained quiet during Sunday, but early the next morning his threat was put into execution, and then he quietly withdrew. Thus began the open rupture, and though opportunity was given for Heke quietly to compromise the offence he had committed, he determined to follow out the course he had entered upon, and endeavoured to strengthen his cause by stirring up all the tribes over whom he had any influence. Many joined him, but happily that division of Ngapuhi, to whom he looked especially for support, was either opposed to him or remained neutral. They saw that his proposals were unreasonable, and when the people of Whangaroa, among whom his own brother-in-law, the son of Hongi, was a leading chief, came over to the Bay of Islands to join him, giving as their reason that they were being deprived of their country by the Treaty of Waitangi, they were met by Archdeacon Henry Williams with the treaty in his hand; and when the three clauses it contained were read over, they declared that there was nothing there for them to object to, and that, if this was the grievance Heke complained of, they would return again to their homes.

It is not our purpose to enter into any particulars of this war, excepting so far as it affected the Christian character of the Maoris. It was a war especially against the flagstaff as the sign of their subjection, and against the military who were there to protect the flag. Little violence was done to the settler, and at Kororareka the natives said to the civilians, "Why do you carry arms? we are not come to fight with you." And when the town was abandoned they urged the settlers to come and fetch away their property, and many of Heke's men actually assisted them in carrying goods to the boats. On a subsequent occasion, when the seat of the war was near Waimate, two drays, under the escort of four soldiers, were met by the Rev. R. Burrows, on the road from Kerikeri to Waimate. He had not proceeded far when a party of armed natives started up from the bushes. They spoke of the drays, and said they could easily have killed the soldiers, and carried off the property, but they did not like treachery. These incidents show an honourable and chivalrous spirit, which unhappily has not been adhered to in later proceedings. At length peace was restored. The natives were not required to make any reparation, except to replace the flagstaff, and all again settled down in quietness.

The effect of this outbreak was serious upon the body of professing Christians. Regular instruction was of necessity suspended, on whichever side the natives were ranged. Their minds were filled with other subjects, and there was a return to the scenes which they had learnt to delight in before Christianity was brought to them, though happily the war was free from those acts of cruelty which they had practised in olden time. The moral field, which had been green and promising, and from which indeed much fruit had been gathered, was now trampled under foot. We may ask, why was this permitted by the great Ruler of the Church? We must look for an answer to the history of the Church of God from the beginning. A falling away had been perceived for some time, and the love of many had waxed cold. That reaction was taking place which our Lord has taught us to look for. Many, who had received the word gladly, were afterwards offended when they found the course of events was not according to their own wishes. The evil passions of many had been let loose, and the trials of war were permitted as a chastisement. It was a trial, however, which God would make productive of good to those who were really Christians.

The depressing influence of the war continued after peace was restored. Many who had fallen back were glad to withdraw from the restraint of Christian discipline. A downward course is always easy. After the danger was over it was only the sincere Christian who continued stedfast. But this apathy was showing itself also in those parts of the island which were remote from the scene of these disturbances. This must, therefore, be attributed to other causes. The novelty of first impressions was beginning to wear away. The baptized natives began to feel that Christianity is more stringent in its requisitions than they had expected, and the frequent repetition of truths in which the heart was not proportionably interested, often induced a weariness. The excitement which followed upon the first introduction of the Gospel was unnatural, for nearly the whole population became attendants upon Christian worship. It could not therefore be expected that this state of things should be permanent.

Where Christianity had been more recently introduced, the number of baptisms continued to be large, until a great proportion of the population had been received into the Christian community. It may be thought perhaps that the examination of candidates was not sufficiently strict, but when a native came recommended by his teacher for consistency of conduct, and it was found, after repeated examinations, that he was fully acquainted with the whole scheme of redemption—the fall of man—his recovery by

Christ—the need of the Holy Spirit to make him "meet for the inheritance of the saints in light;" when it was found that he professed with apparent sincerity "repentance toward God, and faith toward our Lord Jesus Christ," it would have been a matter of serious responsibility to say, "I have no doubt of your present sincerity; but in order the more fully to test it, you must wait another year before you can be received into the Church." The record of the proceedings of the early Church leads to the belief that the apostles would not have hesitated to receive such an one.

There were many cases in which it was clear that the desired change had already taken place. One instance may be mentioned. In June, 1846, the Bishop of New Zealand was on his way to the station of the Rev. R. Maunsell to open a church, and in a distant part of the district met with a little boy, about thirteen years of age, who was suffering much from a deep abscess in the side. He placed him in his canoe and carried him to the station. His mild and patient demeanour under his sufferings was striking. When Mr. Maunsell conversed with him about the Saviour, he was much surprised to find that he was well acquainted with what he had done for him, and with the means by which he might obtain an interest in him. His aged and feeble mother had, it appeared, been induced, by his means, to acknowledge the same Lord, and had learned from him the leading truths of the Gospel. On being asked what he prayed for, he repeated a prayer of his own composition, which was remarkably simple and appropriate; and the poor little fellow repeated it with much earnestness and devotion. This, it appeared, was the form that he had been in the habit of using with his mother; and when he became weak the poor old woman prayed for him. After he had been about six weeks on the station, a proposal was made that he should be baptized, which gave him much joy, and on the following Sunday he was admitted with his mother into the fold of Christ. About a fortnight afterwards his strength was rapidly failing, and his friends determined to remove him, that he might die at his own home. He was placed in a canoe, and after they had pulled about four miles, he became much weaker. One of his relatives asked him when he thought he should die; he simply replied, " Let me go to my Saviour," and expired. How cheering is it to reflect that amidst so many adverse circumstances which tended to depress the cause of religion, God was carrying on His own work in the distant parts of the vineyard, and raising plants which will flourish for ever in the paradise of heaven.

Christian principles often exercised a salutary influence in restraining the violence of those feelings, which otherwise would have led to serious consequences. In Manukau a quarrel was going on about the boundaries of land. Before the introduction of Christianity, that district had been for years deserted

but when there was no longer a fear of attack from
Ngapuhi, the different tribes returned to their own
localities. After this the colonization of the country
gave value to land which had before been useless,
and hence each tribe was ready to secure to itself all
that it could claim. The boundary between Ngatiteata and Ngatitamaoho was now the subject of dispute. The former tribe built a fortification near the
contested spot, and Ngatitamaoho went by night, and
marked their boundary by digging away a part of the
cliff. This night movement was an infringement of
the native rule in such matters, and excited much
displeasure among Ngatiteata. Mr. Maunsell was
spending the night at a little distance from their Pa,
and was roused before daylight by a violent knocking
at the door. "We are off," said a native; "Ngatitamaoho are come." Mr. Maunsell proceeded with
them, but they had not gone far when it was remarked that they had not had prayers. They therefore drew up on the slope of a rising ground, in
number about two hundred. All laid down their
guns, and joined reverently in the service, while
their teacher urged them to show the sincerity of
their Christianity by their actions. Mr. Maunsell
then hastened on to the other party, with whom he
found Mr. Buddle, the Wesleyan missionary from
Auckland. In a short time Ngatiteata appeared
upon the ridge of the hill, and came onward until
their first rank was close to that of their opponents.
Both parties sat down and remained in perfect

silence for about an hour, while the two missionaries, getting between them, took the opportunity of urging them to make peace. One or two chiefs on each side then spoke briefly, and having remained some time longer they quietly separated. There was a promise that all would end well, but a few days afterwards, upon some sudden excitement, a collision took place, and many lives were lost. One young man who was mortally wounded was the first native whom Mr. Maunsell had baptized. He had always maintained a most consistent character up to this late event. On being carried from the field, he observed to his bearers, " God has now given me the fruit of my works." The combatants were not yet satisfied, but called together their allies from a distance, and after some displays of force, the accidental discharge of a gun brought on a general engagement, which ended in the defeat of Ngatipo and Ngatiteata. The effect of their losses was most surprising ; all their high vaunts ceased. Self-defence and prayer were now the only thoughts which engaged their attention, and they proposed that a fast should be observed in consequence of the humbled state of their tribe. It was generally agreed to, and throughout the encampment there was no food cooked until evening. Those who had been quite indifferent to religion before, and who either did not attend the services, or made a practice of being disorderly if they did attend, might now be seen reverently engaging in them. It was a cause for much thankfulness that these severe trials of sincerity did not lead to any relinquishment of their Christian profession, but that it rather caused a more strict attention to religious duties. The victors used their success with great forbearance, and as soon as their opponents indicated a wish to discontinue the contest, they laid aside their arms, and joined in mutual lamentations with the defeated party.

In the district of Rotorua there was a similar dispute between two tribes about the possession of a small quantity of land. A quarrel ensued, in which two individuals were slain, Rangitoheriri, a heathen chief of Ngatiwhakaane, and Paora, his nephew, a Christian chief, and principal teacher of Epeha, a newly-formed Christian Pa. These two relatives were on opposite sides in the conflict. Paora was shot dead; his uncle was wounded, and, when hobbling away, was cut down by Paora's tribe. In consequence of this, Epeha was besieged by the hostile tribes in considerable numbers. The son of Rangitoheriri, whose name was Iharaira, a Christian man, was second teacher in his father's Pa. Arriving at the spot where his father lay dead, he thus addressed the corpse : " Here you lie, my father ! Three times you used every effort in your power to induce me to put aside my belief in God, and three times I tried by every argument to persuade you to cast away your dependence in Maori superstitions. There— there is the end of your refusing to listen to truth ! My grief is great, but I say no more." On Iharaira hearing, a day or two after this, that a party nearly related to his father, living on the opposite side of Rotorua Lake, were meditating revenge, he immediately mounted his horse, and rode round to the place, and charged the people with the report he had heard, stating that his hasty visit to them on the Sabbath-day was to forbid their acting so wickedly as to murder any one on account of his father's death. He stayed some time, urging them to remain quiet, and then proceeded round the other half of the lake, stopping a short time at each village to urge all parties to preserve peace, and to hold on to their Christian profession. But the anger of the people was not to be allayed without, at least, a hostile demonstration. Rotokakahi, a neighbouring lake, was the scene of warfare. The lake was calm and peaceful, nothing moving upon it save two or three light canoes passing to and fro from the island in the centre to Epeha, the besieged Pa. But soon the scene was changed. The war party were now gathering together, and, as those from Maketu came up, their allies who were on the spot fired a volley of welcome. Then those from Maketu rushed forward with horrid yells, brandishing their spears and muskets, and finished their proceedings with the war-dance, the most diabolical thing that Satan ever invented. Much discussion followed; but the natives from Maketu would hear nothing of peace. It was strange to see Wiremu Hikairo, an old warrior, and their leader in former wars, at the head of the Christian party, who were all pleading for peace, and declaring their intention, if peace were not made, to go into the besieged Pa, and remain there. This many did, to the annoyance of their warlike friends, as, in the event of fighting, they might shoot their own relatives. By noon all was quiet. It was Saturday, and by common consent all parties prepared for observing the morrow as a day of rest. Mr. Chapman writes that "the next morning had all the stillness of the Sabbath. Protestant, papist, and heathen, all seemed to acknowledge it as a day of rest. It was fine, and we assembled to the number of about two hundred. A quiet, solemn service followed, and I was much impressed with the peculiar suitableness of many parts of the Liturgy to our situation. In the afternoon I visited Epeha. As I approached it from the island, in a canoe, the prayer-bell rang. I landed, and walked slowly up to the chapel, saluting no man by the way. My heart was too full to desire any converse or salutation. ' And is this Epeha, so named by themselves?' said I, as I looked around upon the parapets ; ' and was Paora, once your warm and zealous teacher, now in his cold grave, hurried thither by an untimely end, and his village the theatre of war?' I saw all this as I turned into their neat chapel to weep, to pray, and to exhort. The chapel was full, but Paora's place was occupied by another. It was a solemn duty to tell the truth; but, through the grace given me, I did so. I reminded them of the responsibilities they incurred when they became the soldiers and

servants of the Lord Jesus Christ. They were now
engaged in a carnal warfare. ' See to it,' I said, ' and
pray that you may be delivered from the present
evil.' " Such were the scenes which were of frequent
occurrence in old times; but now Christianity had
its influence among them. After a little desultory
skirmishing, they made peace.

The Eastern District, extending from Hicks's Bay
to Cape Palliser, was more removed from those ex-
citements, which arose out of the colonization of the
country, and here there was a more quiet opportunity
for Christianity to become developed. But while the
advance of religious profession was remarkable, so
that it had come to be generally made, there were
the same evils at work which have always been in
operation from the beginning. There was that offence
which is ever attendant upon the religion of Christ,
which will account for many, who had received the
word gladly, having gone back again; so that in
several villages the congregations were diminished,
while those who remained stedfast might be regarded
with more satisfaction, they having endured the trial
under which others had fallen The average amount
of the congregations in 1845 was 6,060; and the
number of persons who, during the year, had been
partakers of the Lord's Supper was 1,484. This was
a large proportion, but they were not admitted indiscriminately to this ordinance. It was the usual practice of the missionaries to converse individually with
the communicants, who had thus an opportunity of

unburdening their minds, and of receiving that counsel and advice which their cases might require.

The Bishop was at this time engaged in a visitation of the southern and eastern parts of the island, which extended over a period of five months. The preparation for confirmation, followed by the rite itself, was attended with marked benefit. It seemed to stir up the people from a state of lethargy, and some, at least, were led to feel the importance of those vows which they had made in baptism, and then renewed before the congregation. Those only were brought forward to be confirmed who maintained a general consistency of conduct, and they were about half the number who had been baptized.

While the progress of Christianity was healthy and vigorous at the South, the blighting influence of the late war, and of other causes which tended to draw aside the infant Church, still continued at the North. The friendly natives had been much mixed up with our soldiers; they had daily intercourse with them, and they saw much and heard much which was in direct opposition to the instructions which had been given them by their teachers. There was little, then, to lead them to suppose that Christian worship should be attended to with strict regularity. Many gave up the observance of the Sabbath, and alleged as a reason that the troops had taken possession of Ruapekapeka (Kawiti's Pa) on that day. When confidence was restored, many were glad to enter the service of the government as policemen, and others resorted to the town for the purpose of earning money by working on the roads. These occupations were innocent in themselves; but, on their return to their homes, it was found that they had contracted habits of intemperance and immorality, which they introduced to their friends as the custom of the white people. They went back with abundance of clothing and money, but with an increased indifference to religion. Then followed upon this a revival of their heathen feasts, and particularly that on occasion of laying out the bones of their deceased relatives, at which ceremony large assemblies were gathered together, and every evil passion was stirred up by the relation of old grievances and wrongs.

Amidst the general apathy about religious duties, there were many cases to cheer the missionary and to encourage the Christian flock under their depression. Ana, the widow of Te Koki, the principal chief of Te Kawakawa, was a person of dignified bearing, and in the early days of the mission, when the Ngapuhi had many slaves, which they collected in their frequent wars, she always kept her dependents in close subjection. When her tribe began to listen to Christian instruction, she was one of the first to promote the movement, and her example had a good effect upon her people. After Heke's war, she went to live at Paihia, where a boarded house was erected for her. Though naturally of a violent temper, she now showed the simplicity of a child, wishing in all things to order her walk and conversation by the precepts of the sacred volume. Her influence among the young people was great, and she took quite the part of a matron in the girls' school. Thus she continued in an even course, giving clear evidence that her faith in Christ was stedfast, until she was called away to enjoy the Christian's rest.

At Kaikohe there was a poor old woman sinking rapidly under the effects of hooping-cough, which was fatal to many. She was blind also, and living in a destitute condition, with little clothing, in a house which was neither wind nor water-tight; but she seemed to be in possession of the true riches. Without self-confidence, she was enabled to rest upon the Rock of Ages. When she was questioned as to her hope, she replied: " Perhaps I shall go to Christ, and He will say, ' Are you a believer?' and if I answer, ' Yes,' perhaps He will say, ' I never knew you. Depart from Me ; you have been a worker of iniquity.' " But being reminded of Christ's invitation to sinners, she answered, " Yes, I shall look to Christ ;" and it was in this dependence she shortly after departed.

Another instance is mentioned by the Rev. R. Maunsell, which occurred at Waikato. Nopera Hamini a young man, was apparently near his end, being far gone in consumption. When asked of his hope for eternity, he replied, " My only hope is in Jesus my Saviour." He was reminded that eighteen months before he was known to be a wicked young man ; he had run well for a time, but his goodness had passed

VIEW OF PAIHIA.

away as the morning dew.   " Have you repented and fled to Christ as your only refuge ; the mere assent of the lips is not sufficient ; do you feel your need of him ? "   He answered, " Yes ; my dependence is on Christ alone."   It was remarked that his conduct for the last year had been consistent, that he had been constant in attending worship, but that perhaps he depended upon that for salvation.   " No," was his reply ; " in Jesus is my hope.   My trust for the pardon of my sins and the salvation of my soul is not in anything I have done, but in Jesus alone."   He was often engaged in secret prayer, and there was every reason to believe that he was really a member of the Christian family.   In the midst of much evil there was a silent work going on, and those who were occupied in delivering the Gospel message were assured that they had not laboured in vain nor spent their strength for nought.

CHAPTER XVII.

1847.

GATHERING AT WHANGANUI—MANIHERA AND KEREOPA SET OUT
ON A MISSIONARY TOUR TO TAUPO—MURDERED BY THE HEATHEN
NATIVES—MR. TAYLOR GOES TO SEE THE MURDERERS—REACHES
PUKAWA AND TOKANU—INTERVIEW WITH HEREKIEKIE—PEACE
MADE—PERSEVERING EFFORTS OF ROMANISTS AT WAIKATO AND
TAUPO — OPPOSITION TO A NATIVE MARRIAGE — NATIVES RE-
TALIATE BY REVIVING THE PRACTICE OF TATOOING—WHATA, A
HEATHEN CHIEF, INTRODUCES A ROMANIST NATIVE TEACHER—
ROMISH PRIEST GOES TO TURANGA AND CALLS FOR A DISCUS-
SION—THE PRIEST WITHDRAWS—TESTIMONY OF REV. J. F. LLOYD.

AT an interesting gathering at Whanganui at
Christmas 1846, there was a congregation of 2000
persons met for worship, when the Rev. R. Taylor
administered the Lord's Supper to 382 communicants·
On the morrow a missionary meeting was held, at
which it was proposed that some of the Christian
teachers should go and carry the Gospel message to
their heathen countrymen.   Two were chosen for this
work, Manihera and Kereopa, of the tribe Ngatiruanui,
and they selected as the special field for their labour
a tribe at Taupo, with whom their own people had
been at war.   They were advised by a near relative
of the tribe they were going to visit, to defer their
journey until he should have gone before to ascertain
the feeling of the people.   It does not appear that
they acted upon this advice.   They first visited

Rangihaeata, the famous warrior, in his stronghold,
and endeavoured to persuade him to give up his
aggressions upon the English, that war might cease
among them. The old chief replied to their address
by laying his hand edgeways on the back of his own
neck, intimating the danger to which he considered
he should be exposed if he fell into the hands of the
white people. They then bent their way towards
Tokanu, where lived Herekiekie, another celebrated
warrior. On the part of this chief and his tribe
there had been a long standing enmity against the
tribe of Manihera, for the father of Herekiekie had
been killed in battle by the latter tribe, and his widow
still survived, and was instigating her people to seek
revenge. On their way they preached at Motutere.
The people of this place, fearing for their safety, endeavoured to persuade them not to visit Herekiekie's
Pa; or at any rate to go first to Pukawa, where they
would find Te Heuheu, who they said was a good
man, and would give them a welcome. Manihera
replied that he ought to go to Herekiekie's Pa first,
as he came to preach to the wicked. In the course
of his preaching, Manihera said that he apprehended
the time of his departure to be at hand; that either
on that day or the next he should be an inhabitant of
the unseen world. But he pursued his journey. We
cannot but think that these good men were going
beyond the line of duty. While our Lord instructed
his disciples to be harmless as doves, they were also
to be wise as serpents. If persecuted in one city

they were to flee to another. They were not to run into danger where there was no necessity for doing so. In the present case, according to native usage, the avenger of blood would take his first opportunity to wreak his vengeance ; and it was not to be supposed that a party of heathen would in any way be influenced by a change which had come upon their enemies. Timely notice had been given to them, and another course was wisely recommended by their friends, which would either have prepared for their approach, or have shown that the way was closed against them. Ten natives belonging to Taupo, of the Christian party, accompanied the teachers. Some heathen, however, of Tongariro, who had declared their intention to waylay them, sent out thirty of their people to secrete themselves in the bush ; and as soon as the Christian party approached, they fired upon them. Kereopa was shot dead on the spot ; Manihera was wounded, and the enemy rushed upon him, striking several blows upon his head with their hatchets. One of their ten Christian conductors was the foremost, and his cheek was grazed by a bullet. The other nine were a short way behind, and upon hearing the report of the guns, they rushed forward, when the murderers made off. Poor Manihera was tying his head, which was dreadfully cut, with a handkerchief. He gave to Wiremu, the man whose face was grazed by a ball, his Testament and some papers he had with him, telling him that his Testament was indeed great riches ; and, shaking hands with them, he leaned his head aside and died. Thus fell these Christian soldiers, having their harness on, and prepared for the battle.

A month after these tidings reached Whanganui, Mr. Taylor determined to visit the district, with a view of allaying the excitement which these murders had occasioned. Apprehensions for his safety were felt by many friendly natives, and threats against him were uttered at different stages of his journey, but he determined to proceed. The party halted at the small village of Poari, in order to send notice to Te Heuheu of their approach, a rumour having preceded them that Mr. Taylor was coming at the head of four hundred men to avenge the death of Manihera. The next morning they reached Pukawa, and were kindly received by Te Heuheu.* " The great and the lofty have fallen," said this chief ; " we are all cast down on this account ; but I bid you welcome, whether your object is to cover up or uncover the crime. This land has been polluted with blood from the time of our ancestors to this day." Mr. Taylor told him that this was his second visit on account of the dead ; first for Te Heuheu, now for Manihera and Kereopa : that the falling of the mountain crushed the one by the visitation of God, but that the others had been basely murdered, when they only came as messengers of peace. His object now was to put an end to the

* Old Te Heuheu had been buried alive by a landslip at the side of the lake ; and upon his death, Iwikau, his younger brother, took the name of Te Heuheu.

quarrel : that the old feud with Ngatiruanui might
be done away, since all excuse for keeping it open
had been removed by the blood which they had shed.
Te Heuheu said he approved of their proposal, and
thus far there was every encouragement to proceed.
An hour's pull on the lake the next morning brought
them to Tokanu. On the way they passed the spot
where the great Te Heuheu had been overwhelmed
by the landslip. The grass was not yet grown over
the common tomb of his tribe. That part of the
lake was strictly sacred, and the wild fowl, as if
conscious of their security, allowed the canoes to pass
without taking wing. They now entered the Pa of
the murderers, and received a suspicious welcome
from a few females. They sat down in silence opposite to Herekiekie, and the murderers of their friends.
At length Hemapo, the chief next to Herekiekie
arose. He acknowledged the crime which had been
committed, and deplored that his relatives should
thus have to visit him without the interchange of the
usual welcome. Another said, " We suppose you are
on your way to Auckland to fetch Wherowhero to
come against us ; but we are all united and prepared
for the worst. We are sorry for the deed, but we
could not forget the death of our own friends." Te
Huiatahi, who killed Manihera, said, " I am not at
all sorry for what I have done ; but I do not wish to
continue the evil or to carry it further. What I have
done is according to our custom." Mr. Taylor then
replied, that they had not come to judge, but to pre-

vent further shedding of blood;—that the dead were the servants of God, and had died in doing their duty;—that vengeance was left to Him who has said, "Vengeance is mine; I will repay, saith the Lord;" but he trusted that they would see the enormity of their crime and repent of it;—that now the blood of Kereopa and Manihera had been shed, they could not be brought back again to life: they were in the enjoyment of their reward, and it was great;—that sufficient blood had been shed, and their friends did not wish that any should rise up to avenge their death. It had been said that he was coming with several hundred men to avenge their deaths. He had come, and they beheld his party, with one only weapon, the Word of God! It was then arranged that two of Mr. Taylor's companions should return to Whanganui, accompanied by one of Herekiekie's people, and ratify the peace which was thus favourably progressing.

Mr. Taylor proceeded thence to Waiariki, where their departed friends had last slept, and near to which place they were buried. A neat double fence inclosed the sacred spot. They sang a hymn standing around it, and Mr. Taylor then addressed the party from the words, "Blessed are the dead which die in the Lord from henceforth." Many a tear was shed. They knelt down and offered up prayer, that the same hope which had sustained Manihera and Kereopa might support them also in their dying hour and that their precious blood, here poured out, might not fall to the ground in vain, but lead to the conversion of those by whom it was shed.

While the preachers of the simple Gospel of Christ were toiling onward in their vocation, the emissaries of Rome were assiduous also in their endeavours to disseminate their tenets. They lost no opportunity of turning to advantage any event which was passing. After peace had been made with Heke at the north, while the natives were yet sore by reason of their discomfiture, a priest lately arrived from France paid a visit to Heke, bearing with him the present of a gown for his wife. "John Heke," he said, "the Queen sent you missionaries, and the Queen has sent soldiers to destroy you." Thus they tried not only to prejudice the Maoris against the missionaries, but also against the government. They had tried their utmost at Hokianga, and in the Bay of Islands, but the Gospel was there before them, and the Scriptures were in extensive circulation, and they gradually withdrew from a contest which did not promise much for them. At Waikato they obtained a stronghold, particularly at Rangiawhia. But when God's word is allowed to speak, it is quick and powerful as of old. Tihinui, a young chief of influence who had joined the Romanists, determined to leave them, and at the close of the Protestant service at Ngauhuruhuru, he stood up and openly renounced the errors of Popery. He was soon followed by many others. This caused much irritation among the Roman Catholic party, and they sent a challenge to the Protestant teacher to meet them in open discussion. The priest wrote out a list of subjects to be brought forward, which were agreed to by the Rev. J. Morgan, but it was arranged that natives only should be present. Four days were to have been occupied, but at the end of the third day, Kahawai, chief of the Romanist party, proposed to Hori Te Waru, the Protestant chief, that they should discontinue the discussion, to enable them to prepare for starting on the morrow for a visit to Taupo.

Wise in their generation, the priests turned to the open district of Taupo. The natives there had long been asking in vain for missionaries to reside among them, but there were none available for the post. Promises had been held out, and expectation grew impatient. A second Romish Bishop had lately arrived at Wellington, accompanied by sixteen Priests of the order of Mary. They were thus in a position to gain a footing on the Western side of the lake, where they preached, as elsewhere, not the Gospel of Christ, but that of Mary.

It was much to be regretted that those who seemed ready for instruction should thus have another Gospel pressed upon them, which indeed is not the Gospel ; but let us not forget that there is One who orders and overrules all things for his glory, and the strenuous efforts of the Roman Catholics had the good effect of stirring up the Protestant missionaries to more activity. The spirit of emulation ought not to be needed, but our weak nature requires it. After a while a missionary was found for Taupo. The two systems of instruction were thus brought side by side. In this way a spirit of inquiry was called forth among the people, and they were led to look into the difference which exists, and the grounds upon which the respective systems rest. This is the very thing which is wanted, and there is no fear that when Scripture is made the criterion, the truth will speedily prevail.

The advance of Christianity on the East Coast had hitherto been without interruption, but a circumstance occurred in the year 1847, which appearing at first to be of little account, afterwards produced a great amount of evil, not however without its attendant good. It was one of those cases, which are the fertile source of trouble among uncivilized tribes, the arrangement of a marriage connexion. A young woman had become a widow, and her husband's relatives wished her to marry her late husband's brother. This she refused, under the sanction of that liberty which had lately followed upon the introduction of Christianity, and at the same time she declared the name of a person of another tribe, that of Ngatimara, whom she would prefer. This only increased the opposition which was made to her wishes, until at length she ran away to the tribe where the young man lived upon whom her affections were placed. Not only was she gladly welcomed by him, but the whole tribe, which was a powerful one, espoused her cause. This produced a general gathering, and a numerous body were under arms for the purpose of demanding the restoration of the lady.

The chief of Ngatimaru went over to the aggrieved party before the tribes had met, taking with him a very handsome greenstone "mere," which was the payment he had received for a large war canoe, and might be valued at about one hundred pounds. Entering the Pa he threw down this "mere" before the chief. His object was understood, and the man replied, "I do not wish for your 'mere,' only let the woman be sent back to us." There was much angry altercation throughout the day, and both parties continued under arms. It was in vain to urge that the woman was free, and ought to be allowed to choose for herself. At length the demand was modified, and those who felt themselves aggrieved, said that, if the woman was now given back to them, and then should a second time make her escape, they would not offer any further hindrance to her marriage with the person of her choice. This proposal was agreed to, and the people soon dispersed. All went on quietly for a fortnight, when early one morning there was a general clamour in the Pa of Ngatimaru. The lady had suddenly made her appearance in a way which showed the strength of her determination. She had been removed to a village at some distance, and all the intermediate ground was occupied by those who were interested in preventing her escape. But she avoided the usual road, and swimming the deep river twice, she contrived to throw herself once more on the protection of those who were watching for her return. At the end of the week, I paid a visit to the party who had lost the prize. Three chiefs, all of high rank, were at work in the woods, with a number of their followers. I told them that as the woman had been given up on certain conditions, and had now fled a second time, Ngatimaru proposed that the banns should be published on the morrow. The chiefs replied angrily, that they would not consent; that some unfair means had been used to decoy the woman away, and that they would not stand to the agreement. I reminded them that the stipulations had been fulfilled, and that it was wrong in them to oppose any longer. They continued obstinate, and at length it became necessary to tell them that the banns would be published on the morrow, whether they approved or not. When Sunday morning came there was much excitement. The people assembled in large numbers, and the church was thronged. It was clear that a disturbance was contemplated, and both parties were equally urgent to have their own will gratified. Towards the close of the second lesson there were evident marks of anxiety; one side triumphing in expectation of the wished-for banns, and the other ready to make a disturbance. Another course was adopted, the service proceeded without the publication at the usual time, and now again there was a change of feeling, and the dissatisfied natives thought they had gained the victory; but it was of short continuance. When the sermon was ended, the banns were duly published, and the hymn which followed tended to prevent the confusion which other-

wise would have taken place. As the congregation
was dispersing there was some angry altercation, but
it was hoped that all further trouble was at an end.
This however was not to be. On the morrow we were
startled by the report of a small cannon. This was
the signal for strife. The discontented party had laid
their plan. "Let the woman be married as she likes,"
said they, "but we will have our revenge." The
firing of the gun was to give notice that the heathenish
practice of tattooing was going to be revived, for the
purpose of annoying the members of the church, and
a young man was that morning submitted to the
operation. They continued the tattooing daily for
some weeks, and so strong was the inclination of the
young people to be made like their elders in appearance, that very many went off to receive the marks,
in spite of the opposition of their friends. The
Christian party made a vigorous effort to prevent their
relations from falling into the snare, and subsequently
they refused to hold intercourse with them, when
those efforts had proved fruitless. This state of
things continued more than six months, and the
separation which it was necessary to make drew
together more closely a number of the more disrepu-
table part of the community. At length they expressed a wish for reconciliation. They had gained
their object, and would now like to be received again
by their friends. Some of the number might perhaps
feel regret for what had taken place, but in many a
spirit of apathy and indifference had taken deep root.

Te Whata, one of the leading men in this late movement, was a heathen chief, but all the members of his family, and his wife also, had embraced Christianity. He now expressed a wish to join them, but after a while he cast off his wife and took another woman. His relatives remonstrated, but to no purpose, and when they withdrew from his company, he went off to Wairoa, where there was a small party of Papists, and there took refuge under a more lenient discipline, which allowed him to throw aside the restraint which had been put upon him. In a few months he returned to Turanga, bringing with him as his chaplain, a shrewd Roman Catholic native from Ruatahuna, which was the stronghold of the Romanists. Renata, a chief of Ruatahuna, living at Turanga, went to this teacher, who was his near relative. When he entered the house it was supposed that he would go through the usual ceremony of crying, and his relative made a motion to him to do so. " We will dispense with that," he said ; " it is sufficient that I look at you, and that you look at me. I am come to send you away ; why do you come with your rotten seed to the farm of another man ? " He replied, " There is no fault in what I have done ; it is your missionary who has neglected to fill the whole of the ground." "No, our missionary has been urging this man for these ten years, and it is his wickedness which has kept him back." " But why do you call our seed rotten ; we belong to the true Church, and yours is the rotten one ? "

Renata replied, "Yours is rotten, because it teaches you contrary to God's word. Why do you pray to Peter, when Cornelius was not allowed to do so? Why do you pray to angels, when the angel would not allow John to do so?" Whata then said, "I will not suffer my teacher to go. Your religion is a bad one. Your people would not hold intercourse with me because I had taken a second wife, but now my sins are all gone. Look at David who sinned; the prophet released him directly from his difficulty." Renata answered, "David sinned and he repented, but where is your repentance?"

A few months after this, I was absent on a journey in the Heretaunga district. On my way home I received a letter, stating that a Romish priest, M. Lampiller, was at Turanga awaiting my return, hoping to convince the natives that hitherto they had been under a false teacher. "I will wait," he said, "for your missionary's return, even if he is six months away." Being unable to go home direct, I wrote to request the natives by all means to detain the priest, in order that the discussion proposed by him might take place. At the different villages on the way, the people were frequent in their remarks about the priest, and it appeared that he had been busily occupied for some weeks endeavouring to establish his own case, and the anxiety of the natives to hear what was to be said in reply to him was becoming intense.

It was late at night when I reached home, but at

daylight a messenger was sent to apprise the priest of my arrival. Arrangements were made for the meeting to take place on the following day, and the people were invited to come together from the surrounding villages.

By eight o'clock in the morning they began to assemble, and two small tents were pitched under the shade of the willow trees, one being for the accommodation of the priest. A table was placed in the midst, upon which were arranged the Scriptures in the original languages, with the Vulgate and Douay Bibles, and the Maori New Testament. The priest admitted the authority of all except our translation, saying of the Vulgate, " Ah, this is mine." It was agreed that each speaker should occupy half-an-hour alternately. The priest declined to begin the proceedings. It therefore rested with me to repeat what I had been told, that he had proposed that the truth of our respective creeds should be tested by the trial of fire. This he at first denied, but when a number of the people corroborated my statement, he asserted that this was the only way to arrive at a true conclusion ;—that this was the course adopted by the Prophet Elijah when all Israel had turned away to the worship of Baal. " If your missionary," he said, " will agree that two oxen shall be provided, we will then each call upon God to send fire to consume the sacrifice which He is pleased to accept. Or, if it be preferred, let two piles of dry wood be prepared, and let your teacher and myself each ascend his pile; then let fire be applied, and God will interfere for the rescue of his true servant." I replied, that the Prophet Elijah acted under the authority of God, but that authority was wanting here; and therefore it would be an act of presumption to make the experiment;—that we had a sure test, by applying which we could be sure of arriving at the truth. "To the law and to the testimony," saith the Prophet; "if they speak not according to this word, it is because there is no light in them." I then attacked the infallibility of the Church of Rome, and spoke of the absence of authority for asserting Peter's superiority to the rest of the Apostles. When he spoke again, he still adhered to his first proposal, expressing his willingness to expose his body to the flames, and quoting as authority that "the good shepherd giveth his life for the sheep," while he declared that I was afraid to expose myself to danger. The natives became very impatient while he was upon this subject, and it was difficult to keep them from causing serious interruption. The priest now spoke of miracles, which he said were wrought in his Church, and were a proof that the truth was with them. He was challenged to mention any that had been performed since his residence in the country: and some amusement was caused by a lame man hobbling up to him, and begging that he would restore his limb. The worship of the Virgin Mary and the saints was then brought under discussion, and my references were made to the

Douay Bible and to the Vulgate to show the absence of authority for such a practice, while the natives were referred to the same passages in their own New Testament. The priest spoke of tradition, and holding the Vulgate in one hand, and our New Zealand Testament in the other, he exclaimed, " I do not find fault with your book ; both my book and yours are the Word of God, but do not think you will obtain salvation from the book. It is to the Church you must look, and to those traditions which the Church has carefully preserved. The Protestants have only one eye, but we have two." The priest speaking of the Apostle Peter as the head of the Church of Rome, and declaring that the authority of the keys was delivered to him, I remarked that there was no proof that Peter ever went to Rome, unless it is admitted that where he says at the close of his first epistle, " the Church which is at Babylon saluteth you," Babylon was intended for Rome, as being the chief city in the world. " Of course it means Rome," he said, " and Peter was at Rome when he wrote his Epistle." This was an admission the force of which had not occurred to him, and I directed the audience to refer to the 18th chapter of Revelations, where they would read something about Rome under the name of Babylon, from which it might be gathered that the time was hastening on when her end would come, and the cry would be uttered, ' Babylon the great is fallen—is fallen." It was at the end of the year 1849, and I was able to add,

" We have just received news from Europe which
tells us that a large body of troops from the nation to
which this priest belongs has lately entered Rome,
and it is possible that the doom of Babylon is at this
very time being carried out." Every time the priest
rose to speak he did not fail to recur to his first proposal, the appeal to the trial by fire. The day was
advancing, and again I said that an appeal to fire
would be an act of presumption, but that if the
priest wished to try the experiment he was welcome
to do so, and if he received no harm we should all
be ready to acknowledge that there was a super-
natural interference in his behalf. The natives at
once rushed forward to a fence which was near at
hand, and brought together a large heap of wood, to
his great annoyance. At length, after the lapse of
nearly ten hours, their patience was exhausted, and
the assembly was broken up in much confusion, the
people being abundantly satisfied that the priest was
unable to make good his cause.

The priest remained at Turanga for some months,
and kept around him a few of those who from different causes were inclined to favour him. In his
chapel he had images of the Virgin Mary, and of
some of the Apostles, and with a view to impress his
disciples the more with the reality of the affection
which Mary feels for those who depend upon her, he
said, that sometimes she shed tears of love for them.
They were led to expect that such a miracle might
be wrought now for the strengthening of their faith,

and while they were upon their knees, the priest directed their attention to the flowing tears. But one of the congregation had detected him pouring water into the head of the image, and after the service was over the trick was exposed, to the great dissatisfaction of his followers. The priest's position was now becoming uncomfortable, and he took an early opportunity of announcing to his supporters that he had received a letter from his bishop, to say that all the priests were to leave New Zealand for some other part of the world, and under this pretext he quietly withdrew, and the Romish party, with very few exceptions, joined the Protestants.

With respect to the spiritual aspect of the Maori Church at this period, it may be well to cite the testimony of the Rev. J. F. Lloyd, who, having recently arrived in the country, had accompanied the Rev. O. Hadfield to Otaki on his recovery from a protracted illness, which had kept him away three years from the scene of his labours. Mr. Lloyd's testimony is the more valuable from the fact which he mentions that on his voyage out, and on his first arrival in New Zealand, he had heard so much to the disadvantage of the Maoris from many apparently well-informed persons, that he was almost tempted for a time to think that the accounts he had read of them at home were highly coloured, and not altogether to be depended upon. After a particular description of the villages of Waikanae and Otaki, with a general notice of the people, he gives the fol-

lowing account of the Sunday which he spent there :
—" It was the day appointed for the administration
of the Lord's Supper. There was a congregation at
each of the three services of between seven and
eight hundred. The large church was filled to over-
flowing. Most of the vast assembly sat upon the
ground in the usual native posture, and were closely
packed together, presenting a dense mass of human
faces. Those who adopted European costume sat
upon benches, at the east end and along the sides of
the church. Never have I seen in any English congregation more reverence or devotion than I witnessed
upon this occasion ; and I may safely say the same
of all the public services that I attended at Otaki,
and the other villages along the coast. The responses
of our beautiful service were given with a fervour and
unanimity, such as I have never heard in any church
in our own favoured country. The hymns that have
been printed at the end of the Maori version of our
Prayer Book were sung by the whole multitude, with
a heartiness which rendered them much more grateful to the ear than better performances, which are
confined to a few individuals in the congregation.
And as I looked along the dense mass of human faces,
and saw the eagerness with which they drank in
every word of the discourse which was delivered to
them, I could not but wonder at the marvellous
change which by the grace of God has been effected
in so short a time in this people, once notorious
through the world for their savage ferocity. After

the midday service was concluded one hundred and
thirty individuals were admitted to the Lord's Supper.
These were the choice and most approved members
of the flock, and the solemnity, devotion, and intelligence with which they joined in the sacred service
was most impressive and affecting.

" The change that has been effected in the social
and religious condition of the natives at Otaki, has
not been confined to that one locality. I found the
same great work going on, though not perhaps with
the same rapidity, in all the villages that I visited in
the surrounding district."

CHAPTER XVIII.

DIFFICULTIES WHICH BESET THE NATIVE CHURCH — PROGRESS IN THE EASTERN DISTRICT FOR TEN YEARS — CENTRAL SCHOOLS— EFFECT OF CHRISTIANITY UPON MANNERS AND CUSTOMS — INCREASE OF AGRICULTURE—ADOPTION OF ENGLISH CLOTHING AND THE COMMON APPLIANCES OF CIVILIZED MAN — ERECTION OF CHURCHES—ENDOWENT FUNDS—MAORI SYNODS.

THE state of the Eastern District at this period was peculiar, and yet there seemed to be a gradual advancement. At Waiapu, which was the most populous part of the coast, the work had long been carried on by native teachers only. Three missionaries had resided there in succession, but two had been much interrupted in their duties by ill health, which obliged them to relinquish their post ; a third was removed by death. The Church Missionary Society were proposing to withdraw their mission gradually from the country, on the ground that New Zealand was now become an English Colony, and that provision would be made for religious instruction from other sources. But it was felt necessary to press upon them the importance of keeping up, for some time longer, the full strength of the mission, for the very existence of the native Church seemed to depend upon this step.

Much of the country was likely to remain long beyond the boundary of colonization, simply because it was not worth colonizing, and such districts seemed still to be a proper missionary field. The natives were not in any degree nearer to the desirable condition of supporting a ministry among themselves, than when they first made profession of Christianity. All that could be expected from them for some time was that they should erect their own places of worship. The Maori Church was in its infancy, and it had at once to struggle with serious difficulties before it could attain to any settled organization. Those natives who were within reach of the colonists were in the way to acquire property, but they were bewildered oftentimes by the sudden change which had come upon them, and instead of turning their attention to the support of the Church, they were more likely to become indifferent to religion altogether. There was the greater reason then that the fostering care, which had brought them a little way on the road, should be continued to them. If they had been left to their own resources, the worst consequences might have been apprehended. Important measures for their benefit were set on foot by the Government, and many of the settlers were anxious to promote their welfare, but there were under currents which no forethought could guard against.

Yet notwithstanding all, after making a fair allowance for the backsliders and the lukewarm in such proportion as they are to be found in every community, there seemed to be a large number who walked as became the Gospel. They were not matured Christians, but there were many babes in Christ, who were anxious to be instructed. The steady progress which had been made in the Eastern District, extending from Waiapu to Wairarapa, from the time of the commencement of that mission, was remarkable, and gave much reason to hope that the change would be lasting. In the year 1840 the Christian Church consisted entirely of persons who had gone there from the Bay of Islands, principally as teachers. The number of communicants at that time was :—   29

In 1841 they amounted to	133
„ 1842	„	451
„ 1843	„	675
„ 1844	„	946
„ 1845	„	1484
„ 1846	„	1668
„ 1847	„	1960
„ 1848	„	2054
„ 1849	„	2893

The communicants might be regarded as the fruit of the tree. They were those members of the congregation who were supposed to be walking in the narrow path. In the course of ten years there had been time for the novelty of Christianity to wear away; many had gone back again, but the number of those who held onward in their course was large.

The New Zealanders are not to be compared with the early Christians of Greece and Rome in the

Apostles' days, many of whom were ready almost immediately to become teachers of others. There is a degree of dulness in elderly people, whose minds have not been subjected to any kind of discipline in youth, of which those can form no idea who have not been in the habit of trying to instruct such persons. Hence it would have been in vain to seek from among them for men competent to fill up the vacancies occasioned by the death or removal of the first missionaries.

The question may be asked why had not the missionaries done more to bring forward the young, many of whom exhibit no ordinary degree of intelligence. The answer to this is that there was not a staff of teachers to carry on such a work. Owing to the causes which have been already mentioned, the charge of an immense district was often left to one individual. The case would be somewhat parallel if a clergyman were required to itinerate between London and York on foot, and then between London and Southampton, officiating at places on the road varying in distance from ten to twenty miles; and then when he is at home, having charge, in addition to other matters, of three hundred candidates for baptism, and of seven hundred regular attendants at Bible classes, who had been left in the interval, not to the care of competent curates, but to teachers who themselves required to be taught "which be the first principles of the oracles of God."

Much attention was given to schools of a simple

character, from the earliest days of the mission. It was the custom in every village to attend for an hour after morning prayers, and the result was that at one period the larger part of the population was able to read and write, but after a time the novelty wore off, and then there was the greatest difficulty in getting the children together for instruction. The parents who were able to read were indifferent about securing the same advantages for their children. With a view to counteract this evil, and in order to have centres of operation at some of the leading points which might be as beacons to show the benefit of education to the community, Central Schools were established at Waimate in the Bay of Islands, at Auckland, at Otaki in Cook's Straits, at Waikato, and subsequently at Poverty Bay and at Tauranga, under the care of missionaries of the Church Missionary Society, the expense for the scholars being defrayed by the Government. The principal aim has been to give a general education to the most promising which might fit them to become useful members of society, and also to raise up a superior class of teachers who might carry on the work of schools in the villages, as well as to prepare candidates for the ministry. Being conducted upon the industrial system, the men and boys have had to attend to the work of the school farms, ploughing, reaping, threshing, &c. A certain number too have been instructed in carpentry, and have made good proficiency in the art. The women and girls, in addition to direct school instruction, have taken their regular share in those duties which belong to their sex, and which are calculated to give them the civilized habits of the English. The greatest drawback which has been experienced in all the schools has arisen from the independence of the Maori character. The benefit of instruction is not sufficiently appreciated, and the children are allowed too much to follow their own inclinations. If by dint of persuasion they are sent to school, the slightest incident, whether it be a quarrel with a school-fellow, or the novelty of the arrival of strangers to visit their friends, or only a simple disinclination to the partial restraint of school, is sufficient to induce the scholars to run off to their homes, and it is very seldom that the parents think of sending them back. For this reason there are few of the scholars who have remained steadily, except those from a distance. There is not therefore the same amount of encouragement which is to be met with in an English school ; there is the frequent disappointment of seeing a youth of great promise drawn away, when he was just beginning to reward his instructor by the steady progress he had made. Still, out of the number taught, there are a few who have done well.

It will be interesting to inquire into the effect of the new religion upon the manners and customs of the people. Christianity and civilization are intimately connected, though not always united : civilization is often found without Christianity, but

Christianity will invariably produce a progressive advancement in civilization, because education is an essential part of it—it opens the mind to new pursuits, and creates a wish for an improved condition. There is, indeed, a spurious kind of civilization, which consists in the promiscuous adoption of foreign ideas, in which there is often a larger proportion of evil than of good. This was now being forced upon the acceptance of the Maoris who were living in the vicinity of the newly-established towns, and religion was needed to modify those evils, and to fortify the native mind by the inculcation of right principles, preparing it to reject the evil and to choose the good.

The first effect of Christianity was to induce the people to give up that system of warfare which for generations had made every tribe the enemy of its neighbours. In any part of the country where danger was apprehended, the population was not scattered over the district, but, for mutual protection, they lived in fortified villages, and their cultivations were carried on so near at hand, that, upon a sudden alarm, they could speedily rush into a place of safety. The traces of this practice are to be seen in the neighbourhood of Auckland. Nearly all the volcanic hills, which are numerous, were occupied as Pas; and the little terraces which are noticed on their sides are the clearings upon which their houses were built. As soon as the fear of these incursions was removed, the inhabitants became scattered in small parties and every man was able to reap the fruit of his own labour without molestation. One natural consequence was a great increase of agriculture, which was promoted by the demand for wheat and potatoes in the English towns. In their purely native state, every family had within itself its own resources. Their food, their clothing, their habitations, were all provided by the different members of the family; and the only interchange in the way of barter was in the purchase of canoes, and the finer kind of mats, which were made in perfection by a few only of the tribes. But now, in proportion to the facility of obtaining the coveted articles of foreign clothing and agricultural implements, the New Zealander was stimulated to raise twice as much produce as he required for his own consumption; and by traffic he supplied his wants at a much easier rate. This alteration, then, had its beginning in Christianity, which introduced a state of peace previously unknown, together with the opportunity of giving attention to quiet pursuits; and it was further promoted by intercourse with civilized man. The mind of the Maori, by nature active, is continually pushing forward to some new object. The sight of something which had not been seen before often created a desire to obtain it; and the effect, to a certain extent, was salutary, inasmuch as it urged the people to habits of greater industry. A very few years brought about a vast change in their general appearance and pursuits. English clothing superseded the native garment, and,

next to the immediate necessaries of life, the proceeds
of labour were successively spent in the purchase of
steel flour-mills, horses, cattle, ploughs, and threshing-
machines. Large sums of money have been expended
on water-mills, which have generally cost from five
hundred to seven hundred pounds; but these have
for the most part proved a failure, for as soon as they
have got out of repair they have been abandoned.
At one period, small vessels of from thirty to forty
tons were purchased for the conveyance of their produce to the towns, they being quite alive to the
advantages of going to market for themselves. These
vessels continued to run frequently, until the breaking out of the war put a stop to their trade.

That a radical change should be produced in the
customs of a people is hardly to be expected. Our
own experience will tell us that habits formed in
childhood are seldom entirely shaken off; a new
generation must spring up before a decided improvement will show itself. But in New Zealand, while in
the domestic life of the Maoris there is little difference
to be observed, they will sometimes show an aptitude
to adopt even the refinements of civilized life. The
natives have at all times been fond of great gatherings
in time of peace. On these occasions a feast was
given of a very costly character, where food was laid
out with most barbarous profusion, the great bulk
of it being eventually carried away by the guests.
But of late years they have endeavoured to regulate
these matters after another manner, and it has been

common to have a marriage feast where four or five hundred guests have been entertained, in successive parties of perhaps a hundred persons, where all were seated at tables, and provided with plates, and knives and forks, the greatest order and decorum being observed.

But there is a desire for imitation not merely in those things which mark a transition from the rude habits of their ancestors to the customs of civilized nations, but happily, under the influence of Christianity, they have been ready to bestow much labour and expense upon the erection of places of worship. It was the remark of Bishop Selwyn, during his early travels through the country, that the best building in every village was that which was dedicated to the service of God. At Otaki, in the year 1840, when Te Rauparaha and Te Rangitaake had been involved in a serious quarrel, the peace-offering which was given by Te Rangitaake was a large piece of timber, prepared as a ridge-pole for a church; and the building which now stands at Otaki never fails to excite the admiration of the passing traveller. The boarded churches which have been erected on different parts of the coast in the neighbourhood of East Cape, though they may not have been finished so well as an English carpenter would have done them, are yet most respectable buildings, and have become regular landmarks for English vessels which pass along the coast. The church at Tauranga, built entirely by the natives, affords a specimen of the most elaborate

Maori carving which is to be found in the country; and, at the most moderate calculation, they have expended upon it, in labour and in the consumption of food during its erection, not less than two thousand pounds. Four years ago I was travelling along the Bay of Plenty, in company with the Rev. Rota Waitoa and Mokena, the leading chief of Ngatiporou. At Maketu, when the people of the place came together, Mokena spoke to them about the want of a church for their village. The answer given was:—"We are waiting for the pakeha to build it for us. We are looking to the Bishop and to Archdeacon Brown." This was just the key-note for Mokena. " I will tell you what we have done at Waiapu," he said. " We began at first with chapels of raupo, which soon decayed and fell to pieces; but seeing that the pakehas built with wood, we thought we would have churches like theirs. We had no money to pay English sawyers with, so we went into the woods ourselves and cut down timber, and I took charge of one of the pits myself. Then came the difficulty about the erection. Carpenters' wages are high; but the planing of boards seemed to be a simple process, so we bought planes and other tools, and, having cut the timber, we then became our own carpenters; and there the buildings stand for you to look at. Now, I recommend you not to wait for the pakeha to build your church for you, but go and put it up yourselves."

Among the East Coast natives a further proof has been given of sincerity, in the desire shown to have clergymen resident among them. At Waiapu, after the health of several missionaries who had successively occupied that part of the island had failed, the natives again asked for another English clergyman. I told them I was ashamed to apply to the Society again, having so often done so; and I explained to them the principle of the Church Missionary Society, that when Christianity had been received by any people, the rule laid down by the Apostles should be followed, and that persons from among themselves should be prepared to become their pastors, for whose maintenance they should provide. At that time there were several superior men in the Central School at Turanga, who were under training as teachers, and the people at once assented to the justness of this proposal, and set about collecting money for an endowment fund. The result has been that in the Diocese of Waiapu seven different districts have completed the required sum, and two others have collected more than half the amount, making a total of 1,678*l.* In addition to this, they had made two other collections, which were altogether spontaneous, as an endowment for the Bishopric. Of the sum of 589*l.*, there was collected at the opening of a church at Te Kawakawa, in Hicks's Bay, in the year 1861, the sum of 257*l.*, and on a similar occasion at Turanga, in 1863, the sum of 332*l.*, nearly the whole of which was from the Maoris. This money is independent of what has been given in other dioceses in

New Zealand, in which not less than 1,300*l.* has been raised for the support of clergymen.

The experiment of a Maori Synod has also been tried successfully. The fourth meeting was held in January, 1865, at the native village of Te Kawakawa near East Cape. Arrangements had been made in 1863 for holding it at Tauranga, but this was prevented by the breaking out of the war. Much interest was shown by the natives when it was found that the constitution of the Synod gave the power of self government in many things to the members of the Church. The introduction of the lay element in the Colonial Synods has succeeded admirably, and it will be well for the Church at home when in this respect she follows the example of her offspring in the Colonies.

CHAPTER XIX.

We have seen that when Christian Missionaries began their labours among the New Zealanders, they were in a state of the wildest barbarism. The blessing of God had accompanied the effort made, until nearly all the inhabitants had made profession of Christianity. In the meantime the aspect of the country was changed. The casual intercourse with whaling vessels which resorted to the harbours for supplies in early days, was followed by an extensive trade with New South Wales for flax, the staple commodity of the country; but in the year 1840 the islands became a dependency of the British crown, and the country was beginning to be largely occupied by settlers. This altered state of things brought with it many advantages, and the natives gladly welcomed the change. But there were many circumstances connected with it which tended to draw off their minds from the simplicity of their first profession. They acknowledged that religion gave them much benefit, and that it led the way to the acquisition of those comforts which had improved their present condition, but their intercourse with civilized man brought with it complications which could not be guarded against. The Maori had possessed the entire control of his actions, and he was in the habit of settling all differences after a manner of his own. But now there was another race, whose ways were different, beginning to settle down among them, and misunderstandings often arose, which sometimes it was not easy to remove. If a case occurred in a town, or where the English population was predominant, it was settled according to the customs of the stronger party, and if dissatisfaction was felt it was not allowed to show itself; but it was not so in a Maori district: there the natives felt their strength, and took the law into their own hands. The reasoning adopted was, the white man has his own way in the towns, but here we will settle our own affairs.

There was at the same time another influence going on, the effects of which were not apparent. Large quantities of land had been sold in many parts of the country; but most of it was waste land, and amounted altogether to but a small portion of what the natives could dispose of without doing injury to themselves. As the settlers became more numerous, the demand for land increased also, and in their desire to meet the wishes of a clamorous public, the agents of the government often displayed an intemperate eagerness

to make purchases. Contracts were sometimes made
with a few only of the proprietors, which gave great
dissatisfaction to the tribe; and as these cases were
not unfrequent, there grew up a feeling of jealousy in
the minds of the people, lest if this course were continued the whole country might soon be alienated,
and nothing left for themselves. There were many
instances in which violent feuds had sprung up either
about disputed boundaries, or because purchases had
been made from those who were declared to have only
a limited proprietorship in the soil. The chief cases
which had occurred were at Manukau, at Taranaki,
and in the province of Napier. The quarrels were of
a serious character, and many lives were lost, and
these evils led to a determination not to part with any
more land, and this was the beginning of the Land
League. Renata Tamakiterangi, of Napier, in a letter
to the Superintendent of that province, writes :—" All
our troubles have arisen from the improper manner
of conducting land purchases, and on this account
the sale of land was stopped. Whenever the government shall have laid down some equitable system of
land purchase, and when calm is again restored, the
tribes who wish to sell will dispose of their land
under a properly regulated system." There was much
interchange of ideas among the tribes on this subject,
and the determination to keep the land in their own
hands gathered strength.

The relations between the Maori race and the
government have been further complicated by the

native Runanga, which was for a time an exceedingly good arrangement. Upon the introduction of Christianity it was fixed upon as a substitute for the barbarous mode of settling by brute force those differences which must always arise in every community. The Runanga was a quiet assembly of the tribe, and the avowed course of proceeding was to settle disputes by peaceable arbitration, and in case of offences to levy a fine according to a prescribed rule. This was a great improvement upon the old system. One case will serve as an illustration. A young chief of some rank at Opotiki had committed some misdemeanour, which led the Runanga to impose upon him the fine of a horse. He set them at defiance, saying that he was a chief, and he would have no more to do with the Runanga. He would be " puta ki waho," walk outside their jurisdiction. " You declare yourself to be no longer under the Runanga?" said the authorities ; " Yes, I do." " Then we will deal with you according to our old custom." They then took from him two or three horses, a canoe, and all the property he possessed. This system of Runanga prevailed throughout the country, and sometimes matters were arranged fairly, but often it was not so. They claimed also the right of jurisdiction over the scattered settlers who were living among them. Blame has often been cast upon the government for not having taken the initiative in these affairs, but those who are disposed to censure show their ignorance of the real state of the country. An English-

man has no other idea from his childhood than that
the law is paramount. He knows that it is vain to
make resistance; he therefore quietly does what is
required of him. It is not so with a native offender
living among his own people, with other tribes around
him ready to support him in the course he means to
pursue. Were a Queen's officer to show himself
there unaccompanied by force, he would be told to go
back to the place from whence he came. The first
unhappy attempt at Wairau, in the year 1841, when
Captain Wakefield and many others lost their lives,
was a lesson to show that the undertaking was one
of difficulty.

There was a similar case at Tauranga in 1842. A
feud had broken out between the tribe Ngatiawa, and
Te Arawa the tribe of Maketu. The Ngatiawa considered themselves the aggrieved party, and asked the
government to interfere. Mr. Willoughby Shortland,
the acting governor, went to Tauranga, accompanied
by a force of 200 soldiers, who were encamped at
Maunganui. It was then found to be impracticable
to use any coercion against the Maketu natives, and
when Pekama Tohi, their chief, came to Mr. Shortland
to inquire into their object, this prudent answer was
given: "We are here to prevent you from attacking
Tauranga, and to prevent Tauranga from attacking
you."

At Manukau, in the year 1845, a serious quarrel
broke out, and application was made by one party for
the interference of the government. The manner in

which the difficulty was disposed of showed that it would be extremely inconvenient to the government to do anything. They wrote to the Rev. R. Maunsell to say that they were prevented by the disturbances in the Bay of Islands from taking any step at Waikato, and that as his influence with the tribes had been exercised heretofore with such good effect, they must depend upon him to use his best endeavours to bring about a reconciliation.

The working of the Runanga continued, but it was often very partial in its decisions, and the better disposed among the natives saw the superiority of the English mode, and asked to have magistrates located among them, but the majority of the people were opposed to this course. A resident magistrate was appointed to Turanga on the arrival of Governor Brown, in consequence of a wish expressed by a few chiefs that the government would take some steps to stop the importation of spirits into Poverty Bay. But the magistrate's arrival excited much uneasiness. The system was tried with great caution there and in many other places, but with the same result; the aggrieved parties were always ready to prefer their complaints in the hope of obtaining redress, but the aggressors were unwilling to submit to a legal decision, and there was no power to compel them to do so. This was particularly the case if an Englishman had suffered wrong from a native. What could the government do ? It is not correct therefore to say, "The government took no trouble to help them to

have useful English laws where the Maoris live."*
In the meantime the idea was instilled into the
native mind, that they would do well to unite themselves under one head. A story is related that Te
Heuheu, the chief of Taupo, was receiving hospitality
in Auckland in the year 1857 ;—that a candle was
placed upon the table, when the following dialogue
ensued :—

"What is the use of this candle?"

"To give light."

"What is it which causes the light?"

"It is the fat."

"Will the fat give light by itself?"

"No; it requires a wick in the middle of it."

"Yes, and this shows you what you require; if you
are gathered round a king, you will become a great
people, and your light will extend far and wide." This
suggestion was at once acted upon.

"Let us have a king to be at the head of our
Runanga, and let his authority be established throughout the country."

This was the origin of the king movement, and soon
the watchword of the party was, "He puru toto, he
pupuri whenua:" "Stop the effusion of blood, and
keep possession of the land." The Waikato chief
Potatau was fixed upon, though much against his
will, to hold the regal office, but being a very old
man he was passive under the name of the dignity,

* See Address to the Maoris, by the Aborigines Protection
Society.

and left all action to others. Every exertion was used by the promoters of the scheme to extend their influence through the country, and the most specious arguments were resorted to in order to gain adherents. In April, 1859, there was a large meeting at Pawhakairo, near Napier, at which Tamihana Te Waharoa was present with seventy of his followers from Waikato. The Napier chiefs were strongly recommended to take back into their own hands all the land which they had leased to the sheep farmers, and for which they were receiving a large rental. But they rejected this advice, saying that they were quite satisfied with the arrangement they had made with the settlers. This was before the first outbreak at Taranaki, and it hence appears that the promoters of the movement were making strenuous efforts to strengthen their cause.

Upon the withdrawal of the troops from Taranaki during the interval which occurred after the return of Sir George Grey to the country, a meeting was held by the natives at Peria, in Waikato, for the discussion of the governor's proposals in the year 1862, the result of which was that the majority of the people became more determined than before to follow their own course. A Waiapu native, Hoera Tamatatai, was present at the meeting, and returning home with a king's flag, became a zealous advocate of the cause, and as he travelled along the Bay of Plenty he proclaimed, that the recommendation of the Maori king was, that every white man should be sent away from the native districts, and that not even the missionaries should be allowed to remain. It appears then that there was a strong party at Waikato, who for the sake of preserving their nationality and the exclusive control over their lands and persons, were willing to forfeit all the advantages to be derived from commercial intercourse, and even to forego their religious instruction. The missionaries had always advised them to receive without hesitation that which appeared to be the will of God, and was clearly for their benefit, a union with the English under the common government of the Queen ; many therefore were ready to look with suspicion upon their teachers, and to say that they had only been sent before to prepare the way for the government. After the so-called peace had been concluded at Taranaki in 1861, the road to Whanganui continued to be stopped, and a board of tolls was put up demanding the sum of five pounds from all settlers who should travel that way, but fifty pounds from any minister of religion, whether native or English.

Meanwhile the party in Waikato, bent upon carrying out their extreme views against the English, made every preparation for combined action. In 1862 a deputation from the Thames was sent to Poverty Bay to summon the natives to join them in a general rising, stating that Waikato would very shortly become the scene of conflict. The invitation was not responded to, and in April, 1863, a further attempt was made at a large meeting held at Turanga, on occasion of the opening of a church, when the Waikato deputation were much disconcerted by the rejection of their proposal that all should join the king movement.

When hostilities began in Waikato, Tamihana sent to the natives of the East Coast, to desire that they would remain quiet, and leave him to settle his own quarrel with the government. He had been previously joined by a party from Waiapu, about fifty-five in number; but after the battle at Rangiriri he wrote a letter to Opotiki, to be passed on to all the tribes to the Eastward, requesting them to rise up in a body. Up to this time the people of Opotiki had declared their determination to take no part in the war, and had sent a communication to the government to that effect. But they at once responded to Tamihana's appeal, and it was not long before the most unsettled of the natives hastened to the scene of conflict. As the troops were advancing into the heart of Waikato, messengers were sent along the coast in quick succession, and every device was resorted to, in order to obtain the support of those who had remained behind. Each conflict was reported to be a most unheard of victory gained by the natives, and those who had no wish to engage in the war were told that there would be no share for them in the spoils, unless they went at once to join their comrades. While the troops were gradually working their way through upper Waikato, it was said they had been driven back to Auckland, and that the town itself would be an easy conquest. The consequence was that all their worst passions were roused, and a thirst for plunder and blood was stirred up, such as it had been in olden times. They tried to persuade themselves that their cause was just, and that to fight was the only cause by which they could save themselves from being crushed by the oppression of the white man. They began by looking to God as their defence, but when reverses came upon them, there were many who threw up their religion, saying, that as God had not given them victory, they would worship Him no longer.

The Tauranga natives had been beaten at Te Ranga, and had made their submission to the governor. Waikato was now in the hands of the troops, but the tribes of that district had fallen back into the interior. In the meantime Satan was not wanting in expedients. Having possession of the hearts of his votaries, he kept them back from accepting terms of reconciliation, lest they should slip away from his dominion. His next device was to frame the Hauhau or Paimarie superstition, with the promise of complete success to those who should follow it.

A Taranaki chief, Horopapera Te Ua, having shown strong symptoms of insanity, his people considered that it was dangerous for him to be at large, and bound him with ropes. In a little time he contrived to gain his liberty. He was then secured with a chain, which was securely padlocked, but he broke the chain asunder, and was again free. "The angel

Gabriel," he said, "had appeared to him to give him his release." The next achievement of Te Ua was still more marvellous. It is related that, in a fit of frenzy, he severed his child's leg with an axe; but when the people gathered around to pour forth their lamentations, they found the child playing before the door, with only a scar visible, showing where the amputation had taken place. From this time Te Ua was no longer regarded as a maniac, but as a great prophet, one who was raised up for their deliverance. He then related to his people a remarkable dream, which was interpreted to mean that victory was near at hand. Soon after a party of soldiers, under Captain Lloyd, being out on a reconnaisance, their retreat was cut off by the natives, and some of the number, including that officer, fell into their hands. The report was at once circulated that this success had been achieved under the protection of the angel Gabriel; that the natives, only thirty in number, had been attacked by a large body of soldiers, and that without fighting, but only by the use of Horopapera's magic wand, the soldiers all fell before them. Horopapera then sent a letter to Tamihana Te Waharoa, and to the New Zealand chiefs generally, instructing them to sheathe the sword of war, "that the Lord of Hosts has given to the natives the sword of Sampson and of Gideon, the sword by which the Philistines and the Midianites were overpowered. This is Gabriel the archangel. He has come down like a mighty flood upon his people, and upon the ruler

who is anointed to be over them. He commands
you to stay the four winds of heaven, and that all
the people shall take upon them the solemn oath
(Kia tomo katoa tatou ki ana pooti).* If you obey
this command your God will come down upon this
land. It is because he loves his people, and is about
to restore you to your rock, which is Jehovah."
Here was a recognition of the Divine Ruler, but
there was a strange admixture of fanaticism, and, in
order to secure the adhesion of the people, it was
necessary to give them a new system. Their case
bore some resemblance to that of Israel of old, when,
the ten tribes having raised the standard of rebellion,
Jeroboam made the golden calves for the people to
worship, lest by going up to Jerusalem they should
return to their allegiance. The Christian religion
had taught them quiet submission to the powers that
be, and under the instruction of the missionaries
they had been accustomed to pray for the Queen,
and to acknowledge her authority. The Scriptures
therefore were to be laid aside, together with all the
books they had received from the missionaries. They
were directed to return to their native customs, including the tapu and polygamy, and a new form of
worship was prepared, which seems to have been
borrowed in part from the Romish Missal, one portion
being headed, " A song of Mary for the people who

---

* Pooti is the term used for the ceremony which is performed
around the pole when the people are brought under a mesmeric in
fluence.

are standing destitute on the island, which is divided into two ; " but it is worded in a jargon which the natives say they do not understand.* It is written partly in English, as an untaught Maori would pronounce the English words, with a sprinkle of Latin also.   One line will be sufficient as a specimen :—

Koti te pata mai merire.

God the father miserere mei.

At the same time the form is repeated with an intensity of earnestness, which is calculated to work powerfully on the feelings.   When the worship of these fanatics was practised at Poverty Bay it was followed by a most bitter lamentation, unlike anything ever witnessed before.   It was a mourning on account of those who had been slain in the war with the English, and for the land which had been taken from them in Waikato.   It was commenced by the Taranaki natives, but the effect was overpowering upon the bystanders, who joined in by degrees until there were very few who did not unite in the chorus.   There was a chord touched which vibrated in the native breast.   It was the " arohi ki te iwi," *amor patriæ,* and they could not resist it.   In their harangues, the evils of their condition were magnified to the utmost, and the sympathies of the people were enlisted to such an extreme degree that they seemed to be hurried along as by a mighty torrent.

* At Poverty Bay the question was put to Watene, a Tiu, or Priest from Waikato ; "Do you understand the words you are using?" " No I do not, but I suppose Horopapera does."

The Hauhau emissaries, who were sent through the country in the early part of the year 1865, left Taranaki in two bodies. The one was to pass by Whanganui and Taupo, and thence to Whakatane, Opotiki, and East Cape, after which they were to proceed to Poverty Bay, by way of the coast. The other party was to go through the centre of the island by Ruatahuna and Wairoa, and both were to meet at Poverty Bay. The instructions given by Te Ua were, that they should travel peaceably, carrying with them the human heads, which they were to deliver to Hirini Te Kani, a Poverty Bay chief. The object of this expedition was not fighting, but to obtain the adhesion of all the tribes through which they passed. It appears however that on the arrival of the first party at Pipiriki, on the Whanganui river, their purpose was changed, and they proceeded thence with the intention of murdering any missionaries who might come in their way. This purpose was announced at Whakatane, but there were no means of warning those who might be exposed to danger. On their arrival at Opotiki they found the tribe already in a state of extreme excitement. They had been induced to rise at the call of Tamihana twelve months before, and on their way to join that chief they received a check at Matata from the Arawa tribe, and lost several of their people, among whom was Aporotanga, a leading chief, who had been taken prisoner, and was afterwards shot by the wife of Tohi, the Arawa chief, who had fallen in the battle. Returning home they were reduced to great hardships from the scarcity of food, which had all been consumed in fitting out their unsuccessful expedition. Upon this there followed a virulent attack of low fever, which carried off about a fourth-part of the population. Smarting under their losses they were still endeavouring to obtain the help of their neighbours to raise another force for an attack upon the Arawa. The ravages of the fever had not yet ceased when the Hauhau fanatics came upon them. They were at once assured that all they wished for was within reach. The boasted success of the Hauhaus on the western coast, which had never yet had any existence, was related to them, and they were told, that if they confided with implicit faith in the directions of the new prophets, they might march without fear to Maketu against the Arawa, and thence to Tauranga and to Auckland, for that no power could withstand them. These declarations were supplemented by the exercise of a mesmeric influence. They erected a pole, upon which the Paimarire flags were hoisted, and the whole body of the people, men, women, and children, were made to go round it for a length of time, until they were brought into a state of giddiness, when they were easily operated upon by the Tiu. The English settlers who were living there all agree in describing their condition as one of raving madness. At this unhappy juncture the Rev. Messrs. Volkner and Grace arrived in a small schooner, the former having

with him a supply of medicine and nourishing food
for the sick. They crossed the bar, and when they
were in the river they were entirely within the power
of the fanatics. The Taranaki Hauhaus gloated on
their prey, and the Opotiki natives were ready to
pay implicit obedience to their new teachers. The
miscreant Kereopa declared that it was the will of
the god, speaking by the human head, that Mr.
Volkner's life should be taken, and all the Opotiki
chiefs in succession gave their consent to the barbarous murder which followed.

When we look at all the circumstances, it is difficult to account for this tragedy. Mr. Volkner had
been living for more than three years among the
Whakatohea tribe, and he had earned for himself
very much respect by the uniform kindness of his
manner, by his anxiety to promote their welfare in
every way, not merely by his religious instructions,
but by looking after their temporal interests, and
particularly by his unremitting attention to the sick.
They seemed to regard him as a friend who really
had their welfare at heart. Mr. Volkner wrote to me
on the 22d of January, a few days after visiting
Opotiki, " I found that during my absence the natives
had most carefully abstained from touching any
property belonging to me, and when I made my
appearance again among them, they gave me a most
hearty welcome." It was this conduct of the natives
towards him which put him off his guard, when he
was warned that there might be danger in going back

to Opotiki. The murder was an act of savage madness, hurried on at the instigation of the evil one, and though there were a few among the Opotiki natives who grieved at the time of the crisis, they were afraid to open their lips. They saw the body of the people powerless in the hands of the fanatics, they were themselves unconsciously imbibing the same spirit of fanaticism. They did not dare to speak, lest they might be made to suffer for their interference. But the majority were hurried along by the torrent, and had brought themselves to the belief that what they were doing was right. They inflicted a most cruel death upon one who in every way was their kindest earthly benefactor. His own immediate friends, who knew his earnest desire to promote the welfare of the people of his charge, were amazed at the tidings of the deed, and the whole Christian world was aroused to the recollection that such deaths were frequent in olden times ; and yet the martyrdoms of former days do not bear a parallel to this, because they were the work of men who never professed the religion of those they sought to destroy. Following the example of that Saviour whom he had endeavoured to serve, Volkner prayed for his murderers that they might be forgiven, for indeed they knew not what they did. And quickly he passed away to join the multitude of those who "came out of great tribulation, and have washed their robes and made them white in the blood of the Lamb."

The rapid spread of this new superstition altogether disappointed the expectations of those who were best acquainted with native character, but still it was not to be regarded so much as a religious movement; it was rather an expedient, which had been adopted for the purpose of recovering their national independence, and in order, as they supposed, to gain this end, multitudes formally renounced the Christian faith. How truly are the words of the Apostle fulfilled in them: "Even as they did not like to retain God in their knowledge, God gave them over to a reprobate mind to do those things which are not convenient." Many were hurried onward to their own destruction.

We have seen that the occupation of the country as an English colony excited the jealous feelings of the natives. The Land League and the king movement gradually grew out of this jealousy, and the war which followed shook the native church to its foundation. Many have not endured the sifting to which they have been subjected. But in all this we only see another instance of what has been the experience of the Church in all ages. Whenever persons take up a religious profession under the influence of excitement, they will fall back as soon as that excitement ceases. In our own day we have had revivals in America and in England, and there seemed to be a wonderful reformation for a little while, and then the effect suddenly disappeared Plants of exotic growth will not endure the rude blasts of the common world. If Christianity be sound in character, if the fabric of our faith is built upon a true foundation, the floods may come, and the winds may blow, but it will not fall, because it is founded upon a rock.

Where, then, is the Christianity of the native Church? What are the results of all the labour that has been bestowed? Where is the field of promise that has been so much talked of? There are many who think it will be difficult to answer these inquiries; but there might be the same difficulty if we were to institute a close examination into the condition of many favoured districts in England. Oftentimes there would be all the outward appearance of religion, and even a zeal for many things that are good, but a fearful absence of that deeper principle which leads the Christian to delight in the knowledge of Christ as the one thing needful. Our Saviour tells us of the kingdom of God, " Ye cannot say, Lo, it is here, or, Lo, it is there," because " the kingdom of God is within you." We see a something which is external: it promises fair, and we think surely it is there; but, after all, we may be mistaken. Where there is the greatest sincerity in religion it will most shrink from observation. When we see the fruit upon the tree, we then believe it to be a reality; but its quality has yet to be tested. If in those who profess to be Christians there is that consistency of life which Christianity requires, we are then bound to believe that it is sincere. In the native Church, that sincerity is to be met with, just as it is in other parts of the world. During the period of fifty years in which the gospel has been proclaimed to the New Zealanders, who can say how many have received it in sincerity? Of this we are certain, that the multitude is large of those who, after having afforded during life a sufficient reason for believing that they were true converts, have in their last moments given a clear testimony that they died in the Christian's hope.

While we lament over the sad convulsions by which the Maori Church has been torn asunder, we must bear in mind that the missionaries from whom the New Zealanders received the knowledge of Christianity, came to them from that nation with which they have since been engaged in an unhappy conflict. This fact has been industriously put forward by some whose interest it was to withstand the progress of the Gospel. Then, too, the failure of their attempts to drive back their enemies, followed by the introduction of the Paimarire superstition, has tended to test their professions to the utmost. These trials have come upon them, like a flood of waters, with overwhelming force; but it will be found that there are many sincere Christians scattered over the country at the present time, although they may not come under general notice. When the prophet Elijah had fled into the wilderness, through fear of the vengeance of Jezebel, he declared before God that the prophets of the Lord had been all slain, and that he only was left. But God said to him, "Yet have I left me seven thousand in Israel, all the knees which have not bowed unto Baal."

Great numbers have fallen away; but it is a cheering fact that there are twelve native clergymen, supported by the contributions of their flocks, amounting to upwards of three thousand pounds, who are labouring with diligence and zeal to lead their countrymen in the right path. The present period is the sifting-time of the Church, a sifting which will be for its benefit.

The Gospel was to be preached in all the world for a witness unto all nations. It was brought to New Zealand, and has been accepted by great numbers. But because there are many also who reject it,— because many have, apparently, received it gladly, and after that have renounced it,—this is no sign of failure in the object first proposed by those who undertook to bring the offer of Christianity before them. There is no falling short in the beneficent purposes of God in this. We only witness here what is seen in every other part of the Christian Church. The external fabric is large and beautiful, and within there is room for all. Many do not enter; and why? because they will not. Of those who do, there is still a large proportion who are satisfied with outward conformity, but who fall short of those higher spiritual qualities which are required in the Gospel.

There is yet a mighty change to be effected in the whole Christian world before it will have reached that condition which is promised. The wickedness which now prevails on the earth has to be removed from it; wars are to be made to cease, swords are to be beaten into ploughshares, and spears into pruning-hooks, and the nations shall learn war no more. Never was there a period when the violent passions of men were aroused to more deadly strife; yet the course of the world is hastening on, and though many ages have rolled away since the purposes of God were revealed to Nebuchadnezzar in Babylon, they will soon receive their accomplishment. Much has been fulfilled, and what yet remains must also be accomplished. " Thou sawest till that a stone was cut out without hands, which smote the image upon his feet, that were of iron and clay, and break them to pieces. Then was the iron, the clay, the brass, the silver, and the gold broken in pieces together, and became like the chaff of the summer threshing-floor, and the wind carried them away, that no place was found for them; and the stone that smote the image became a great mountain, and filled the whole earth." It is added : " And in the days of these kings shall the God of heaven set up a kingdom which shall never be destroyed; and the kingdom shall not be left to other people, but it shall break in pieces and consume all these kingdoms, and it shall stand for ever." That kingdom will have within it a countless multitude from all people and nations and kindreds and languages ; and there, too, will be found the New Zealand Church, composed of a goodly company of those who once were savages, but who, having been called out of darkness into the marvellous light of the Gospel, will be made partakers of the heavenly inheritance.

APPENDIX.

RÉSUMÉ OF NEW ZEALAND AFFAIRS.

THE following table of dates is appended, to facilitate the reader's better understanding of the events which are summed up in Chapter XIX.

A question arises about a block of land, in the vicinity of Taranaki, on the west coast, known as the Waitara block. This land having been sold to the Government by a native whose right to do so was disputed by the chief, William King, he protests against the sale, as being in violation of the " mana," or tribal right. The policy of the Government had hitherto been to decline having to do with land of a disputed title. On this occasion the Government resolved to persist, and the first instalment of the money was paid in December, 1859 ; when the chief, William King, appeared in person, and renewed his protest against the sale.

The Government proceeding to survey the land, the surveyors were driven off by the native women.

The Governor arrives at Taranaki, March 2d, 1860, and desires William King to come there for a personal conference.

The chief declares himself afraid to go, because of the soldiers which the Governor had brought with him, but proposes another place of meeting.

The Governor directs Colonel Gold to take military possession of the land.

The war at Taranaki continues until June 4th, 1861, when, a sort of peace being patched up, the greater portion of the troops were transferred to Auckland.

Governor Brown's proclamation to the chiefs of Waikato, demanding that the king movement should be given
up, May 21, 1861.

Reply of the native Runanga, dated June 7th, 1861, in
answer to the Governor's proclamation, in which they
pray him not to be in haste to begin hostilities—" Let our
warfare be that of the lips alone ; let it not be transferred
to the battle made with hands."

Memorandum forwarded to Governor Brown, July 4th,
1861, signed by the Bishop of New Zealand and several
of the Church Missionary Society's missionaries, in which
they express their conviction that there " are not any of the
Maories who desire to be the Queen's enemies," and that
the existing difficulties admitted of a peaceful solution.

Arrival of Sir George Grey, as successor to Governor
Brown in the Governorship of New Zealand, Oct. 1861.

Roads commenced to be made to Maungatawhiri, on the
Waikato river, thirty-eight miles from Auckland.

Imperial control over native affairs abandoned, May
30th, 1862.

Sir George Grey decides that the Waitara block had
been wrested from the natives by the late Government
without any legal title. He resolves on giving it up ; but,
before this was publicly known, takes military possession
of the Tataraimaka block, which the natives held in pledge
for the Waitara. Regarding this as a recommencement of
hostilities, they cut off a small party of two officers and
six men on their way from Taranaki to Tataraimaka.

Renewal of the war at Taranaki, May, 1863.

Early in June, 1863, General Cameron moves the greater
part of the troops from Taranaki to Auckland, in order to
defend that town from an apprehended assault of the
natives.

The population of the native villages between Auckland
and the Waikato ejected from their homes by Govern-

ment proclamation, July 9th, 1863. Military occupation of these districts.

Troops cross the Waikato : various encounters, culminating in the defeat of the natives at Rangariri, November 20th, 1863.

Occupation of the Maori capital, Ngaruawhia, December 8th, 1863.

In his despatch of July, 26th, 1865, Mr. Cardwell expresses his opinion that, on the occupation of Ngaruawhia, a proclamation might with advantage have been issued, stating the terms on which those who had been in arms might return to their allegiance.

Instead of this, the Governor is dissuaded by his responsible advisers from coming to head-quarters, on General Cameron's invitation, and there meeting the native chiefs.

Encounters at Te Rora, Rangiawhia, and Orakau.

The general, turning the native works at Pikopiko, disperses the natives at Rangiawhia, who retreat to Maungatatauri, their mountain fastness, January, 1864.

The subjugation of the delta of the Waikato and Waipa rivers completed.

A body of troops shipped to Tauranga, on the east coast, with instructions to confiscate native lands and property.

The natives, friendly and hostile alike, fly into the bush.

After some delay, a proclamation issued, distinguishing between friendly and disaffected natives, and assuring the former of protection.

Confidence only partially restored : outbreak of war at Tauranga.

Repulse of British troops at the Gate Pah, April 29th, 1864.

Rise of the Paimarire fanaticism at Taranaki, April, 1864. The fanatics threaten Whanganui, at that time bare of troops; but the town is defended by the friendly natives, who repulse the Paimarire at Moutoa, May 14th, 1864.

Defeat of the natives at Tauranga, by Colonel Greer, June 21, 1864.

Battle of Te Ranga, in the Waikato, and defeat of the Maori chief, Rawiri, June 21st, 1864.

Submission of the Tauranga chiefs, July 25th, 1864. Confiscation of one-fourth of their land.

Second battle in defence of Whanganui, between the Paimarire and the friendly natives; the latter under the command of the chief, John Williams, who had been for many years head-catechist to the Church Missionary Society's Mission at Whanganui. Defeat of the Paimarire, Feb. 23d, 1865. John Williams dies of his wounds, Feb. 24th; on the 27th, all the authorities at Whanganui, civil and military, follow his remains to the grave, the British ensign forming his pall.

Another party of the Paimarire visits the Eastern districts. They reach Opitiki. Murder of the Rev. C. S. Volkner, March 2d, 1865.

The Paimarire reach Turanga, March 16th, 1865. The Bishop of Waiapu leaves Turanga for Auckland, April 3d, 1865.

The Christian chiefs from Otaki, Wi Tako and Matene Te Whiwhi, reach Turanga, and resist the action of the Paimarire.

War in the Eastern districts, between the Colonial troops, aided by the friendly natives, and the Paimarire.

The Paimarire defeated: the murderers of Messrs. Volkner and Falloon apprehended, tried, and condemned; five of them have been executed.

Although broken as a political conspiracy, the fanaticism of the Paimarire, a compound of popery and heathenism, is still at work among the natives.